MONSTERS AND MONSTROSITY

MONSTERS AND MONSTROSITY
IN 21ST-CENTURY FILM AND TELEVISION

Edited by Cristina Artenie and Ashley Szanter

Universitas Press
Montreal

Universitas Press
Montreal

www.universitaspress.com

First published in May 2023

ENTERTAINMENT STUDIES / MEDIA MONSTERS

Library and Archives Canada Cataloguing in Publication

Title: Monsters and monstrosity in 21st-century film and television / edited by Cristina Artenie
 and Ashley Szanter.
Other titles: Monsters and monstrosity in twenty-first-century film and television
Names: Artenie, Cristina, editor. | Szanter, Ashley, editor.
Description: Previously published: Montreal: Universitas Press, 2017. | Includes bibliographical
 references.
Identifiers: Canadiana 20230225705 | ISBN 9781988963631 (hardcover)
Subjects: LCSH: Monster films—History and criticism. | LCSH: Monster television programs—History
 and criticism. | LCSH: Monsters in motion pictures. | LCSH: Monsters on television. | LCSH:
 Motion pictures—History—21st century. | LCSH: Television programs—History—21st century.
Classification: LCC PN1995.9.M6 M65 2023 | DDC 791.43/67—dc23

Table of Contents

Ashley Szanter
Introduction   vii

Marylou Naumoff
Loving Monsters: Understanding Horror Fiction Consumption
as a Response to the Uncertainty of American Identity   1

Coco D'Hont
The Enemy Within: Deconstructing Emerging Femininity
in Contemporary Monster Films   22

Erin Casey-Williams and Erika Cornelius Smith
Twice Dead: Gender, Class, and Crisis
in *Pride and Prejudice + Zombies*   39

Kristine Larsen
Monstrous Parasites, Monstrous Selves   59

Tracey Thomas
Spot the Monster: Pack, Identity, and Humanity
in MTV's *Teen Wolf*   91

Heather L. Duda
Sticking Together a Soul: Plato, St. Gregory of Nyssa,
and *I, Frankenstein*   106

Brooke Southgate
"That's Not a Real Dinosaur:" The Indominus Rex and Monstrosity
in *Jurassic World*   128

Alissa Burger and Jenny Collins
"The Shadow of Saint Nicholas:" Dougherty's *Krampus*   139

Tatiana Prorokova
Unmasking the Bite: Pleasure, Sexuality, and Vulnerability
in the Vampire Series   159

Alberto N. García
Zombie Blues: The Depressing Rise of the Living Dead
in Contemporary Television   178

Jessica George
"The Monster at the End of This Book:" Authorship and Monstrosity
in *Supernatural*   199

Notes on Contributors   223

Introduction

ASHLEY SZANTER

Academic discourse on monsters, though not particularly new, still seeks to find its place. While Jeffrey Jerome Cohen's *Monster Theory/ Reading Culture* (1996) built a strong foundation for the discipline, it is only in the last fifteen years that serious scholarly inquiry into the pervasive cultural role of monsters gained widespread respect and attention. But how can this be? With the undeniable proliferation of monsters across all platforms of media, how can we still question the cultural impact of the monster? Though we have left belief in the supernatural and "realness" of monsters in the past, we continue to craft monstrous narratives which delve into the depths of the human subconscious.

Monsters seem to be here to stay.

Upon envisioning what this project could look like, we discussed what direction this could go in: do we want to make a political statement? Should we focus on just film, or just television? What about a specific monster? Instead, we let our contributors span the wide breath of monster texts available—and they took full advantage of the opportunity. We had an overwhelming response to the call for papers on monster legends spanning cultures the world over. The ubiquitous presence of the monstrous on screen evokes myriad interpretations. In certain cases, we love to love the monster. In others, we bond over mutual desire to see it conquered, vanquished. The inherent mutability of the monster provides us with endless opportunities to reimagine, reenvision, and reencounter these creatures.

This volume contains discussions and dissections of monsters across multiple media and geographical origins. However, the notable shifts in how we engage monsters and monstrosity feature heavily in this text. Our contributors tackle resurrections of previous series and conversations through films like *Jurassic World* and *Krampus*. Others gravitate towards the rebirth of some of the older, tried and true monsters like the vampire and the zombie, including analyses of *Pride*

vii

and Prejudice + Zombies, The Originals, The Vampire Diaries, iZombie, and *Teen Wolf* – all of which reinterpreted and reinvented these creatures for the modern, Millennial audience. While the text serves to address these new iterations of the "Classic" monsters in the canon, others take a look at stranger, more fringe monster narratives like *Pan's Labyrinth, The Village,* or even the very real parasitic monstrosities of *Monsters Inside Me.*

Though many of these chapters will analytically address particular texts, like the long-running series *Supernatural,* others will take on the metanarrative surrounding trends within monster studies, such as the construction of identity, creation or representation of the soul, or the ongoing questions of authorship and agency within a particular story world. In its entirety, this volume endeavors to examine how 21st-century media presents and contends with the body and mind of the monster. What do they reveal about us culturally, individually, as a community? What can we learn from them?

Providing answers to these questions are our contributors: Marylou Naumoff, Coco D'Hont, Erin Casey-Williams, Erika Cornelius Smith, Kristine Larsen, Tracey Thomas, Heather Duda, Brooke Southgate, Alissa Burger, Jenny Collins, Tatiana Prorokova, Alberto Garcia, and Jessica George. Together, they provide the meat of the text you know hold in your hands.

Opening the volume, Marylou Naumoff tackles questions of evolving American identity through the figures of vampires and werewolves in "Loving Monsters: Understanding Horror Fiction Consumption as a Response to the Uncertainty of American Identity." Contending that America is now at a crossroads of identities, many of which are fractured and unable to coalesce as they once did, Naumoff presents two ubiquitous monsters (vampires and werewolves) in order to articulate how popular culture is using them to face situations of uncertainty from a safe distance. The recent uptick in horror fictions saturating the market speaks to a growing cultural desire to grapple with horror in safer spaces. American horror consumption, as Naumoff argues, enables both a resistance to and embracing of inevitable change towards conceptions of national and personal identity.

Coco D'Hont's "The Enemy Within: Deconstructing Emerging Femininity in Contemporary Monster Films" breaks down two contemporary forest monster films: M. Night Shyamalan's *The Village* and Guillermo Del Toro's *Pan's Labyrinth.* Her analysis traces the evolution of the forest as an antagonistic presence when juxtaposed

viii

with civilization—the kinds of forests that house many of our oldest fairy tales. However, D'Hont goes a step further and equates these specific stories, both with young, female protagonists, and posits that they also stand to examine emerging femininity and critique traditional, patriarchal institutions. The forest monster film, as a subgenre, often questions deeply political institutions and uses the act of entering the forest as a metaphor for communal disruption and individual transgression—both of which are fundamentally monstrous acts in their respective contexts.

Erin Casey-Williams and Erika Cornelius Smith analyze the inherent questions of class and structure in "Twice Dead: Gender, Class, and Crisis in *Pride and Prejudice + Zombies* (2016)," arguing that scholars and horror critics rarely discuss the zombie film in terms of how it challenges and deviates from traditional conventions of the horror genre. While there are some predictable horror tropes in most zombie films, the 21st century has already seen some significant changes to the zombie monster, which reveal shifting cultural attitudes towards identity, gender, and class. Casey-Williams and Smith posit the 2016 mash-up adaptation *Pride and Prejudice + Zombies* as a new kind of zombie film that embodies distinctly modern conceptions of identity in terms of social structures. Through their analysis of this film, readers encounter how American tendencies towards soft horror are at play with attitudes of belonging and the self.

Kristine Larsen scales down her examinations of monstrosity to take into consideration the parasitic monster in "Monstrous Parasites, Monstrous Selves." Taking both a literal and a metaphorical reading of the parasite, Larsen begins by tracing our fascination with parasitic monsters, including mentions of *Alien* and the popular Animal Planet series *Monsters Inside Me*. A literal reading of the parasite incorporates several scientific analyses of the innate, cross-cultural human fear of the parasite, but Larsen then transforms her analysis into a broader context, drawing parallels between our fear of microscopic parasites and our general invasion anxiety. Post-9/11 concerns frame her analysis and lead to discussions of fear of the "Other" in regards to ideological, religious, and biological difference. Her treatment of the term "parasite" serves to examine the interconnectedness of our biological fear of infection with our deeply, and often culturally, ingrained fear of invasion by those we deem "foreign."

Tracey Thomas discusses the evolving roles of the werewolf in contemporary culture in "Spot the Monster: Pack, Identity, and

Humanity in MTV's *Teen Wolf*." The werewolf is oft-derided in the monster pantheon—usually acting as a foil or antagonist in narratives which place other supernatural creatures (i.e. vampires) as their superiors. Whereas vampires represent human desires for wealth, beauty, and status, werewolves occupy the other end of the spectrum, representing our innate fears about the line between human and animal. Thomas explores the MTV hit show *Teen Wolf* for how it transforms the figure of the werewolf in contemporary American culture. Specifically, she looks at how the show deals with evolving identity at the human/monster divide—how can our protagonist be both a monster and a hero exhibiting deep humanity? Through her discussion of *Teen Wolf*'s brand of lycanthropy, Thomas explores how this show represents the line between human and other.

Heather Duda presents "Stitching Together a Soul: Plato, St. Gregory of Nyssa, and *I, Frankenstein*" wherein she breaks down our cultural tendency to transform the monstrous creature into a hunter of its own kind. Citing such examples as Blade from *Blade* and Nick Knight from *Forever Night*, Duda contends that we aim to rehabilitate the monster to facilitate its transformation from villain, or "Other," into a protagonist and, occasionally, potential love interest. Acts of humanity and emotion often allow for the character to change in order to become a creature we root for—but what of the soul? Duda presents the interesting case of Stuart Beattie's 2014 film *I, Frankenstein*. Attempting to adhere to the trope of the "redeemed monster," what Beattie's film does differently is discuss earned humanity in terms of the soul. Pulling from Western philosophic and religious traditions, Duda argues this film provides a new and provocative look at the power of the soul in the humanization of monsters.

In "'That's Not a Real Dinosaur': The Indominus Rex and Monstrosity in *Jurassic World*," Brooke Southgate tackles the 2015 film by posting the mythical, scientifically created dinosaur, the Indominus Rex, as a metaphor for spectacle consumerism. Though dinosaur films predating *Jurassic World* deal with similar ideas, the resurrection of this concept proves an even more scathing critique of contemporary consumerism—particularly in regards to explosive, blockbuster filmmaking. Our tendency towards "monstrous attractions," says Southgate, indicates that we cannot see the line where our corporate manipulations of nature should end. So long as there is a spectacle at the end of the exploitation of nature, there seems to be no push back among either real life moviegoers or the fictional spectators within the film.

Drawing a connection between the dinosaur as natural and as cyborg, Southgate explores how our contemporary appetite for monstrous attractions serves as a poignant critique of contemporary appetites.

Alissa Burger and Jenny Collins address one of the newest preoccupations of popular culture in "'The Shadow of Saint Nicholas': Dougherty's *Krampus*." The Krampus, a centuries-old Bavarian folk villain, functions as a foil to the Saint Nicholas, or Santa Claus, figure. Rather than bringing toys and gifts for good children, Krampus punishes those who have misbehaved or proved themselves unworthy of reward. However, as Burger and Collins note, the message in Dougherty's *Krampus* is less about simply punishing children than it is a tool to reinforce the patriarchal institution of the nuclear family. Through an examination of the human characters and their behaviors throughout the film, Burger and Collins argue that the "loss of Christmas spirit" is the family's ultimate crime as it threatens to upend Western notions of the family — particularly the nuclear family who celebrates Christmas, the ultimate expression of Western values and institutions. Though not as tried or true as the figure of the zombie or vampire, Western culture resurrected the Krampus as a figure of punishment and an enforcer of social order.

Tatiana Prorokova unpacks the visual portrayal behind the vampire's bite in "Unmasking the Bite: Pleasure, Sexuality, and Vulnerability in the Vampire Series." When examining our cultural need to humanize monsters, the vampire exists at the forefront of this action. Prorokova provides detailed examinations of vampire bites in the popular television shows *The Vampire Diaries* and its spinoff, *The Originals*. While also considering implications of gender in the two shows, she emphasizes how they also focus on the vampire's bite, not as a necessary action required to feed, but as an action which brings the biter sexual pleasure and fulfillment. Whereas many vampire films present the bite as a gruesome act, Prorokova argues there is a nuanced power dynamic which exists between vampire and victim. Though the visual artistry of "the bite" in these two shows furthers her claim of its inherent sexual pleasure, the shows' focus on the victim's body increases the vulnerability of the act. Through analyses of specific scenes, Prorokova unveils the cinematographic nuances of vampiric bites in both *The Vampire Diaries* and *The Originals*.

Alberto N. Garcia's chapter, "Zombies Blues: The Rise of the Sorrowful Living Dead in Contemporary Television," addresses the rapid changes happing to the zombie creature. While many could

xi

easily imagine the traditional zombie, shows like Britain's *In the Flesh*, France's *Les Revenants*, and America's *iZombie* have collectively changed how modern audiences react and interact with the zombie monster. Garcia argues that, while the horrific zombie still remains in the cultural consciousness, this new zombie is undergoing a stunning transformation wherein they develop deeply emotional characterizations—empathy, kindness, a sense of justice, and interpersonal connections. Ultimately, Garcia claims that the zombie no longer embodies the abject horror of Romero's or Snyder's iterations. Instead, these new zombies demand compassion and understanding, leading to the question of which creature will come to replace the horror once embodied by the old-fashioned zombie.

In "'The Monster at the End of This Book': Authorship and Monstrosity in *Supernatural*," Jessica George attempts to breakdown the television monolith that is The CW's *Supernatural*. Taking a deeply theoretical approach, George breaks down how the horror serial presents the notion of authorship: who, or what, is an author? What is legitimate or illegitimate authorship? The massive popularity of this particular show created a widespread fandom that participates in the show through "paratexts," or fan-made narratives. As a result, the show writers adopt a tendency towards "meta episodes" which force the protagonists, the monster-hunting Winchester brothers, to encounter in-universe fictions about themselves. George argues that this forces both the show's characters and its audience to figure out who authors fact/fiction as well as whether or not the author could be a god or, potentially, a monster.

Though varied in scope and cultural backgrounds, we believe these authors engage with monsters and monstrosity in new and innovative ways. As you encounter the chapters in this volume, we hope you find yourself captivated by the vibrant, interdisciplinary conversations happening within monster studies. This volume on monsters and monstrosity in 21st-century film and television sets the stage for future scholarship and asks us to consider how the monsters we know, love, and sometimes fear manage to reinvent themselves, slowly saturating popular culture with every new iteration.

xii

Loving Monsters: Understanding Horror Fiction Consumption as a Response to the Uncertainty of American Identity

Marylou R. Naumoff

Vampires and werewolves are arguably the most iconic monsters in American fiction. Never has their presence been as ubiquitous. Not only is America embracing monsters but it seems to *need* them in a way that surpasses mere entertainment value. Veronica Hollinger, citing Rosemary Jackson, explains that "fantasy has come to function as an expressive rather than escapist or compensatory mode of writing" where fantasy's "role is to hold up the mirror to our own human desires and anxieties" (199). Americans are managing and being confronted with a great amount of uncertainty regarding their identity and the future of their nation. The country's primary logic of liberal universalism, which has historically structured national identity, systems of power, and codes of conduct, is atrophied and failing. This troubled universal has been subjected to a multiplicity of assaults from numerous sources that have greatly compromised its authority and ability to contain and speak for the populace. As a result, we currently exist as a fractured collectivity that can no longer be seamed together rhetorically. This causes strife and uncertainty over American identity, and what the future holds for the nation's citizens. The anxiety produced by such disparate visions simultaneously competing to define national identity creates a longing for ways to work through, and perhaps formulate answers for, these challenging times.

An historical and alluring space for such contemplations to occur is through the consumption of horror fiction. This essay considers the renewed American appetite for the genre as paradigmatic of the national subject's need to process, manage, and confront uncertainty at a safe distance. In 2013, Marina Levina and Diem-My T. Bui observed that

> monstrous narratives of the past decade have become omnipresent specifically because they represent collective and social anxieties over resisting and embracing change in the twenty-first century... And while monsters always tapped into anxieties over a changing world, they have never been as popular, or as needed, as in the past decade (1-2).

Many of the more popular texts — *True Blood,* the *Twilight* saga, *The Vampires Diaries, The Originals*, and the *Underworld* series — share many of the same themes. By reading vampires and werewolves with an eye toward understanding the subjects they come to represent, I demonstrate that America is simultaneously resisting and embracing change, which not only accounts for the nuanced form monsters take but also for the state of transition and/or emergence of nuanced identities in the populace.

An Uncertain Nation: Exploring Contestations over American Identity

The United States is confronted by a great deal of uncertainty. Factors such as the 9-11 attacks, war, accusations and proof of torture, the failing economy, the appointment of our first black president, the uprising of the Tea Party, mass shootings, continued terrorist threats or attacks, and the persistence of multiculturalism all coalesce, leaving Americans anxious about the U.S. and its future. This uncertainty produces competing and contradictory rhetorical texts that seek to speak for or represent the country. Debates such as that over healthcare reform, the repeal of "don't ask, don't tell" in the military, new voter registration requirements, the institutionalization of marriage equality, and immigration policies have revealed tensions over who can and who should get to count in America. The looming dominance of China and our debt to them greatly compromises our notions of economic security and hegemony, while simultaneously undermining the capitalist structure and the concept of American exceptionalism. The middle class is disappearing as our nation struggles to determine and form the structure and make-up of the twenty-first-century job market. Examples such as these reveal that Americans are simultaneously managing and negotiating the comfort and limitations of clinging to a mythologized

Loving Monsters

past, as well as the possibility and fear that change presents. What voices get heard, what sensibilities prevail, and what face(s) represent the nation will determine what it means to be American in the 21st century.

Benedict Anderson accounted for how individuals come to see themselves as belonging to a nation in *Imagined Communities*. Individuals will never become acquainted with all of their fellow countrymen but they must believe that they know them and in this imagined knowing a sense of communion is formed. Carroll Smith-Rosenberg asserts that "few nation-states or national identities are as artificially constructed" as the United States and that "few have been more successful in imbuing generation after generation of immigrants with a deep sense of national belonging" (1). Such imaginings become increasingly difficult to maintain in a diverse populace. Samuel P. Huntington states that America is "less a nation than it [has] been for a century" due to "Globalization, multiculturalism, cosmopolitanism, immigration, subnationalism, and antinationalism" resulting in a "battered American consciousness" (4-5). Huntington fears Americans may indeed face a similar fate as Sparta or Rome—"Historically the substance of American identity has involved four key components: race, ethnicity, culture (most notably language and religion) and ideology. The racial and ethnic Americas are no more. Cultural America is under siege" (12). One explanation for the state of American identity is that many of these intersecting factors are illustrated and informed by the influx of immigrants to the United States. Huntington's point is illustrated by Dina Gavrilos as she notes that the "unprecedented levels of immigration from Mexico, as well as other Latin American and Asian countries over the past three decades" has resulted in a public discourse that points to a decline of the sense of a unified national identity (95).

While immigration is nothing new to the United States, the contemporary influx of immigrants presents challenges to national identity that differ from those of previous eras. While immigrants have always informed American culture, dominant identity maintained its dominance because historically immigrants attempted assimilate to the white mainstream. However, the rise of identity politics in the 1960s and 1970s created a climate of multiculturalism and the embracing of subnationalisms. Americans are also no longer fitting into tidy identity categories. One way of managing difference was for a society to be able to clearly define the substance of those differences. As we persist in

3

an increasingly multicultural society we must also acknowledge that our categories of identification are becoming increasingly messy and ill-suited to define the individuals contained within the populace.

Naturally, these developments produce a sense of discomfort among the large segments of Americans that still identify with more traditional Anglo conceptions of national identity. The political and cultural divisiveness evidenced by the formation of the Tea Party, and heard in the political speeches of Donald Trump, illustrates a resistance, if not a direct rejection, of a diversified American populace and culture. Even as public discourse celebrating post-racialism circulates, Frederick Lewis astutely notes that, "The reactive identity of 'real Americans' taking back their country from what they seem to perceive as a federal government dominated by urban 'elitists' and racial minorities is palpable" (193). In sum, it is becoming increasingly difficult to agree on what constitutes and structures American identity.

Traditionally, to investigate matters of citizenship and national identity one would look to political discourse. It is not, however, only overtly political texts that inform our notions of national identity. Increasingly, popular culture has come to be the vehicle through which we negotiate who we are as a nation, as well as many other cultural and political topics, and as such these texts provide great insight into the tensions described above. As David Magill explains,

> Monster tales, in print or digital frame, also serve as a central space for processing the anxieties and fears of American culture and its identities. . . . Studying the monster then is to study the human and its identity constructions. We understand our monsters to understand ourselves" (81).

I propose that via an examination of vampire and werewolf fiction one can find some of the most significant representations and rearticulations of American identity because the horror genre provides a safe space to confront and work through fears and anxieties that other genres do not provide. As Jonathan F. Basset explains, "From a psychodynamic perspective, the horror genre is frightening, yet fascinating, because it gives expression to deep-seated and taboo psychological concerns that are typically repressed and denied cultural expression in other mediums" (15).

American Identity and Liberal Universalism

> The monster has its tentacles wrapped around the foundations
> of American history, drawing its life from ideological efforts to
> marginalize the weak and normalize the powerful, to suppress
> struggles for class, racial, and sexual liberation, to transform the
> "American Way of Life" into a weapon of empire.
> W. Scott Poole, *Monsters in America: Our Historical Obsession with
> the Hideous and the Haunting.*

To understand how vampires and werewolves are reflecting and
aiding Americans in working through anxieties over national identity
we need to begin with the founding of the nation. In the United States
national identity has been informed by a brand of universalism that can
be classified as liberal universalism. Simply defined, the liberal universal
is a mode of universalism that privileges an American understanding
and employment of liberal theory and accounts for the constituting
qualities of the American citizen-subject.

The Founding of American Liberal Universalism

To understand how national identity was initially formed and to
appreciate how this legacy impacts structures of power, and resistance
to these structures, a brief history of liberal universalism is necessary.
The founding fathers of the United States were greatly influenced by
the philosophical orientation of the time, namely the Enlightenment.
The order of the day on this continent was following suit with what
was occurring in Europe. French scholars, Roger Celestin and Elaine
DalMolin describe French universalism as:

> French exceptionalism [which] originates in the Enlightenment
> and the Revolution of 1789. The *philosophes* of the eighteenth
> century, among them Voltaire, Rousseau, and Diderot,
> perceived themselves as the harbingers of a new world in
> which arbitrariness, injustice, and the irrational . . . would be
> vanquished by the forces of reason and progress. This would
> be true not only of France, but also of the rest of the world,
> for these notions of reason and progress were perceived
> as being universal. . . . The republic created by the French

> Revolution was perceived as the particular embodiment of the Enlightenment's abstract universalism, a "universalist republic." The sovereignty and specificity of a particular nation were thus inextricably linked with principles that were considered universal. (3)

This notion of universalism further popularized a deferral of the body and glorification of the mind. The glorious mind was European and then by extension, American. As Laclau explains, "the universal had found its own body, but this still was the body of a certain particularity – European culture of the nineteenth century. So European culture was a particular one, and at the same time the expression—no longer incarnation—of universal human essence" (97).

For the purpose of this project I will be restricting my discussion of the liberal universal to its interpretation and application in the United States. The classic Cartesian mind-body split was used as justification for the exaltation of white males and the subjugation of women and those who were not perceived as white. This system of power greatly shaped notions of rights and citizenship in the United States and its influence is still apparent today. White men, of a certain economic class, were viewed as being possessed of the mind and women and non-whites as being more bodily. By extension women and non-whites were perceived to be more susceptible to their desires and urges, rendering them unfit for civic and political life. Citizenship, and those capable of exercising the rights associated with it, was initially conceived as a disembodied abstract. This abstract, philosophically speaking, required no body to function. This of course did not, and arguably still does not, play out as theory would have it. While a claim of rational disembodiment is proffered there is most definitely a body attached to these "rational" minds and it was those very bodies—white, male, Christian, wealthy bodies—that enabled them to claim disembodiment in the first place.

The disembodied liberal subject is also the impetus for the division of the private and public sphere in the United States. Raced and gendered bodies were relegated to the sphere of the private, the home (Lister 194-198; Norton 126-137). This resulted in white males dominating public space. Their rational minds, which were not compromised by their desires and urges, were therefore capable of pursuing issues of politics, economics, international relations, and nation building. As Wendy Brown explains,

Loving Monsters

> The liberal subject—the abstract individual constituted and addressed by liberal political and legal codes—may be masculine not only because his primary domain of operations is civil society rather than the family, but because he is presumed to be morally if not ontologically oriented toward autonomy, autarky, and individual power. (*States of Injury* 183)

It then follows that our nation's identity naturally was founded by those, and continues to be embodied by those, who are white, male, Christian, capitalist, and heterosexual. The defining qualities of being Christian, a capitalist, and heterosexual establish this list in addition to being white and male because these qualities were favored by those in power. Given that these individuals were in positions of power and authority the systems they created led to the protection and perpetuation of their power. Therefore laws, values, and norms that were disseminated by various adjudicating and cultural bodies such as the government, the legal system, schools, churches, and cultural artifacts all served the privileging of the liberal universal as the ideal citizen-subject.

In the U.S. context two popular discourses that grew out of Enlightenment philosophy are of particular significance for national identity: notions of equality for all and its consummate counterpart the sovereign subject. By exploring these two discourses it becomes evident how liberal universalism discursively excludes those falling outside its purview and how such exclusion is justified. Ironically, these discourses privilege certain identities over others even though their creation was in the service of the noble ideals of freedom, justice, and equal treatment for all. Conversely, these narratives can be framed in such a way as to condone oppressive power structures and alleviate said power structures of their culpability in the limiting of those falling outside the purview of the liberal universal. These narratives also create an impossible perfection that will never be realized but will constantly be pursued.

Liberalism in theory is designed to allow for differences among citizens in a pluralistic society because liberal states are comprised of "free institutions" that allow for varying conceptions of the good life; it is the job of the justice system to create the conditions for a "stable society of free and equal citizens, who remain profoundly divided by reasonable [differing] doctrines" (Rawls 4). These differing doctrines also produce different notions of the good life among citizens. The ability

7

to seek and fulfill your own version of the good life is a foundational principle of liberalism. Kymlicka explains it is a theory that gives

> an account of what people's interests are, most comprehensively conceived, and an account of what follows from supposing that these interests matter equally. According to liberalism, since our most essential interest is getting these beliefs right and acting on them, government treats people as equals, with an equal concern and respect by providing for each individual the liberties and resources needed to examine and act on these beliefs. (13)

As much as the individual, and the freedom to pursue one's own notion of the good life, is championed in American discourses, the reality, some scholars argue, is quite different. Differences among the nation's people can cause disruptions in equality and the distribution and enactment of rights. In her work *States of Injury*, for example, Wendy Brown engages in a series of gender analyses to demonstrate, in part, that equality as sameness, one of the foundational pillars of America, simply is not feasible:

> In liberalism, equality is defined as a condition of sameness, a condition in which humans share the same nature, the same rights, and the same terms of regard by state institutions. Individuals are guaranteed equality – the right to be treated the same as everyone else – because we are regarded as having a civil, and hence political, sameness . . . while equality is cast as a matter of sameness, gender in liberalism consistently emerges as a problem of difference, simply *as* difference: there is *human* equality on the one hand, and *gender* difference on the other. (153; emphasis in the original)

The problem of difference that Brown notes is an important one. The narrative of equality is structured in such a way that it is believed that its opposite is inequality. The problem Brown has with this formulation is that our equality is premised on the notion that all Americans are equal because all citizens are all the *same*. This is certainly not the case because when one is *different* from the standards of the liberal universal they are rendered unequal. It follows that under the tenets of liberalism, injustice is when one who is the same is treated differently but "ontological

8

Loving Monsters

difference" is a problem "outside the purview of justice" (*States of Injury* 153). Brown suggests that equality as sameness, as it is defined and operates within the United States, cannot and does not function. Again she uses gender as a way to illustrate her point: "Equality as sameness is a gendered formulation of equality, because it secures gender privilege through naming women as different and men as the neutral standard of the same" (*States of Injury* 153). As mentioned above liberal universalism is premised on masculine sameness and this sameness must maintain its difference from women to exist. It must be everything that is not woman, everything that is not irrational, subject to desires of the flesh, emotional, and confined to the private sphere. This point becomes tremendously important when considering how Enlightenment theory encouraged and provided the justification for stratifying humans by the dictates of the mind/body split. The conclusion that Brown ultimately draws is that liberty cannot be universalized. For liberty to exist within the liberal confines of the United States others must lack liberty, just as for man to exist he must maintain his difference from woman. In the end the United States seems to "sustain rather than break with the explicit belief of the ancient citizens of Athens: some must be slaves so that others might be free" (Brown, *States of Injury* 156).

Equality for Some: Multiculturalism and the Troubled Liberal Universal

> Since tolerance was coined to manage eruptions of the particular against the imagined universal, the marginal against the mainstream, the outsiders against the insiders, it is little wonder that tolerance has made a *revenue* as the Enlightenment narrative of history has faltered. The universal lies in tatters, the normal is under constant challenge, the outsiders are all inside now but without cosmopolitan sophistication or aspirations the result is hardly harmonious.
> Wendy Brown, *Regulating Aversions.*

It can be argued that the vampire and werewolf figures are needed when liberal universalism is losing its ability to rein in difference and national identity has become such a contentious issue. These monsters become particularly relevant given the contestations over national identity and our inability to reach a consensus about, to use Samuel P. Huntington's words, *who we are*. The number of discordant voices that cannot or do not wish to embody the liberal universal (coded as

9

white, male, heterosexual, Christian), or who may simply view it as an unethical representation of American identity, has become impossible to ignore. The long history of inequality in the United States has come to haunt the U.S. as Judith Butler explains in "Restaging the Universal":

> The universal can be the universal only to the extent that it remains untainted by what is particular, concrete, and individual. Thus it requires the constant and meaningless vanishing of the individual. . . . The all-encompassing trajectory of the term is necessarily undone by the exclusion or particularity on which it rests. There is no way to bring the excluded particularity into the universal without first negating the particularity. And the negation would only confirm once again that universality cannot proceed without destroying that which it purports to include. Moreover, the assimilation of the particular into the universal leaves its trace, an inassimilable remainder, which renders universality ghostly to itself" (23-24).

This excerpt from Butler's essay speaks to Laclau and Mouffe's work *Hegemony and Socialist Strategy* while also revealing how this work is helpful in understanding the functioning of liberal universalism. All of these authors point out that for the universal to achieve its goal of producing a cohesive identity "particulars" (aspects or individuals that differ strongly from the components of the universal) must constantly be deferred, dismissed, or delegitimized. These particulars, however, become impossible to silence or eliminate completely and their "trace" dirties the purity and by extension the legitimacy of the universal. That is why Laclau and Mouffe theorize that it is *only* at the moment when a particular emerges that hegemony becomes necessary. Hegemony functions to silence or remove the presence of a particular to maintain the reputability and power of the universal. Because the complete removal of the particular *is* not achievable the universal itself is never pure and is constantly working to maintain itself.

Monstrous Americans

The U.S. it can be argued is witnessing a real crisis of "particulars." This crisis is precisely why the figures of vampires and werewolves provide the cathartic space needed to work through how the nation is

Loving Monsters

to negotiate the diversity of a populace that will no longer submit to the hegemonic force of the liberal universal. The majority of the vampire and werewolf texts explored in this essay feature a human woman that has an amorous relationship, or at the very least flirtation, with a vampire, and at times a werewolf as well. When examining these texts in relation to national identity it is important to note that women, namely white women, have served as a metaphor for the nation ("motherland"). Amy Kaplan explains in her essay "Manifest Domesticity" that even though men were expected to do the work of nation building while women were to do the labor of home building, women still played an important role in the founding and growth of the nation. As mothers and wives, women serve as the bastion of the nation's morality and also the perpetuation of the populace. Keeping this in mind I assert that the human women in *Twilight, Vampire Diaries,* and *True Blood* represent the nation and its relation with the proliferation of "particulars." The predominant choice of these characters to pick/prefer vampire paramours rather than werewolf mates communicates a preference for a certain type of subject. Exploring what type of subject vampires and werewolves represent in society provides us with insight into how the battle over universalism is being staged, who stands to win this battle, and how the nation might carry on from here.

Vampires: The Rational Subject

The vampire has enjoyed a prominence in Western culture since the publication of Bram Stroker's *Dracula* in 1897, and has managed to travel through the ages as he is, to use Keith Scott's description, a post-modern subject in that he is "protean . . . a perfect example of the free-floating signifier, ready and able to stand for anything we might wish him to represent" (22). Vampires stay with us because they are traditionally human in form, making them relatable and extremely adaptable so that they reflect our fears and enable us to explore the human condition (Peacock xviii; Clements 5). In Nina Auerbach's influential work, *Our Vampires, Ourselves,* she states that one can read vampires as a reflection of the time in which they emerge. Historical and cultural factors directly influence the form and qualities a vampire takes. Auerbach asserts that vampires are so much a personification of their age that her book can be read as a "history of Anglo-American culture through its mutating vampires" (1). This also accounts for why vampires seem to change so much as their appeal is generational (Auerbach 5). Susana Loza, citing Bellin, states that contemporary constructions of vampires should be deconstructed because "these texts 'give image to historically determinate anxieties, wishes, and needs, they simultaneously function by stimulating, endorsing, broadcasting the very anxieties, wishes that give image'" (92). Late twentieth- and twenty-first-century vampires have come to represent such figures as "rebellious outsider, as persecuted minority, as endangered species, and as member of a different race" (Carter 29). The vampires found in contemporary fiction are more human than ever, leading them to be characterized as "domesticated, de-fanged," and "re-souled" (Moffat and Schott 3).

Human women find not only vampires with no bite, but also vampires that are good citizens. It is no coincidence that the undead that win the hearts of the living are also those vampires that long for their humanity to be restored and also attempt to be productive members of society. In other word, today's "good" vampires all display the qualities — rational thought, restraint, and morality — of the disembodied, liberal universal, of an ideal American citizen-subject. These qualities are exemplified by Edward Cullen (*Twilight*), Bill Compton (*True Blood*), Stefan Salvatore (*Vampire Diaries*), and Elijah Mikaelson (*The Originals*).

One of the ways in which the Enlightened subject is superior to others is that *he* is capable of rational thought and is not ruled by his desires or emotions. Vampires exhibit this quality most clearly when they make the choice to abstain from human blood, or at the very least not to take human life to survive. Edward Cullen and Stefan Salvatore do not consume anything but animal blood. The Cullen family refer to themselves as vegetarians because of their absolute rule that they are to never drink human blood (*Twilight*).

Edward demonstrates his self-control and love for Bella when he shares with her that he initially was rude to her and avoided her because her blood smelled so good to him. He likens the scent of her blood to heroin. Edward finds it evil to consume human blood and when asked why he only hunted animals he responds that he did not want to be a "monster" (Meyer 187). His vampiric nature is forgiven when he shamefully admits to Bella that when he was a young vampire he stalked criminals as an act of rebellion against his father/maker, Carlisle Cullen (*Breaking Dawn: Part I*). Bella comforts him and reassures him that he has probably saved lives by only killing those humans that would harm others. This demonstrates that Bella is willing to dismiss

Loving Monsters

or minimize any qualities that mark him as a vampire, never fearing for her safety. Indeed this is an argument that Edward and Bella have throughout the series until Bella eventually becomes a vampire herself; Edward is constantly insisting that he could hurt her and she always retorts that she trusts him. This blind faith emphasizes to readers/ viewers that Edward is more human than vampire, more like us than not like us.

Stefan Salvatore chooses not to drink human blood because when he does give into the bloodlust he becomes a "ripper" that gorges himself on human life. This decision comes at a cost because he is not as strong as other vampires. This sacrifice is one Stefan is willing to make because he wants to preserve his humanity. An original vampire, Klaus, seeks to use Stefan as a tool for his own purposes by commanding Stefan to stop fighting his urges to feed on human blood ("The Reckoning"). After killing one human Klaus then commands Stefan to feed from Elena. Rather than be afraid Elena confidently tells Stefan he will be able to resist because he loves her. Stefan is able to resist but then Klaus compels him to turn off his humanity so that he will turn into the "ripper" and only then does Stefan bite Elena. The ability to control, and even be ashamed by one's bloodlust demonstrates that Edward and Stefan are not animals, but rather men that desire love and the restoration of their humanity.

These moral vampires are always contrasted with those vampires that embody more violent characteristics. These counterparts often crave blood and killing. Bill Compton is tormented by his maker, Lorena, that wants Bill back in her life again, not only out of a possessive type of love, but also because she misses the killing sprees her and Bill used to delight in ("Release Me"). They mock and provoke the moral vampires to indulge their urges and return to being killers. This reminds viewers that even though these characters may be loving and romantic they are still vampires, they are still other, and it is only through concerted effort, through their desire to be human, that they are able to emulate humanity.

These characters all seek to not only regain their humanity but also their standing in society. In *Twilight* the Cullen family live as the perfect nuclear family with a patriarchal father-figure that is a successful doctor, despite being a vampire. Stefan Salvatore participates in founders' activities in the town of Mystic Falls. But perhaps the most striking example of a vampire's desire for citizenship can be found in the series *True Blood* where a synthetic blood allows vampires to "come out of the

13

coffin." One theme that is consistent throughout the series' seven seasons is the battle fought by vampires that have "mainstreamed" to be granted the rights and privileges afforded American citizens. This demonstrates a strong desire to not only be "de-fanged" and "re-souled," but to also be embraced and accepted as humans, as fellow citizens.

In many ways the vampires humans love ultimately represent those subjects that seek to assimilate to dominant culture. Not surprisingly this also results in moral vampires becoming coded as white and emulating white normative standards and sensibilities. The majority of vampire love interests inhabit white bodies and a white world (Hobson 25). These vampires do not only emulate white identity but also American identity. Ewan Kirkland acknowledges the tendency of scholars to assert that vampires represent a racial other but that is less of the case today (104). For example the patriarch of the Cullen family (*Twilight*), Carlisle, was present at the founding of the nation, Bill Compton (*True Blood*) is a Civil War soldier and a founder of his town, and the Salvatore brothers (*Vampire Diaries*) are participants in the founding of the fictional Mid-Atlantic town of Mystic Falls. Kirkland notes that the "Valorization of White vampire privilege is also presented in the reformed modern vampire, struggling to retain or regain his humanity to assimilate into human society" (104). Poole notes that this practice of humanizing vampires results in a loss of vampires' monstrous appeal and effect (214).

A concurrent motif is the romanticization of the past. Recall earlier I state that Americans are struggling with uncertainty and the longing to cling to a mythologized past. Hannah Priest notes that in romantic vampire fiction, particularly YA fiction, the values and norms of the era from which the vampire lived as human tend to affirm the "fictionalized societal structures of the period and the implications this has for the construction of female identity and sexuality within the novels" (57). This gives readers and viewers a way to return to a simpler time when the world was a less frightening place and it was believed that people had values. Edward Cullen is the most obvious example of this tendency. He brings into the twenty-first century the respect and expectations of a young man born in the early twentieth century. He insists on marrying Bella before he will consent to turning her into a vampire. Bill Compton (*True Blood*) and Stefan Salvatore (*Vampire Diaries*) demonstrate their chivalry derived from the eighteenth and nineteenth centuries. A return to these earlier eras does not only promise the return of certain morals and values but also returns us to a time of unquestioned white privilege and authority.

Loving Monsters

The "de-fanged," "re-souled" vampire becomes cast as white by never permitting a vampire love interest to be non-white in well-known, popularized fiction. Kirkland points out that "While Black vampire Blade resorts to technology and narcotics to subdue the vampire within, these White vampires have the inner ability to control and transcend their bodily instincts and desires" (105). Another example can be found in *Twilight* when audiences encounter the only non-white vampire in the film, Laurent. He is part of a triad of vampires that drink human blood. We discover later that Laurent was attempting to live the "vegetarian" vampire lifestyle with the Cullens' "family" in Alaska. Laurent is not capable of staving off his bloodlust and gives into his animalistic tendencies. This characterization is further fostered by creating a foil for vampires, and this foil can be found in the form of a werewolf.

Werewolves: The Savage

Werewolves have been part of our collective imagination far longer than vampires. The first reference to a werewolf appears in *The Epic of Gilgamesh* in 37 B.C.E. (Sconduto 2). The wolf has historically been feared and loathed in Western culture so much so that wolves have been exterminated from America (exception Alaska), Britain, Germany, Switzerland, and France (Armstrong 128). One reason individuals fear wolves is because of the way they reflect humanity's dual nature— "the beast within" (Armstrong 127). American psychologist Nandor Fodor notes that individuals appear as wolves in dreams and "the transformation is used symbolically as self-denunciation for secret deeds, fantasies, and desires" (qtd. in Armstrong 132). As vampires have become more human, werewolves have remained beasts. This opposition between man and beast, as well as between the mind and the body, is naturally staged as vampires and werewolves have long been framed as enemies. Priest notes that,

> Often a werewolf's very existence is predicated on their antagonism towards vampires; almost always, a hierarchal relationship is created between the two species, with vampires embodying power, culture, civilization and colonization, and werewolves depicted through primitivism, victimization, infantilization and "underdog" heroism (213).

15

This antagonism extends into a series of binary oppositions, particularly in regards to race and class. Feuds between vampires and werewolves are major plot lines in *Twilight, True Blood, The Originals,* and most explicitly in the film franchise *Underworld.* Consistently vampires are portrayed as aristocratic while werewolves are seen as bestial, as well as often being portrayed as poor. In the film franchise *Underworld* this class distinction is most striking where the lycans, former slaves to the vampires, live in sewers while vampires live in castles or mansions. McMahon-Coleman and Weaver assert that these storylines "provoke comparisons with racist colonial expectations that Indigenous groups would 'die out,' or bring to mind policies of forced assimilation" (104). The *Twilight* saga harnesses the colonial history of the United States by pitting white vampires against the indigenous Quilete tribe. The Cullens' wealth is contrasted with the Quilete wolves' relative poverty, and this often occurs via the main human heroine's eyes, Bella Swan. McMahon-Coleman and Weaver assert that Bella "wants the vampire life because it is Edward's life, and thus it is privileged to the reader over any alternative" (101). Werewolves in both *The Originals* and *True Blood* are characterized as occupying a lower socio-economic bracket. The wolf pack in *The Originals* lives in a wooded bayou area outside of New Orleans that appears to have few comforts of modern life.

If vampires are relatable, and able to be assimilated into mainstream society, werewolves cannot be assimilated due to their animal form. The animalistic aspect of the werewolf is often stressed and viewed as something that cannot be controlled. In *Twilight* readers and viewers are expected to fully trust Bella in the hands of a vampire but Edward constantly stresses how much he fears that Jacob will lose control and harm her because wolves have no self-control.

The contrast between the rational vampire and the animalistic werewolf is illustrated quite well in *Vampire Diaries*, as McMahon-Coleman and Weaver observe: when Caroline is turned, she is effectively coached on how to control her hunger by using her mind to self-discipline. This is contrasted with newly activated werewolf, Mason Lockwood, "who can only rely on chains and manacles to limit the danger of lupine shapeshifting" (107). Rosalind Sibielski notes this tendency as werewolf characters are reduced to their animalistic drives whereby there is nearly always "libidinous behavior in women and aggressive behavior in men" (119). These kinds of characterizations hark back to staid and dangerous myths depicting slave women as wanton and slave men as brutes. The werewolves in *Twilight* are further

Loving Monsters

removed from their humanity by a process called imprinting where a wolf becomes completely devoted and loyal to another. The way it is described, the individual has no control over it and often imprinting serves the purpose of making the genetic line stronger. This idea robs the imprinted individuals of freewill and true love as they are reduced to breeding machines driven by instinct.

Werewolves ultimately represent not only subjects that have not been assimilated into mainstream American culture but also those that do not desire to do so. Shapeshifting creates the possibility to move beyond fixed boundaries and thus has the potential to destabilize understandings of identity (McMahon-Coleman and Weaver 108). The liminal space werewolves occupy challenges the authority and centrality of white normativity embodied by the vampires. Good wolves remain loyal to their pack and this often equates to adhering to the rules and cultural practices of their collective. Werewolves then are reflective of those subjects that refuse to dilute their cultural expressions to accommodate a majority that may feel confusion or discomfort when confronted with individuals that differ from them.

Miscegenation and The Nation

Racial codes and markers have been highly constructed and contested over the course of America's evolution. There was an obsession with cataloging racial categories and bloodlines in the United States as recently as the early twentieth century, as evidenced by the Johnson-Reed Act of 1924 (Ngai 69). At the turn of the current century America once again is faced with the loss of the white majority, as well as a destabilizing of other identity markers. This creates conflict and uncertainty over how American culture will be altered by the changing makeup of the nation. This sense of conflict and urgency is present in the narratives of the films and television series explored in this essay. While conflict is a necessary element of the plot, many of the storylines bring viewers to the apocalyptic edge of existence. This conflict is visible in the 2016 presidential election race as Americans passionately disagree over what the direction of America should be: do we look back to a past that we should restore or to a future of change?

To understand how the nation is responding to these challenges we can turn to its representation, the human woman. The humans of *Twilight*, *True Blood*, and *Vampire Diaries* are drawn to vampire lovers,

17

and while there may be a flirtation with, or brief relationship with a werewolf the characters ultimately give their hearts to the undead. This communicates to viewers that the nation can love a monster if only they assimilate and emulate the qualities of the traditional citizen-subject.

The formula is not as tidy as that, however. The characters reflect the struggle and ambivalence felt by the nation. Bella (*Twilight*) moves to Forks, Washington, where she is accepted by the popular crowd, but having always felt like an outsider Bella welcomes her transition to being a vampire. In her new immortal form she feels like her true self with extraordinary powers. Even though Bella's happy ending consists of a heteronormative family complete with miracle child she still only feels comfortable within her supernatural body.

Sookie Stackhouse (*True Blood*) is no mere mortal, her lineage includes fairy blood. This supernatural forbearer gives her the ability to read minds. Sookie's attraction to vampires, and later shifters, is largely due to the fact that she cannot hear their thoughts. This ability has always made it difficult for her to connect with people but she finds refuge within the supernatural community. Sookie, unlike Bella, craves normalcy. She deeply loves Bill Compton but struggles with the prospect of a future with no children or morning breakfast with her husband. The series finale concludes with Sookie living an average human life having given away her fairy powers, the thing which made her different, and being free of the conflict of loving Bill (Sookie ends his existence at his request). While Sookie may still be surrounded by supernatural beings she herself chose and desired to be "normal."

Elena Gilbert (*Vampire Diaries*) appears to be a normal high school cheerleader grieving the death of her parents when she meets and falls in love with Stefan Salvatore. As the series progresses it is revealed that Elena is a supernatural being, a doppelgänger of the vampire that turned Stefan and his brother Damon. Although she loves and trusts Stefan, and he does all he can to protect her, she is still inadvertently turned into a vampire. Elena does not thrive in her new form as Bella does, rather she is initially uncontrollable, her humanity turned off, and then she grieves the loss of her human form and potential to have a "normal" life.

These stories not only explore how these mortal women, read the nation, are working through the presence of monsters in the world but also the change in the populace this presence brings. Contemporary vampire and werewolf texts all feature a hybrid, a being of mixed blood, in their storylines. Some of the hybrids are purely supernatural such

Loving Monsters

as the werewolf-vampire hybrids of *Underworld, Vampire Diaries,* and *The Originals*. Other stories feature human-supernatural hybrids such as Sookie (*True Blood*) and the daughter of human Bella and vampire Edward, Renesmee. One consistency across storylines is that hybrids are superior beings. The vampire-werewolf hybrids are stronger and faster than both of their constituting elements. The supernatural-human hybrids possess powers that exceed not only human, but also supernatural capabilities. The presence of these hybrid beings reflects the nation's feelings towards an increasingly diverse America facing the loss of white centrality and cultural determination. Is this change to be feared? Embraced? These questions reflect American's twenty-first century struggle with the changing nature of the nation and scholars can continue to track the managing of these anxieties by continuing to explore the monsters we love, fear, and perhaps become.

Works Cited

Anderson, Benedict. *Imagined Communities: Reflections on the Spread and Origin of Nationalism*. London: Verso, 1991.

Armstrong, Edward Allworthy. *Legendary Creatures and Monsters*. New York: Cavendish Square, 2014.

Auerbach, Nina. *Our Vampires, Ourselves*. Chicago: The University of Chicago Press, 1995.

Basset, Jonathan F. "Ambivalence about Immortality: Vampires Reveal and Assuage Existential Anxiety." *Fanpires: Audience Consumption of the Modern Vampire*. Eds. Gareth Schott and Kirstine Moffat. Washington: New Academia Publishing, 2011. 15-30.

Breaking Dawn: Part I. Dir. Bill Condon. Summit Entertainment. 2011.

Brown, Wendy. *Regulating Aversion: Tolerance in the Age of Identity and Empire*. Princeton: Princeton University Press, 2008.

————. *States of Injury: Power and Freedom in Late Modernity*. Princeton: Princeton University Press, 1995.

Butler, Judith. "Restaging the Universal: Hegemony and the Limits of Formalism." *Contingency, Hegemony, Universality: Contemporary Dialogues on the Left*. By Judith Butler, Ernesto Laclau and Slavoj Žižek. London and New York: Verso, 2000. 11-43.

Carter, Margaret L. "The Vampire as Alien in Contemporary Fiction." *Blood Read: The Vampire as Metaphor in Contemporary Culture*. Eds. Joan Gordon and Veronica Hollinger. Philadelphia: University of Pennsylvania Press, 1997. 27-44.

Celestin, Roger & Eliane DalMolin. *France from 1851 to the Present: Universalism in Crisis*. New York: Palgrave Macmillan, 2007.

Clements, Susannah. *The Vampire Defanged: How the Embodiment of Evil Became a Romantic Hero.* Grand Rapids: Brazos Press, 2011.

Gavrilos, Dina. "Becoming '100% American': Negotiating Ethnic Identities through Nativist Discourse." *Critical Discourse Studies* 7.2 (2010): 95-112.

Hobson, Amanda. "Brothers under Covers: Race and Paranormal Romance Novel." *Race in the Vampire Narrative.* Ed. U. Melissa Anyiwo. Rotterdam: Sense Publishers, 2015. 23-43.

Hollinger, Veronica. "Fantasies of Absence: The Postmodern Vampire." *Blood Read: The Vampire as Metaphor in Contemporary Culture.* Eds. Joan Gordon and Veronica Hollinger. Philadelphia: University of Pennsylvania Press, 1997. 199-212.

Huntington, Samuel P. *Who Are We? The Challenges to America's National Identity.* New York: Simon & Schuster, 2005.

Kaplan, Amy. "Manifest Domesticity." *American Studies: An Anthology.* Eds. Janice A. Radway et al. Oxford: Wiley-Blackwell, 2009. 17-25.

Kirkland, Ewan. "Whiteness, Vampires and Humanity in Contemporary Film and Television." *The Modern Vampire and Human Identity.* Ed. Deborah Mutch. New York: Palgrave Macmillan, 2013. 93-110.

Kymlicka, Will. *Liberalism, Community, and Culture.* Oxford: Oxford University Press, 1989.

Laclau, Ernesto. "Universalism, Particularism, and the Question of Identity." *The Identity in Question.* Ed. John Rajchman. New York: Routledge, 1995. 93-108.

Laclau, Ernesto and Chantal Mouffe. *Hegemony and Social Strategy: Towards a Radical Democratic Politics.* 2nd ed. New York: Verso, 2001.

Levina, Marina and Diem-My T. Bui. "Introduction: Toward a Comprehensive Monster Theory in the 21st Century." *Monster Culture in the 21st Century: A Reader.* Ed. Marina Levina and Diem-My T. Bui. New York: Bloomsbury, 2013. 1-14.

Lewis, Frederick. "The Impact of Transformations in National Cultural Identity upon Competing Constitutional Narratives in the United States of America." *International Journal for the Semiotics of Law.* 25.2 (2012): 177-195.

Lister, Ruth. "Sexual Citizenship." *Handbook of Citizenship Studies.* Eds. Engin F. Islin and Bryan S. Turner. Thousand Oaks: Sage Publications, 2002. 191-207.

Loza, Susana. "Vampires, Queers, and Other Monsters: Against the Homonormativity of *True Blood.*" *Fanpires: Audience Consumption of the Modern Vampire.* Eds. Gareth Schott and Kirstine Moffat. Washington: New Academia Publishing, 2011. 91-117.

Magill, David. "Racial Hybridity and the Reconstruction of White Masculinity in *Underworld.*" *Race in the Vampire Narrative.* Ed. U. Melissa Anyiwo. Rotterdam: Sense Publishers, 2015. 81-90.

Meyer, Stephanie. *Twilight.* New York: Little, Brown and Company, 2005.

Moffat, Kirstine, and Gareth Schott. "Every Age Has the Vampire It Needs: An Introduction." *Fanpires: Audience Consumption of the Modern Vampire.* Eds. Gareth Schott and Kirstine Moffat. Washington: New Academia Publishing, 2011. 3-13.

Loving Monsters

Norton, Anne. "Engendering Another American Identity." *Rhetorical Republic: Governing Representations in American Politics*. Eds. Frederick M. Dolan and Thomas L. Dumm. Amherst: University of Massachusetts Press, 1993. 124-141.

Peacock, M. Jess. *Such a Dark Thing: Theology of the Vampire Narrative in Popular Culture*. Eugene, OR: Resource Publications, 2015.

Poole, W. Scott. *Monsters in America: Our Historical Obsession with the Hideous and the Haunting*. Waco: Baylor University Press, 2011.

Priest, Hannah. "Pack versus Coven: Guardianship of the Tribal Memory in Vampire versus Werewolf Narratives." *Undead Memory: Vampires and Human Memory in Popular Culture*. Eds. Simon Bacon and Kataryna Bronk. New York: Peter Lang, 2014. 213-238.

Rawls, John. *Political Liberalism*. Expanded edition. New York: Columbia University Press, 2005.

"The Reckoning." *Vampire Diaries: Season 3*. Writ. Kevin Williamson et al. Dir. John Behring. The CW, 2011.

"Release Me." *True Blood: Season* 2. Writ. Alan Ball et al. Dir. Michael Ruscio. HBO, 2009.

Sconduto, Leslie A. *Metamorphoses of the Werewolf: A Literary Study from Antiquity through the Renaissance*. Jefferson, NC: McFarland, 2008.

Scott, Keith. "Blood, Bodies, Books: Kim Newman and the Vampire as Cultural Text." *The Modern Vampire and Human Identity*. Ed. Deborah Mutch. New York: Palgrave Macmillan, 2013. 18-36.

Sibielski, Rosalind. "Gendering the monster within: Biological essentialism, sexual difference, and changing symbolic functions of the monster in popular werewolf texts." *Monster Culture in the 21st Century: A Reader*. Ed. Marina Levina and Diem-My T. Bui. New York: Bloomsbury, 2013. 115-129.

Smith-Rosenberg, Carroll. *This Violent Empire: The Birth of an American National Identity*. Durham: The University of North Carolina Press, 2010.

Twilight. Dir. Catherine Hardwicke. Summit Entertainment. 2008.

Underworld. Dir. Len Wisemen. Lakeshore Entertainment. 2003.

The Enemy Within:
Deconstructing Emerging Femininity
in Contemporary Monster Films

COCO D'HONT

As horror is an indefinitely expanding genre, with a seemingly unlimited capacity to absorb common cultural tropes and transform them into tokens of fear, it can be impossible to "see the forest for the trees." How can horror, or more specifically, its monstrous characters, be read, interpreted, analysed, and understood? While the study of horror and its characters has gradually evolved into a rich scholarly field,[1] the genre transforms so rapidly that academia sometimes struggles to keep up with the newest "trends," such as torture porn and the recent revival of vampire and zombie films. This essay explores a particular contemporary horror trope, namely the forest monster, as a cultural metaphor which enables the metaphorical visualization and narrative deconstruction of obscured but powerful social ideologies including, but not limited to, patriarchy and the nuclear family. It focuses specifically on two contemporary films in which the forest functions as a habitat of monsters which shape and determine the lives of the people they interact with. M. Night Shyamalan's *The Village* (2004) and Guillermo del Toro's *Pan's Labyrinth* (2006) both depict forest monsters as much more than "scary creatures." In these films, monsters acquire the status of, to borrow Judith Halberstam's description, "meaning machines" (21), visualizing and interrogating the inherent problems of the patriarchal family as a central social ideological construct.

The monster in the forest, or the forest as a monstrous space in itself, is not a new cultural phenomenon. *The Village* and *Pan's Labyrinth* are a continuation of a rich tradition in which the forest, the monster, the monstrous forest and the forest monster all interact to construct powerful fictional universes. The origins of forest monstrosity can be

---

1 See, for example, Carroll (1990), Clover (1992) and Jancovich (1992).

The Enemy Within

traced all the way back to the roots of modern civilization, since "the forests were the terrain out of which fairy stories . . . one of our earliest and most vital cultural forms, evolved" (Maitland 6). Forests are dark, hazardous places where travellers can easily get lost and become a prey for the creatures that lurk in the darkness. However, the mythical status of the forest is not restricted to its potential to cause actual bodily harm, but is equally influenced by its ability to function as a canvas for the exploration of the societies it appears to exist in juxtaposition with. Stories such as Nathaniel Hawthorne's "Young Goodman Brown" (1835) depict the forest as a fearful, threatening place, exactly because it highlights the inconsistencies and hypocrisies of the people who enter it, in Goodman Brown's case his ambivalent relationship with the Christian faith. Many twentieth-century horror films have adapted this tradition, with *Deliverance* (1972), *Evil Dead* (1983), and *The Blair Witch Project* (1999) as only a few examples. *The Village* and *Pan's Labyrinth* should be placed within this cultural framework, in which forests and monsters have metaphorical and analytical qualities.

At first sight, both films appear to depict the forest as a natural phenomenon which exists in a strong antagonistic relationship with civilization. The monsters hiding in the forest are suggested to threaten the fragile foundations of the human communities they interact with. *The Village* focuses on a rural community living in an unspecified past—not dissimilar to the seventeenth-century culture of the Pilgrim Fathers—in a picturesque valley surrounded by dense woodland. The villagers have no contact with the outside world because they never venture into the woods, which they believe to be the territory of "those we do not speak of." From the film's very beginning, the threat of these invisible monsters looms over the villagers. It particularly affects Ivy Elizabeth Walker, the daughter of one of the village's Elders. Ivy is blind, and therefore regarded as vulnerable by her peers, because she is unable to see the red painted warning signs the forest monsters leave on the village's houses. A similar sense of vulnerability surrounds Ofelia, the main character of *Pan's Labyrinth*. At the start of the film, she finds herself in a remote village in Northern Spain, surrounded by a forest which looks similar to the one in *The Village*. *Pan's Labyrinth* is set during 1944, shortly after the devastating Civil War, and Ofelia's stepfather is a Falangist determined to defeat the underground republican rebel movement. When Ofelia discovers a mysterious abandoned labyrinth in the forest which surrounds the village, she meets a faun who believes her to be the reincarnated daughter of the Underworld king, and asks

23

her to complete three tasks to prove her identity. Ofelia's adventures cause her to meet terrifying characters such as the Pale Man and the Giant Toad, which profoundly affect her life and personality. In both *The Village* and *Pan's Labyrinth*, forests become spaces of mystery and threat, where the films' protagonists encounter hostility, violence, and possible death.

In many respects, the focus of the films reflects the socio-cultural context in which they were conceived. While arguing that *The Village* and *Pan's Labyrinth* are intended as responses to their complicated socio-political context might be a step too far, the films do discuss key issues which dominated their extra-textual background, such as the division between self and other, inside and outside, and us and them. Both films were released after 9/11, during a period of extreme political turmoil, which caused George Bush Jr.'s Presidency to construct an "axis of evil" that had to be eliminated through a "War on Terror." It could be argued that films such as *The Village* and *Pan's Labyrinth* are more extreme, and self-consciously fictional, versions of the ideological constructions which emerged in the wake of the collapse of the Twin Towers. Critics such as William Chafe have argued that 9/11 invoked "[the] fundamental question of defining successfully a new vision for uniting Americans" (519). A key facet of his "new vision" was the conceptualization of a strict divide between America as an "imagined community" (Anderson 13) in contrast to "evil" enemies. "Either you are with us, or you are with the terrorists," Bush Jr. famously stated in a speech shortly after 9/11, drawing seemingly impenetrable boundaries around an imaginary "us" threatened by an ungraspable "them" ("Address"). One of the images which determined the shape of "us" was a return to a nostalgic conceptualization of the nuclear family as a stable basis for social organization.[2] Horror films such as *The Village* and *Pan's Labyrinth*, with their emphasis on nuclear families, are a fictional reflection of this development. Their father figures fight the dangers that hide in the forest in order to maintain and protect their vulnerable families, and therefore the stability of their own power and social position.

Horror as a genre is well-equipped to reflect and explore the implications of this anxious creation and maintenance of strict social

---

2 This phenomenon is a continuation of a trend which started well before 9/11. Earlier critical explorations by Lerner (1986), Zinn & Eitzen (1987) and Coontz (1992) highlight the political use of the nuclear family as an ideological construct, with Coontz criticizing the nuclear family as "an ahistorical amalgam of structures, values and behaviors that never coexisted in the same time and place" (9).

The Enemy Within

and ideological boundaries. In his exploration of the social function of horror during the 1990s, Noël Carroll argues that: "[t]he present horror cycle and postmodernism correlate insofar as both articulate an anxiety about cultural categories; both look to the past, in many cases with pronounced nostalgia; both portray the person in less than sacrosanct terms" (212). While contemporary forest monster films emerged in a different socio-cultural environment, they similarly complicate the strict ideological divisions drawn in their extra-textual context. They look at the past, both within and beyond fiction, to criticise the present and imagine the future. Their "axis of evil" is rarely straightforward and is suggested to extend into the heart of the communities the films describe. In this, the films exemplify the continuing evolution of horror films as postmodern cultural products, building from the status of horror during the 1990s in which "monsters within postmodernism are already inside – the house, the body, the head, the skin, the nation – and they work their way out" (Halberstam 162). Their protagonists transgress back and forth across the boundaries which surround their homes, and the threat of monsters hiding outside is complemented by the aggression and oppression the main characters face within their own communities. Ofelia, for example, is terrified of her violent stepfather, who has no empathy for her heavily pregnant mother and engages in viciously cruel acts of torture and murder. Boundaries which seem rigid are shown to be fluid, and monstrosity can be found "inside" the community as well as "outside" it. Forest monsters are specific examples of what Cohen calls the ideological "deconstructiveness" of monsters (14). They show what normally remains invisible and provide opportunities for the critical dissection of the social systems they represent. Like other types of monsters, they invoke a fear which is really caused by a "return of the repressed" (Moretti 102).

Forest monster films such as *The Village* and *Pan's Labyrinth* are especially effective as social reflections and interrogations because they explore how stories shape societies, and how the boundary between fiction and fact often becomes blurred in the process. Their criticism of "fictions" and narrative constructions goes hand in hand with a search for "the truth," a quest which reveals that truth can be a fictional construction in itself. Since both films supplement their horror aspects with elements borrowed from fairy tales, they become narrative playing fields where boundaries are explored and problematized in metaphorical form. This marriage of horror and fairy tale is a form of boundary transgression in itself, since both genres differ in their treatment of monsters. "[I]n examples of horror," Noël Carroll argues, "it would appear that the monster is an extraordinary character in our ordinary world, whereas in fairytales and the like the monster is an ordinary creature in an extraordinary world" (16). *Pan's Labyrinth* and *The Village* do not adhere to this strict distinction. Whether their worlds are ordinary or extraordinary is difficult to determine, as is the place monsters occupy in them. In *Pan's Labyrinth* the story contains a faun, an underworld princess, and a dangerous quest to find the truth. Whether these elements are "ordinary" in the context of the story remains ambivalent, as the film never specifies whether they are "real" or mere figments of Ofelia's imagination. *The Village*, on the other hand, fits in more easily with the gothic tradition, reflecting the work of authors such as Edgar Allan Poe and H.P. Lovecraft in its obsession with invisible monsters that threaten an idyllic community. The film thus fits in with a specific American tradition, in which horror fiction reflects the anxieties of its extra-textual context.[3] In both cases, the self-conscious fictionality of the films acts as a critical tool which allows for the dissection of rigid boundaries, both within and beyond the stories. The remainder of this essay focuses on one ideological construction which is especially prevalent in contemporary forest monster films: patriarchy as a model for social organization, and its effects on women and girls.

Observe to Control:
Deconstructing Patriarchy through Monstrosity

Both *Pan's Labyrinth* and *The Village* focus specifically on one important power mechanism which establishes, maintains and perpetuates social inequality. The films extensively discuss patriarchy, reflecting and exploring its impact on women and children, and envisioning alternative social constellations. The central position patriarchy acquires within the films is a reflection of their extra-textual context, in which the paternalistic nuclear family was revived as a central base unit of social organization. The increased visibility of the Christian Right in the political landscape after 9/11 meant that supposed "threats to the family," such as the Equal Rights Amendment, same-sex

---

3 Jancovich (1992) argues that "the canon of American literature is dominated by writers of horror fiction" (34), reading contemporary horror film as a cinematic continuation of a literary tradition which explores the ambivalent nature of ideological constructs such as the nuclear family (85).

The Enemy Within

marriage, and abortion, were once again central topics of debate. The confrontations between young female protagonists and forest monsters, depicted at such length in forest monster films, thus acquire a specific critical value as metaphorical moments in which women explore the effects of patriarchy, resist its oppressive effects, and carve out space to develop their critical agency. This narrative focus is a continuation of a long cultural history in which horror, fairy tales, gothic and supernatural stories revolve around gender-specific dynamics, and do not only reflect but also dissect the power relations of their extra-textual contexts. Whereas psychoanalytic and feminist critics such as Laura Mulvey regard film, and horror film in particular, as a reflection and perpetuation of gendered social inequality,[4] other theorists, including Mark Jancovich claim the opposite, and regard horror films as narrative spaces where gender relations can be re-negotiated.[5] Forest monsters are one branch of an ever-expanding tree of stories which all create fictional worlds in which gender-based power relations are explored, and potentially contested and transformed.

Initially, *Pan's Labyrinth* and *The Village* appear as perfect illustrations of patriarchy as "the manifestation and institutionalization of male dominance over women and children in the family and the extension of male dominance over women in society in general" (Lerner 239). Early in the films this form of social organization, however problematic, appears to result in stable communities where all members know their place. Women are invariably depicted as vulnerable, fragile beings with an extremely limited amount of agency, who need men to protect and dominate them. In this, the films adapt familiar fairy tale motifs such as the damsel in distress, the princess trapped in her castle, and the heroic prince who slays the dragon to save her. The vulnerability of female characters also nods to the position of the "scream queen" in horror films, in which "males and females are not evenly distributed over the categories . . . suggest[ing] that gender inheres in the function itself — that there is something about the victim function that wants manifestation in a female, and something about the monster and hero

---

4 Mulvey argues that the main pleasure offered by film is "scopophilia" (16), or the pleasurable use of observation as an (often gendered) exercise of power. Her application of this theory to the work of Alfred Hitchcock has been expanded into horror territory by theorists such as Clover (1992).

5 According to Jancovich contemporary horror films frequently explore "feelings of helplessness and anxiety" (85) caused by social institutions such as the family, and thus expands gothic fiction's function as "a rejection of patriarchy and repression" (20).

functions that want expression in a male" (Clover 12-13). On the surface of forest monster films, even minor rebellious acts of female characters ultimately confirm their position as "princesses," victims, and "scream queens." In *The Village*, Ivy's sister appears to disrupt the strict rules which determine social interaction within her community. Instead of waiting for Lucius, the man she is in love with, to ask her to marry him, she declares her love to him first. However, she seeks permission from her father before doing so. He seems shocked by her plan and, while giving her permission, urges not to tell anyone about it. When Lucius rejects her, the film frames this as a punishment for her courage. After temporarily breaking free from the conventions which dictate life within the village, Ivy's sister is drawn back firmly within its boundaries, and consoled by Ivy after the rejection. The transgression of patriarchal rules is thus temporary, the transgressor has been punished, and the stability of the patriarchal family is unaffected.

However, forest monster films do not depict patriarchy as a wholly benevolent phenomenon, and instead highlight how it facilitates inequality and oppression. *Pan's Labyrinth* comments explicitly on what Lerner has identified as the patriarchal "commodification of women . . . and female sexuality" (213-216) within the nuclear family, by describing how the reproductive capacity of women is hijacked to install and maintain a position of masculine superiority. The film opens with the arrival of Ofelia and her mother, pregnant with a son, at the remote base where Ofelia's stepfather, Captain Vidal, has set up camp with his Falangist army. Ofelia's mother is visibly struggling, suffering from nausea, and incapable of explaining to her daughter why she is in a relationship with a man she does not appear to love, and even seems to fear. When they arrive at the camp, Captain Vidal greets Ofelia's mother by touching her swollen belly, clearly suggesting that his priority lies with his unborn son and that he considers his wife to be nothing but a reproductive vessel. He urges Ofelia's mother to use a wheelchair, despite her protests that she is capable of walking. Throughout this brief opening scene, the pregnant woman is depicted as vulnerable, weak and insignificant, because the only part of her that really matters is the son she carries inside her. This image of femininity as weak and passive is contradicted by Ofelia's own behaviour. Even though her mother comments on Ofelia's attachment to her fairy tale books, telling her that she is "too old for that nonsense," Ofelia refuses to let go of her books. When her mother urges her to call her new husband "father," because "it's just a word," Ofelia refuses, and seems to take an instant dislike

The Enemy Within

to the man. The first time they meet she offers him the wrong hand because she is using her right hand to hold her stack of books. This brief exchange offers viewers a glimpse of what is yet to come: even though Ofelia appears to be a vulnerable little girl, she is strong enough to resist the patriarchal authority of her stepfather.

This anxiety provoked by the gendered inequality patriarchy creates is highlighted through the introduction of monsters in both films. Monsters, David McNally argues, "are warnings — not only of what may happen but also of what is already *happening*" (9). In *The Village*, monsters are both instruments which maintain patriarchal control, and creatures which embody the artificiality and instability of that control. Little is known about the monsters, since they are not spoken about, and as a result they are frightening *because* they are invisible. The fear the monsters provoke keeps the villagers within the limits of the village and prevents them from exploring the outside world. The film does feature some glimpses of the monsters, and they appear to be humanoid creatures dressed in red cloaks. But ultimately, the appearance of the monsters is less significant than what they *do*, and even their actions are shrouded in mystery. Halfway through the film the monsters invade the village, but because all the inhabitants hide in their cellars, they pass unobserved. The only sign the monsters leave are red marks on houses, and as no other acts than the painting of these warning signs appear to have been committed, the danger the monsters emanate is omnipresent and unspecified. Even though the villagers do not know what the red signs mean, they perceive them as warnings, and destroy every object that has "the bad colour." The film does not elaborate on the symbolic value of red as the colour of (menstrual) blood, but it does implicitly connect the colour red to anxiety, instability, and threat. The colour red seems to suggest that the stability of the village community is somehow endangered, even though the exact nature of the threat remains unspecified.

Pan's Labyrinth draws much more explicit connections between monstrosity and social order. Even though Ofelia's earliest confrontations with monsters occur in the forest, the most important one happens inside her home, reflecting the idea that "[i]t is 'at home', in your house — or in someone else's — that you are most at risk in a fairy story" (Maitland 204). In this regard, the fairy story reflects concerns voiced by some critics of the nuclear family, who claim it facilitates abuse, incest, and other forms

29

of violent control.[6] The most dangerous monster of *Pan's Labyrinth* is "already inside" and is a horrific reflection and interrogation of the patriarchal power which controls Ofelia's family. One of the quests Ofelia has to undertake leads her to the sinister Pale Man, a creature which lives in a secret room in her house. Contrary to the forest scenes, this scene is extremely bright and offers a clear view of the terrifying Man. The Pale Man's masculinity is no accident, the film suggests, when it shows that he eats children, in a horrific adaption of the Cronus myth. When the Pale Man notices Ofelia, he tries to grab her, presumably to make her part of the extensive buffet he is busy consuming. The Pale Man is thus a consumer, a terrifying exaggeration of Captain Vidal's need to "consume" the reproductive abilities of his wife. Moreover, he is an observer and a controller with the ability to inflict great harm onto Ofelia. The Pale Man highlights the connection between observation and control when he reveals that his eyeballs are located in the palms of his hands, rather than in his head. Watching and grabbing become intertwined activities, and patriarchal control becomes a simultaneous process of observation and physical restriction. Whereas the invisible monsters of *The Village* convey a sense that something is not quite right, a feeling which both facilitates and undermines patriarchal control, the Pale Man functions as a much more explicit metaphor for the harmful effects patriarchy provokes. Observation, restriction and control are exaggerated into a form of internalized monstrosity which threatens Ofelia, crucially, *inside her home.*

Even though the monsters initially appear to come from "outside" and threaten stable communities, both films explicitly connect them to the centre of the civilizations they interact with. Monsters become exaggerated representations of the violence existing *within* communities. Patriarchy, *Pan's Labyrinth* suggests, is a violent ideology which controls and represses women and children with devastating effects. *The Village* moves beyond this revelation when it uses the exposure of the "fakeness" of the forest monsters to describe patriarchy itself as an artificial construction. The only villagers who appear to know the truth about the monsters are the village Elders, including Ivy's father. Halfway through the film, her father explains to Ivy that the monsters are not real, but invented by the Elders, and based on old folk tales. He tells her that

---

6 Bell (1993), for example, claims that "[a]s opposed to placing incest on the side of the 'abnormal', feminist contributions suggest that, on the contrary, given the power dynamics of male-dominated society and the understandings of sexuality we live out, incestuous abuse is in a sense unsurprising" (3).

The Enemy Within

the Elders take turns in dressing up as monsters to scare the villagers into obedience, and even shows her where the monster costumes are kept. The monsters are revealed to be nothing but narrative inventions which serve the purpose of controlling the villagers and preventing them from wandering into the forest. For Ivy, the monsters are reshaped into the fictional representations and extensions of her father's power; and they invite her to question to what extent his power, based on a fantasy, is legitimate. This climactic moment, however, is not the end of the film. *The Village* proceeds to map the violent effects the village's paternalistic organisation continues to have on all its inhabitants, not just the women. When, after the discussion with her father, Ivy travels through the forest to find medication to treat her injured lover Lucius, she encounters one of the monsters. After the monster has attacked her, and she has successfully resisted it, the monster is revealed to be her friend Noah, who earlier stabbed Lucius because he was in love with Ivy. Even though the monster has been exposed as a "fake," it does not disappear, but acquires a new meaning as the representation of the continuous harmful influence of patriarchal notions of masculinity and power. Noah's violent acts are inspired by his need to "own" Ivy, and his death suggests that patriarchy does not only harm women, but affects whole communities.

Pan's Labyrinth takes this suggestion even further, after suggesting that its monsters embody the aggression of its masculine characters, and provide opportunities for the visualization and dissection of patriarchal violence. The exposure and resistance of violent masculinity in the context of the family, the film suggests, can function as the analytical basis for the exploration of larger social conflicts. *Pan's Labyrinth*'s Pale Man is a consumer with an insatiable need for more bodies, and appears as a deeply sinister equivalent of Ofelia's stepfather. Captain Vidal symbolically cannibalizes the body of his pregnant wife, blinded by his desire to have a son, and oblivious to her needs and health problems. Just like the Pale Man, he has no empathy and does not register the suffering he inflicts on those around him. Over the course of the film he tortures and kills several political rebels personally, seemingly taking a sadistic delight in inflicting as much pain and suffering as possible. Even when his doctor recommends having his wife transferred to a less remote location with better medical facilities, he rejects this advice, which directly results in his wife's death in childbirth. The Pale Man emerges as a barely disguised representation of Vidal's monstrosity, which turns Vidal's bloodthirst into explicitly depicted cannibalism, visualizing

31

the connection between patriarchy, control, and violence. However, Vidal's aggression is not restricted to his own wife and daughter, and the film extensively reflects his torture of prisoners and his own staff as examples of the atrocities occurring during the Spanish Civil War. The film suggests that making patriarchy into a central social ideology, and the paternalistic family as a model for social organisation, has the deeply problematic potential to legitimize, provoke, and perpetuate war, social inequality and human suffering.

Transgression as Power: Monsters and Ideological Instability

Forest monster films use monsters to visualize the hidden "monstrosity" at the heart of central social ideologies such as patriarchy. Power relations and mechanisms are exposed, and with this exposure comes a potential for criticism and transformation. To what extent forest monster films can provoke radical political change in their extra-textual context remains to be seen and it is likely that, for many viewers, the films are simply an entertaining escape from everyday life. However, a tentative exploration of how forest monster films use their depictions of "monstrous patriarchy" to address larger social conflicts seems fitting, particularly since their focus on the family is such a timely reflection of the post-9/11 cultural landscape in which they emerged. To this end, the final section of this essay looks at the forest explorations in forest monster films, analysing this move beyond the boundaries of the community as a journey into a liminal space where communities can be explored, reimagined, and reconstructed. In both *The Village* and *Pan's Labyrinth*, entering the forest is a transgressive and radical act which disrupts the coherence of the community and puts individual transgressors at risk. Both films suggest that the true danger of the forest does not lie in the confrontation with the monsters that occupy it, but in the break from the community that trespassing its limits entails. Both Ivy and Ofelia leave their safe communities to save the life of a loved one, but this quest comes with great personal danger, not so much caused by the dangers of the forest itself, but by the breaking of the rules their quests demand. Entering the forest thus becomes an act of resistance and deconstruction which functions as a symbolic establishment of individual agency, a dissection of existing ideological structures, and the creation of alternative models of social organisation.

32

The Enemy Within

In forest monster films, the forest comes to function as a liminal space where the strict power relations of the patriarchal system can be renegotiated and critically interrogated, and where women can construct and enact their own identities. For both Ofelia and Ivy, the act of transgressing into the forest carries powerful implications of resistance and rebelliousness. By literally stepping away from the communities that frame them as vulnerable women, they open up possibilities to establish themselves as individuals with the ability to make their own choices. Crucially, the supposed "weaknesses" of the female protagonists become their strengths which help them to navigate the forest safely, a narrative choice which constructs a more powerful form of femininity in the space formerly occupied by dominant masculinity. For Ivy, her blindness becomes a power which sets her apart from her peers. Because she is not distracted by the terrifying image of the forest monsters, she navigates by her own experiences rather than the instructions of others, and does not divert from her physical and symbolic path. Even though her journey through the forest is terrifying and disorienting, there appears to be some truth in Lucius's assertion that "those who are innocent" can navigate the forest safely. Because Ivy does not conform to the harmful patriarchal ideology which regulates her community, stepping away from it does not put her in immediate danger, and offers her the opportunity to revise her own position within the community.

In *Pan's Labyrinth*, Ofelia's transgression into the forest similarly becomes a symbolic journey which takes her beyond the limits of her paternalistic community, and into a space where she can invent a new, more powerful version of femininity for herself. Her transgression into the forest becomes a powerful moment of identity construction and ideological resistance. The film never clarifies whether Ofelia's encounters with the faun and other forest monsters are "real" in the context of the film's narrative universe, or figments of her imagination. Instead, it adopts a form of magical realism which combines harsh depictions of life during the Spanish Civil War with Ofelia's (possibly imagined) confrontations with mythical creatures. In doing this, the film does not depict Ofelia's dreamy nature and love for fairy tales as a sign of weakness or lack of maturity, as her mother does early on. Instead, her imagination becomes her strength, and allows her to envision herself independently from paternal authority. Early in the film, Ofelia is repeatedly ordered to look pretty, behave "well" and is not to let herself be distracted by the fairy tales her mother considers

33

her too old for. Her transgression into the forest allows her to step away from her abusive community, in which women have no function beyond reproduction. The encounter with the Giant Toad, which lives in a muddy nest underneath a tree, is a particularly powerful moment of resistance against idealized femininity. Before entering the Toad's nest, Ofelia takes off the "girly" dress her mother has made for her and continues her quest in her underwear. When she returns after having slain the Toad, she is covered in mud and her beautiful dress has been destroyed by the weather. Ofelia's explorations of the forest allow her to overcome her fears of dirt, disorder, and the unknown, and reinvent herself as a strong girl who is not "pretty," but does have the ability to resist dangerous toads and violent stepfathers.

Ivy and Ofelia use their newly gained powers in different ways, but both girls expose the problems inherent to the societies they originate from and create space for the imagination of alternatives. In *The Village*, Ivy's journey through the forest and her arrival on the other side radically alters the way the viewers perceive the film and invite critical reconsiderations, not only of the film itself, but also of the culture in which the film was conceived. Because the film lays bare how communities depend on the construction of shared narratives to create a shared ideological framework, and exposes the framework in the film as a fictional fabrication, it provokes complex questions about the way in which "us-versus-them" narratives shape our contemporary society. After walking through the forest and climbing over the wall that surrounds it, Ivy suddenly finds herself confronted with a park ranger. The viewers soon learn that she does not live in the nineteenth century, but in the modern era, and that the village where she has lived all her life is an elaborate construction invented and maintained by her father and the other Elders. After experiencing personal trauma, they decided to build a village away from the rest of the world, where they could live with their families without being corrupted by the violence of modern society. Ivy returns to her community with the medication that saves the life of Lucius, and it remains unclear whether she realizes that she has lived in a lie all her life. However, the viewer's perception of the Elders and their community has been profoundly disrupted, and the idyllic but highly regulated life in the village no longer seems as unproblematic as it was early on. Instead of a film about a woman trying to find her feet in a nineteenth-century village, the film becomes a narrative of power, deceit, and ideological construction, and asks complicated questions about the power of narratives and knowledge in relation to patriarchal

The Enemy Within

power and control. Not just monsters, but *stories about monstrosity*, are revealed to be instruments of control that rely on innocence, a lack of knowledge, and the installment of fear in the community. *The Village* implicitly questions the validity of this type of social organization and highlights its vulnerability.

Pan's Labyrinth adds to this sense of "inconvenient truth" when it depicts the potentially violent consequences of narratives and ideologies, and explores opportunities to resist this cycle of violence. The film's final scene revolves around the communication between fiction and fact, and suggests that imagination and reality do not exist as parallel universes, but as interacting worlds. Imagination, the film concludes, can have profound transformative effects which transcends the limits of fiction. At the end of the film, the faun asks Ofelia to kill her baby brother, so that his blood will open a portal to the Underworld and she can assume her position as its Princess. Ofelia refuses, and thus breaks the cycle of violence which has been set in motion by her father. While Ofelia's moral dillema could be described as fictional, it has a crucial effect on her real life, as Vidal chases her into the forest to save his son and ultimately kills her. The impact of Ofelia's choice extends beyond her own life, however, as her distraction of Vidal allows the rebels to conquer the camp and end his cruel regime. In the end, Vidal is shot by the rebels, and his son is saved by Mercedes, his housekeeper, who served as a spy for the rebel army. After Ofelia's death, the film shows how she is welcomed by the King of the Underworld, because her choice to save her brother was the morally right one. Ofelia's transgression of the boundaries between life and death, and fact and fiction, is permanent, but her imagination continues to influence the world she has left behind. Even though the film does not depict the aftermath of Vidal's death, it suggests that the end of his power regime permits the construction of an alternative form of social organisation which does not revolve around fear and violence. Ofelia's explorations of the forest thus result in a very literal "overpowering" of the masculine authority figure and the type of community it created.

Ideologies such as patriarchy, *The Village* and *Pan's Labyrinth* suggest, are both inventions or constructions, and systems that can be disrupted through the power of the imagination. Both films explore the boundary between fact and fiction in an attempt to identify ideologies as narratives, and create new narratives which can support new forms of social order. *The Village* invites a critical perspective on idealized depictions of family life as a basis of social organization, echoing non-

35

fictional criticisms of the patriarchal family as "an ahistorical amalgam of structures, values, and behaviors that never coexisted in the same time and place," which "denies the diversity of family life" (Coontz 9-14). *Pan's Labyrinth* explores the violent implications of using the strictly organized patriarchal family as a model for social organization, connecting alpha-masculinity to violence and even to far-reaching social events such as war. Together, the films reach a twofold conclusion which both praises and criticizes the importance of narratives as the basis of social organization and ideological communication. On the one hand, *The Village* cautions its viewers against taking stories for granted. It advocates individual agency and critical scrutiny to avoid widespread deceit. Even though its elaborate plot may seem unrealistic, the film does comment on the nostalgic idealization of America's past as a rural idyll, and suggests that critical confrontation is to be preferred over the creation of narrative comfort blankets. On the other hand, *Pan's Labyrinth* advocates the use of imagination and stories to resist oppressive ideological structures. While Ofelia's love for fairy tales suggests that she tries to create a dream world in which she can escape from the harsh reality of her life, imagination is also shown to have a more powerful function. It can overthrow oppressive power regimes and facilitate the construction of alternative forms of social organization. Both films thus promote stories as crucial social phenomena which both construct and reconstruct communities and civilizations.

Hiding in Plain Sight:
The Monster as a Central Social Phenomenon

Early on, forest monster films such as *Pan's Labyrinth* and *The Village* suggest that the monstrosity of forests and their occupiers lies in their unknown nature, in the fact that they radically differ from civilizations, and threaten the stability of the communities they are connected to. While both films maintain the idea of the monster as a creature which "incorporates fear, desire, anxiety, and fantasy" (Cohen 4), they proceed to prove Halberstam's point that postmodern monsters are "already inside [and] work their way out" (162). Not only are monsters shown to be constructions, either invented by authority figures to maintain their power, or made up by rebels to visualize opportunities for resistance, they are also firmly located *within* the communities they appear to exist

The Enemy Within

in opposition to. The true monster, forest monster films suggest, is not an outsider but a reflection of forces at work in the heart of the community. Specifically, monsters can function as metaphorical representations of violent patriarchy, or act as tokens of deceit to keep a population in line. In each case, though, they are deeply intertwined with the mechanics of the societies that invent them. The study of forest monsters, and the use of the forest as a horror trope in contemporary horror film, offers valuable analytical perspectives which highlight invisible ideological networks of power, and undermines black-and-white us-versus-them world views. Forest monsters appear as creatures with strong critical potential, not only as visualizations of what normally remains hidden, but also as disruptors of boundaries, social? constructions, and other power mechanisms.

Works Cited

Bell, Vikki. *Interrogating Incest: Feminism, Foucault and the Law*. London: Routledge, 1993.

Bush, George W. "Address to a Joint Session of Congress and the American People." 20 Sept. 2001. *The White House*. Web.

Carroll, Noël. *The Philosophy of Horror or Paradoxes of the Heart*. New York: Routledge, 1990.

Chafe, William H. *The Unfinished Journey: America Since World War II*. 7th ed. New York: Oxford UP, 2011.

Clover, Carol J. *Men, Women and Chainsaws: Gender in the Modern Horror Film*. Princeton: Princeton UP, 1992.

Cohen, Jeffrey Jerome. "Monster Culture: Seven Theses." *Monster Theory: Reading Culture*. Ed. Jeffrey Jerome Cohen. Minneapolis: U of Minnesota P, 1996. 3-25.

Coontz, Stephanie. *The Way We Never Were: American Families and the Nostalgia Trap*. New York: Basic Books, 1992.

Halberstam, Judith. *Skin Shows: Gothic Horror and the Technology of Monsters*. Durham: Duke UP, 1995.

Hawthorne, Nathaniel. "Young Goodman Brown." *Young Goodman Brown and Other Tales*. Ed. Brian Harding. Oxford: Oxford UP, 1998.

Jancovich, Mark. *Horror*. London: B.T. Batsford, 1992.

Lerner, Gerda. *The Creation of Patriarchy*. New York: Oxford UP, 1986.

Maitland, Sara. *Gossip from the Forest: The Tangled Roots of Our Forests and Fairtales*. London: Granta, 2012.

McNally, David. *Monsters of the Market: Zombies, Vampires and Global Capitalism*. London: Haymarket, 2012.

Moretti, Franco. "Dialectic of Fear." *Signs Taken for Wonders: On the Sociology of Literary Forms*. 1983. London: Verso, 2005. 83-108.

Mulvey, Laura. "Visual Pleasure and Narrative Cinema." *Visual and Other Pleasures*. 2nd ed. London: Palgrave MacMillan, 2009. 14-30.

Pan's Labyrinth. Dir. Guillermo Del Toro. Picturehouse, 2006.

The Village. Dir. M. Night Shyamalan. Buena Vista Pictures, 2004.

Zinn, Maxine Bacca and D. Stanley Eitzen. Diversity in American Families. New York: Harper and Row, 1987.

Twice Dead: Gender, Class, and Crisis in *Pride and Prejudice + Zombies* (2016)

ERIN CASEY-WILLIAMS
AND ERIKA CORNELIUS SMITH

"The etymology of the word *monster* has been traced to the Latin notion of *monstrum*...from *mostrare*, meaning to show, reveal, expose, unveil, display" (Castillo 161). Simultaneously foreign and familiar, the "monstrous" or grotesque reveals our gaze and forces us to question fundamental cultural constructs. By destabilizing the binary of "human" and "non-human," zombies and their recent resurrection in *Pride and Prejudice + Zombies* (2016) present new avenues for exploring the categorical ambiguity of race, gender, and social class. Thinking of zombies as a cultural metaphor can help us understand current national, racial, and politico-economic anxieties, and (significantly) how the application of Agamben's theory of bare life can be applied to understanding traditional gender roles and patriarchal family structures. We analyze how Burr Steer's 2016 *Pride and Prejudice + Zombies* film draws upon the zombie cinematic, class-based, and politico-economic history in its portrayal of zombies as those of the working class. We then examine to what degree the film does (and does not) attempt to reinsert the Final Girl trope into a subgenre that has marginalized such figures. In doing so we examine how competing figures of bare life (class and gender) engage in cycles of violence presided over by patriarchal social-space and biopolitical culture.

Why study monsters? According to Jeffery Jerome Cohen's introduction to *Monster Theory: Reading Culture,* monsters appear at sites of cultural crisis and enable the formation of many identities; they lend insight into what it means to be human (ontology, morality, intellect), to be embodied (race, gender, national identity, ethnicity), and to be a

39

part of or excluded from society, politics, culture, the world (6, 8). One could extend Cohen's insights to conclude that *specific* monsters and the way they are presented lend *specific* insights about certain elements of society, culture, history, identity, etc. In the last century, many different monsters have been represented on the silver screen; however, what seems enduring is a formula involving a passive, vulnerable, female (or damsel in distress) victimized by a monstrous male (*Nosferatu* 1922; *King Kong* 1933; Kubrick's *The Shining* 1980) and often saved by a heroic male figure (*White Zombie* 1932; *Creature from the Black Lagoon* 1954).[1]

The genre of horror film remains diffuse and continually splinters into new forms with changing conventions, especially in terms of identity and performance. One of the most popular forms in recent years is the zombie film. One must question what particular insights zombie films—and the popularity of the zombie figure—lend about national, gender, racial, and class identities and embodiments at the start of the twenty-first century. *Pride and Prejudice + Zombies* (2016) allows us to begin to answer this question, but first we must consider the conventions of zombie films in general and their historical situatedness. Although zombie films share many elements in common with other forms of horror—an emphasis on individuality and survival, a disease and deformation of bodily norms, an uncanny threat where the familiar but repressed is made strange and indelible—they remain distinct. Kyle William Bishop explores their pre-history and defining characteristics in *American Zombie Gothic: The Rise and Fall (and Rise) of the Walking dead in Popular Culture*, arguing that zombies are a uniquely American and unprecedentedly visual or cinematic monster (31). And yet, Bishop does not explore the degree to which zombie film (as a subgenre) fits within and deviates from traditional horror conventions, nor does he explicitly engage with their political mimesis, which limits our understanding of how zombie cinema at the beginning of the twenty-first century allows certain understandings of identity and its interplay with society.

---

1 For more on monsters and film theory see Tudor's *Monsters and Mad Scientists: A Cultural History of the Horror Movie*, Paul's *Laughing Screaming: Modern Hollywood Horror and Comedy*, McCarty's *The Official Splatter Movie Guide*, Carroll's *The Philosophy of Horror, or Paradoxes of the Heart*, Crane's *Terror and Everyday Life: Singular Moments in the History of the Horror Film*, Walton's *Mimesis as Make-Believe: On the Foundation of the Representational Arts*, and Grodal's *Moving Pictures: A New Theory of Film, Genres, Feelings, and Cognition*.

Zombie Political and Cinematic History

In zombie literature and film, the original brains-eating fiend was a slave not to the flesh of others but to his own. African scholars trace the ethnobiographic origins of the zombie archetype to Haiti, as the legend mirrored the inhumanity that existed there from 1625 to around 1800. They believe that when slaves were brought to Haiti and the *vodou* religion grew amidst diverse African traditions, the idea of the *zonbi* was born from the Kongo word for "soul," *nzambi*, as a projection of the African slaves' relentless misery and subjugation (Davis *Passage*).

By the time of the French Revolution the population of slaves in Haiti was somewhere between five- and seven-hundred thousand. Most were slaves imported from Africa, predominantly from the west central African region of Dahoumey (Kadish). The hard labor of the plantations along with the epidemics endemic to the tropics kept the mortality rate high. Nearly half a million African slaves perished during the fifteenth and sixteenth centuries, necessitating continuing importation of slaves from Africa (Kadish). The only escape from the sugar plantations was death, which was seen as a return to Africa, or *lan guinée* (literally Guinea, or West Africa). As Amy Wilentz notes, "the plantation meant a life in servitude; lan guinée meant freedom." In an effort to escape this system, enslaved Africans often turned to suicide by means of poisons and powders. Those controlling the plantations viewed this as the worst kind of thievery, since it deprived the master not only of a slave's service, but also of purchased property.

For the enslaved African, this choice also meant great risk in the afterlife. In *vodou*, all people die in two ways—naturally (sickness, gods' will) and unnaturally (murder, before their time). Those who die unnaturally linger at their grave, unable to rejoin ancestors until the gods approve, thus leaving their souls vulnerable. At any time, they may be snatched up by a powerful sorcerer (*boko*) and locked in a bottle which the *boko* uses to control their un-dead but un-living body (Hurbon 190). Zombification represented the worst nightmare of an enslaved Haitian: to be dead and still a slave, an eternal field hand. Some scholars even point to evidence that slave drivers on the plantations, who were usually slaves themselves and sometimes *vodou* priests, used this fear of zombification to control recalcitrant slaves and intimidate those who were despondent. In *The Serpent and the Rainbow,* Wade Davis noted that in the Haitian context, "the fear is not of being harmed by zombis; it is fear of becoming one" (187). William Seabrook's *Magic Island* (1929) reinforces this in discussions with Polynice, who argues that the first reaction to the zombie is pity, rather than fear (100).

Quoting Hurston, Bishop emphasizes that even the educated and the upper classes also feared the prospect of zombification, perhaps more so than poorer Haitians or the enslaved because "they ha[d] more to lose" (*Gothic* 55). Both as a sacred dance and a religion, *vodou* was expressly forbidden in the French colonies, and white colonists initiated multiple campaigns to eradicate the practice. In this context, Swiss anthropologist Alfred Métraux and others emphasize the ways in which *vodou* gave hope to the Haitians (52). Despite rigid prohibitions, *vodou* was one of the few areas of autonomous activity for enslaved Africans. As Carolyn Fick writes:

> As a religion and a vital spiritual force, it was a source of psychological liberation in that it enabled them to express and reaffirm that self-existence they objectively recognized through their own labor . . . Voodoo further enabled the slaves to break away psychologically form the very real and concrete chains of slavery and to see themselves as independent beings; in short it gave them a sense of human dignity and enabled them to survive. (44)

As an ideology, it provided "a kind of intersection between belief systems and political power" and an avenue for enslaved Africans to rebel, short of suicide, "uniting the common people against the central government and the prevailing economic system" (Eagleton 6; *Gothic* 52).

Existing somewhere between mythology and the rituals or social practices of the people, the zombie juxtaposes the social tensions with the political and economic realities of stratified Haitian society. In its roots are the extreme modes of deracination and exclusion from the *polis* and kinship, reconstituted bare enslaved life as a nameless, nonbeing. Giorgio Agamben's *Homo Sacer: Sovereign Power and Bare Life*, urges a reconsideration of theories of sovereignty as put forward "from Hobbes to Rousseau" (109). Responding to Foucault's theory of biopolitics, in which human life becomes the target of the organizational power of the State, Agamben argues that there exists a "hidden tie" between sovereign power and biopolitics, forged in the exceptional basis of State sovereignty (16). Sovereign power establishes itself through the

Twice Dead: Gender, Class, and Crisis

production of a political order based on the exclusion of bare, human life. The paradigm of the bare life captured in the sovereign ban Agamben finds in the figure of *homo sacer* of archaic Roman law (8). Stripped of legal status and expelled from the political community, *homo sacer* is exposed unconditionally to the potential for killing by anyone (183).

Modern democracies offer a new form of inclusion of bare life within the *polis*, established through linking citizenship, nation, and biological kinship. As the 1789 Declaration of the Rights of man proclaims, men do not become equal by virtue of their political association but are "born and remain" equal. Agamben argues that the modern citizen is "a two-faced being, the bearer both of subjection to sovereign power and of individuals liberties" (*Sacer* 125). Democratic citizens are thus bearers of both bare life and human rights, they are at the same time the targets of sovereign power and free democratic subjects.

In his work *Slavery and Social Death*, Patterson argues that a slave's liminality collapses both the political and the existential differences between the human and the inhuman, monstrosity and normality, anomaly and norm, life and death, being and "nonbeing," similar to the status of *homo sacer* in Roman law (Patterson 42, 44; Ziarek chapter 9). Thus in the eighteenth century, there existed in Haiti at least three levels of bare life within the *polis*, shaped by both socio-economic status and a racialized hierarchy. The balance of the population consisted of peoples of European ancestry and of mixed heritage, defined in the law of the colony as "white" or *gens de couleur* (people of color), respectively. The century of domination of white slave holders over African women also produced a subpopulation of *mulattoes*, who because of their white heritage were given special privileges that led to the accumulation of some land and wealth. They did not share equivalent social status with white elite, but were privileged in many ways above enslaved Africans (King).

The political and economic context of seventeenth- and eighteenth-century Haiti, fraught with struggles for representation and rights, endowed zombie lore with a history of displaced persons and racialized hierarchies, as well as anxieties over economy, production, labor, and property. Dendle, who traces the American popular cultural interest in zombies to the American occupation of Haiti between 1915 and 1934, writes: "Ghosts and revenants are known world-wide, but few are so consistently associated with economy and labour as the shambling corpse of Haitian vodum, brought back from the dead to toil in the fields and factories by miserly land-owners or by spiteful *houngan* or

43

bokor priests. . . . The zombie, a soulless hulk mindlessly working at the bidding of another, thus records a residual communal memory of slavery: of living a life without dignity and meaning, of going through the motions" (47).

Although early Hollywood interpretations of the zombie mythology were often oversimplified and exoticized, many show the zombie as a collapse of racial into economic slavery. Victor Halperin's *White Zombie* (1932), starring Bela Legosi as Murder Legendre, vicious *boko*, highlights such an existence in one particularly pitiful scene: in Legendre's sugar factory, Haitians are zombified and human beings are reduced to the role of cogs in a machine (10:46-12:41). Although this scene is set in Haiti, and draws on historical conditions from the island, Bishop points out that it would have also resonated with American audiences of the Great Depression who were often reduced to such mechanized roles in factories, and yet felt trapped by their economic circumstances in a kind of living death (*Gothic* 76). Factory workers and unemployed individuals in America during the Great Depression existed as a permutation of bare life in the biopolitical state: their lives "ceases to have any juridical value and can, therefore, be killed without the commission of a homicide" (*State* 139). As Foucault might put it, the state no longer cares to "make [these individuals] live" and thus is content to "let [them] die" through factory accidents or starving in the bread lines (241). Zombie terror is linked then to one's use-value to the state. As Stratton points out, "In the neoliberal version of that state, where rights are dependent on what people within the border of the state can offer to its economic wellbeing, the degree to which one is reprieved from bare life depends on one's economic worth. In this way, within the state, labour returns as an inverse measure of zombification" (278).

Zombies as Slasher Film Monster-Victims

In George Romero's genre-defining *Night of the Living Dead,* audiences were exposed to realistic horror images of human figures consuming raw flesh or murdering and eating their parents.[2] Romero's film overlaps with the conventions of other horror subgenres, primarily the slasher film. Cynthia Freeland's analysis of slasher films applies

---

2 For a discussion of the realism of Romero's film, see the documentary film *Birth of the Living Dead*, especially 21:00-22:17 and 41:20-42:33.

Twice Dead: Gender, Class, and Crisis

to zombie texts as well: "Characters get less interesting and spectacles of violence become more graphic and prominent," and there is a shift "away from plot to monstrous graphic spectacle" (187, 181). *Night* similarly privileges monstrous graphic spectacle: scenes of zombies tearing into and consuming human flesh are extended and memorable in their lack of musical accompaniment (1:14:30). Carol Clover expands the discussion of slasher films through their privileging of specific weapons like knives, swords, chainsaws that open the body and reflect an understanding of flesh as meat (32). Although guns are the primary weapon in early zombie films, recent additions to the zombie cannon demonstrate a shift toward the use of typical slasher weapons. Selena (Naomie Harris) and Jim (Cillian Murphy) use a machete and baseball bat respectively in Danny Boyle's *28 Days Later* (2002); Shaun (Simon Pegg) and Ed (Nick Frost) use a cricket bat and shovel in Edgar Wright's *Shaun of the Dead* (2006).

Although zombie cinema borrows many distinct characteristics from the slasher subgenre, more telling is the way these films deviate from in the characterization of the monster/villain and the survivor/hero. Zombies are undoubtedly the monsters of such films, but not because they are inherently evil (unlike the monsters Freeland is concerned with). Indeed, zombies have no evil motivation; they are just hungry for brains. But because there are many zombies and because they threaten the *polis*, zombies are able to be killed without repercussions; their bare life status turns them into not just monsters but also victims. Whereas the victim role had, in slasher films, been relegated to young women, it is now visited on any being who bears the visible signs of bare life—ambulation, hunger, unchecked reproduction—but is stripped of any use-value to the state. As Agamben claims, "the biological given is as such immediately political, and the political is as such immediately the biological given" (*Sacer* 148). The biological reality of zombies slides into the political decision that they must be killed uniformly, graphically, without remorse.

As part of this new slasher permutation, zombie films collapse the figure of the heroic male patriarch with the slasher serial killer examined by Clover and Freeland. Slasher villains are realistic male loners who kill primarily young women (Clover 28). Freeland helps us understand these characters' ability to endure and appeal throughout countless sequels: "realist horror creates links between the 'dark side' of male traits (violence, uncontrolled sexuality) and the heroic side (power, independence, and so on) [which] legitimizes patriarchal

45

privilege through the stereotyped and naturalized representation of male violence against women" (187). Serial killer monsters are a far cry from zombies, but do have a great deal in common with heroes of the zombie cannon. Bishop points out in "Raising the Dead" that Ben spends his time in the film savagely "bashing, chopping, and shooting people" and thus "becomes a type of mass murderer" (204). The gender roles of these new hero-killers are exemplified by Brad Pitt's Gerry Lane character in *World War Z* (2013), a patriarch that must protect not just his family but the entire world from the zombie outbreak. Employing a heroic masculinity in selective violence, he demonstrates individuality by separating from his family early on and, at the end of the film, using himself as a guinea pig to test zombie inoculation (1:40:00-1:45:00).

Violent masculine heroes in zombie films are very different from the female victim-hero of slasher films, whom Clover dubs the Final Girl, a character who is "abject terror personified" and "looks death in the face," yet "finds the strength either to stay the killer long enough to be rescued...or to kill him herself" (35). Freeland argues convincingly that we should see the Final Girl as a valuable glimpse of what it means to be *human*, which is necessarily a blend of both victim and hero (66). Both Clover and Freeland emphasize the distinctiveness of the Final Girl trope in slasher films and the interesting ways in which these narratives perpetuate (at least certain kinds of) female agency. If slashers award lone women agency and complexity, zombie films are more concerned with permutations of traditional nuclear families. Zombie films often witness the return of the "damsel in distress" ideology, even if heroic males fail to actually save threatened women: Barbara in *Night of the Living Dead*, Wichita in *Zombieland*, and Selena in *28 Days Later*. Sarah Trimble sees apocalyptic zombie films as acting out a "patriarchal survivalist fantasy" that necessitates male control over "women's bodies and reproductive labor" (295). Zombie films resurrect conventional gender roles as part of their endorsement of patriarchal family structures.

What does the comparison of zombie cinema with slasher subgenres tells us about the role of gender and of women, in particular? Barbara Creed in *Monstrous-Feminine: Film, Feminism, Psychoanalysis* and Sarah Alison Miller in "Monstrous Sexuality: Variation on the *Vagina Dentata*" have pointed out that women have often occupied the category of the monstrous. Women as victims of slashers bleed into the idea of the monstrous and can become, in zombie films, a kind of "third term that problematizes the clash of extremes" between monster-victim and killer-hero; however such a role is not one of liberation but of reduction

Twice Dead: Gender, Class, and Crisis

to another kind of bare life (Cohen 7). If zombies are a metaphor for displaced people that the state has no use-value for, and thus must be killed, then women are the objects on which the state exerts its power to "make live." Women must legitimately reproduce the next generation of killer-heroes even if they are never allowed to occupy such a role themselves: Fran in *Dawn of the Dead*, Lauri in the *Walking Dead*, and most women in the French series *Les Revenants*. This cinematic reflection of our current political ideology lends insight into why recent years have witnessed increasing legislation over women's bodies; such bodies are not seen as people, but as the property of the state and its ability to perpetuate itself. The biopolitical state is, necessarily, a patriarchal state and a patriarchal state slides insidiously into the biopolitical.

The Case of *Pride and Prejudice + Zombies*

Jane Austen's *Pride and Prejudice*, published in 1813, provides social commentary on manners, upbringing, morality, education, and marriage in the society of the landed gentry of the British Regency. The monarch on England's throne during the beginning of the nineteenth century was King George III; however, in 1811, George III was deemed unfit to rule, and became king in name only. Actual political power was handed over to his son, George IV, whose title was Prince Regent, giving the time period the name Regency.

Unlike the peaceful Victorian Era which followed, the Regency period was one of political turmoil. The British Empire had lost the American colonies in the American Revolutionary War, and gained no new territories after suffering defeat in the War of 1812. Meanwhile, Napoleon's rise to power in nearby France created anxiety and fear throughout Britain. In 1803 the Corsican general stationed his enormous "Army of England" on the shores of Calais—a menacing, visible threat to southern England. This prompted Britain to strengthen its own defenses, including increasing the size of the army and navy and building new reinforcements. To fund these efforts, taxes were increased on the British population. Political freedom diminished, as any attempt to expand the rights of citizens of England was generally viewed as treason (White).

Defensive war preparations, costly wars in the Americas, and the broader militarization of the British state exacerbated other economic issues: high taxes, skyrocketing food prices, and widespread

47

unemployment caused by wartime trade restrictions and new labor-saving industrial machinery. Ruth Mather notes that economic struggles forced many men to enlist. In the popular Lancashire ballad "Jone O'Grinfelt," the protagonist illustrates the choice between enlisting and starving: Jone tells his wife he will "fight oather [either] Spanish or French" before he spends another day cold and hungry (Mather).

Britain experienced change in all aspects of life as a result of these political upheavals and the larger Industrial Revolution. Scientific advances and technological innovations brought growth in agricultural and industrial production, economic expansion, and changes in living conditions. Although the first decades of the nineteenth century were marked by wars, financial crises and social unrest, Britain's industrial base grew rapidly, fueled by the expansion of international trade. Between 1809 and 1839 imports nearly doubled, from £28.7 million to £52 million, while over the same period exports tripled, from £25.4 million to £76 million. Ten years later these figures were £79.4 million and £124.5 million respectively (Atterbury).

Already the largest city in the Western world at the beginning of the century, London continued to expand, reaching a population of nearly 1 million by 1800 (Heyck). One out of every eleven Britons lived in the capital (Floud 17-35). National economic prosperity, however, did not evenly extend through British society. While skilled craftsmen and craftswomen such as nailers and weavers worked from their own cottages and purchased their own machines, allowing a modicum of independence, many laborers went into debt to buy their tools, or had nothing to sell but their own labor. Heyck notes that they were able to control the "rhythm of the labor themselves" but they worked long hours doing difficult work subject to the demands of merchant capitalists and the market (62). Most historians of the Georgian period characterize it as a time of contrast and paradox:

> between the majestic stability of the social hierarchy and the unseemly scramble of people for higher rungs on the social ladder; between the warmth of paternalist social relations and the naked lust for power; between the breathtaking wealth of a few and the heartbreaking poverty of the many; between the rituals of deference given by inferiors to superiors and the startling frequency of riots; and above all between the stately calm of agricultural England and the bustling aggressiveness of towns and commerce. (Heyck 47)

Twice Dead: Gender, Class, and Crisis

Anxiety over economic security, individual rights, and participation in the *polis* manifested in Georgian Britain in ways similar to other developing Western democratic governments. Within these shifting political landscapes, Agamben argues that bare life marks the hidden inner borders of modern politics where racialized and gendered targets for exclusion become the new living dead (*State* 130). This is illustrated by reform measures such as the 1832 Reform Act, for example, which increased the electorate from around 366,000 to 650,000 people (Evans 84). This amounted to nearly eighteen percent of the total adult-male population in England and Wales, yet it still excluded women and working class men (Pearce 324).

Writing in this context, Jane Austen's short career overlapped with one of the most transformative and tumultuous eras in British history. In a world marked by revolution abroad and unrest at home, Jane Austen's readers were aware that the she was "doing something new with the novel, that she was using it to describe probable reality and the kinds of people one felt one already knew" (Sutherland). Gillian Russell writes, "The hum of wartime, if not the blast or cry of battle, pervades [Austen's] fiction." This is particularly evident in *Pride and Prejudice*, where the presence of the troops at Brighton and militia officers like Wickham reflect wider concerns about the place of the military in English civil society (Sheehan).

Here, Grahame-Smith saw an opportunity to alter the text: "There's a regiment of soldiers camped out in Meryton for apparently no reason. It's not a big leap to say that the regiment is there to burn coffins and kill zombies" (Hesse). But the rewrite and insertion of zombies does more than simply add putrefaction and gore to the classic novel. As noted earlier in this work, the political and economic context of seventeenth- and eighteenth-century Haiti endowed zombie lore with a history of displaced persons, as well as anxieties over economy, production, labor, and property. The Regency period of Austen's *Pride and Prejudice*, marked by political upheavals and economic struggles, saw staggering unemployment as a result of the state's military policies and anxieties surrounding a potential French invasion. This led to the economic "displacement" of thousands of British citizens in search of employment, living on the verge of starvation, struggling to sustain themselves. In both Austen's original text and Grahame-Smith's rewrite, for example, Mr. Wickham laments, "A military life is not what I was intended for, but circumstances have now made it unavoidable, as they have for so many who intended otherwise with their lives" (68; 77).

49

Virginia Woolf, in writing about Jane Austen and Walter Scott, argued "their model, their vision of human life, was not disturbed or agitated or changed by war. Nor were they themselves. . . . . Wars were then remote, wars were carried on by soldiers and sailors, not by private people. The rumours of battle took a long time to reach England" (130-131). Although Austen references military officers and militia encampments, warfare remains a distant rumor, an almost "unmentionable" experience in her novels. Some scholars argue, however, that Austen's novels are in fact an ideal conduit for discovering the underlying structures and preoccupations of a population experiencing a distant war, living through wartime (Favret). The concern of wartime, as Favret argues, is "not necessarily about whether or not a war is justified or well-run; the concern is how one is to 'sit at home in the evening' and live through a war" (Favret). Mass protests and demonstrations spread fear of revolution throughout Regency England, particularly among the landed gentry, and the "unmentionables" of Grahame-Smith's 2009 literary mash-up bring conflict and war directly to the private homes and "private people" of Austen's world, demonstrating they were in fact always there.

In the *Pride and Prejudice and Zombies* novel, the "unmentionable" zombies conform to the larger themes of zombie literature: "It is a truth universally acknowledged that a zombie in possession of brains must be in want of more brains" (7). Rarely identified or described individually, they typically appear in lowly hordes, spilling out from the "In Between" surrounding the gated communities of London. They are often clothed "modestly," unless specifically noted as a tradesperson in the case of the blacksmith (95). A direct threat to the *polis*, "unmentionables" may be killed with impunity. At one point in the text, Elizabeth provides accompaniment on the pianoforte for Mrs. Hurst and her sister who sing: "When once the earth was still and dead were silent, and London-town was for but living men, came the plague upon us swift and violent, and so our dearest England we defend" (45).

Steer's film version of *Pride and Prejudice + Zombies (PP+Z)* also directly engages the themes of warfare and defense, and but provides greater context and attention to the anxieties of the Regency era subtly woven through Jane Austen's original text. Serving as narrator near the beginning of the film, Mr. Bennett clarifies, "It wasn't always like this my dear daughters. As the century began, Britannia was rich with worldwide trade. From the colonies, there came not just silks and spices, but a virulent and abdominal plague. Naturally many suspected the

Twice Dead: Gender, Class, and Crisis

French are to blame. Are you surprised?" (6:45). The plague afflicting Britain is not the result of Napoleon's actions, but connected to British colonial holdings. Maps and illustrations appearing throughout Mr. Bennett's narration date the period as 1700 to 1800. At the time, British imperial holdings included small sections of India, Central America, and the Caribbean, in addition to large portions of North America. The dual "plagues" of political turmoil and economic insecurity that marked this period, as highlighted in both Grahame-Smith's text and Steer's film, challenged the peace and prosperity of the British Empire. British subjects, as "unmentionables," experienced a form of economic bare life, an inescapable status of bare existence.

While Steer's film may unproblematically adopt the view that individuals of certain socio-economic classes are reducible to zombie-fied bare life, its attitude toward women is more complex. Unlike most of the recent zombie films of the early twenty-first century, *PP+Z* provides a number of different female heroes, or what Freeland or Clover might call Final Girls, who fight successfully against not only the zombie hoard but also traditional patriarchal roles for women. Elizabeth Bennet (Lily James) is perhaps the most obvious permutation of the Final Girl, a female who has been trained not only in the deadly arts and can read *The Art of War* in the "original Wu dialect," but also in the "female arts" of ballroom dance, drawing, and etiquette (28:48). She breaks many horror conventions regarding female behavior, stalking into the woods alone at twilight after rejecting Mr. Collins's (Matt Smith's) marriage proposal and confronting her mother's displeasure, despite warnings earlier in the film that "No one walks alone" (51:50, 37:45). Virginal, or at least discerning in her sexual attachments, Elizabeth functions here as Final Girl, but also places herself in a stereotypically dangerous situation; however, she is not attacked by zombies, nor is she saved by a (male) hero. Instead she meets with Wickham (Jack Huston) and accompanies him to a zombie chapel, to attend service for those zombies who retain some elements of their humanity. Throughout the film, Elizabeth is simultaneously masculinized and sexualized, in her prominently muscular upper torso and heaving bosom; she is seen dressing for a dance, slipping knives and guns into her satin garters; even Darcy (Sam Riley) remarks on both her eyes and her "muscular arms" (18:28, 11:15, 19:00). During her refusal of Darcy's infamous first proposal, she physically attacks him, kicking him across the room, and the subsequent fight results in a ripped bodice and skirt, displaying her whirling legs and undulating breasts (1:07:58).

51

However, this permutation of Elizabeth as female hero faces many of the same contradictions and conundrums that permeate Clover's and Freeland's understandings of the Final Girl. Just because she is a woman-hero does not make her a champion of feminist ideals or necessarily a threat to the patriarchy. The sexualization of Elizabeth throughout the film remains worrisome in its objectifying gaze; moreover, she does not demonstrate the fear or insecurity that Clover's Final Girl succeeds in spite of, or that Freeland finds so telling of the human experience. Steer's Elizabeth Bennet remains, rather than a fully developed or complex Final Girl character, a mash-up of traditional feminine and masculine traits. One way this can be understood as distinctly *not* enabling toward women is the suggestion that ideal women must adhere to traditional female roles in that they can sing, dance, remain serenely beautiful and virginal until marriage, *but also* be physically fit, trained in various self-defense techniques and methods, and know at least as much if not more about traditionally masculine hobbies and pursuits as the men in their lives. And yet, it is undeniable that the characterization of Elizabeth as mash-up of violent heroine places distinct stress on the traditional zombie film formula of male heroes and domesticated females. In the climax scene of the film, it is Elizabeth who saves Darcy from the villainous Wickham (a zombie passing as human) in a subversive reversal of the damsel in distress blueprint, even riding into the scene on a white horse (1:32:13).

Elizabeth is not the only interesting rewriting of female agency — and subversion of cinematic stereotypes — in the film, nor are all the characters reproduced faithfully from Grahame-Smith's novel. In the novel, Charlotte accepts Mr. Collins's proposal because she has been infected by the zombie plague; this is often read as a metaphor for women's situation in Austen's time, and marriage as a kind of living death and thus a feminist criticism of this patriarchal institution (Beard 3, Nelson 346). However, in the film, Charlotte (Aisling Loftus) remains uninfected and Mr. Collins becomes lovable comic relief. In this way, the film loses the biting satire and feminist criticism of marriage in patriarchal society, but also suggests that getting married is not quite the feminist-death and patriarchal-living-death that it seems. Given that she is able to survive the zombie apocalypse and marries a goofy, ultimately likable, non-traditionally attractive clown (played by Matt Smith of *Doctor Who*), Charlotte presents an alternative to either the Final Girl or zombie-victimization for women and suggests a valuable new perspective.

Twice Dead: Gender, Class, and Crisis

Although the novel suggests a feminist critique of marriage in its portrayal of Charlotte, such does not extend to additional agency for Elizabeth. Grahame-Smith portrays Darcy on a horse, saving an unarmed and outnumbered Elizabeth from "a fast-approaching herd of unmentionables" at Pemberley, preserving the damsel in distress formula (203). Additionally, Darcy saves the Bennets in general from Wickham's machinations via physical violence (264). The novel critiques marriage but does not offer any alternatives to preserve female agency. The film, in contrast, presents two endings to the traditional story; in the first Elizabeth marries Darcy and Jane (Bella Heathcote) marries Bingley (Douglas Booth) and the quartet seem to live happily ever after in traditional (patriarchal) marital harmony. And yet, after the screen goes black and the credits roll, lulling the audience into thinking the story is over, the movie restarts and the wedding party is attacked by a new hoard of the infected. Elizabeth and Darcy's eyes meet as they are confronted with this threat to their traditional arrangement and must decide if Elizabeth will take on her newly acquired role of domestic angel to be passive and protected at all costs, or whether she is to fight by Darcy's side as an equal (or perhaps even better) hero (1:42:08).

In a final alternative to either married zombification or isolated heroism, the film presents Lady Catherine played by Lena Headey of *Game of Thrones*. In the novel, Lady Catherine remains a threatening figure to Elizabeth and her future with Darcy—even engaging in a physical fight to the death (293). Elizabeth intimates that she herself is a better fit for Darcy since Lady Catherine's daughter is neither "fetching," nor "trained in the deadly arts," nor has "strength enough to lift a Katana" (292). Grahame-Smith's novel preserves and foreground the division between women in patriarchal cultures where they must compete—either physically or socially—for the most eligible man: "you shall live. And for the rest of your days, you shall know that you have been bested by a girl for whom you have no regard" (296). In contrast, in Steers's *PP+Z*, Lady Catherine is presented as a slightly older version of Elizabeth herself; they both have dark hair, dress in leather pants, and fight zombies. Although she begins the film set against Elizabeth, and again confronts her about her rumored engagement to Darcy, Elizabeth refuses to engage her: "To take arms against you, my Lady, would be to take arms against England" (1:16:40). When Elizabeth defeats Lady Catherine's surrogate—an immense bald man—and refuses to stop pursuing Darcy, Lady Catherine accepts her: "I do not know which I admire more, Elizabeth Bennet; your skill as a warrior or your

53

resolve as a woman" (1:18:15). She then offers her home to Elizabeth's family, providing her protection and acceptance even of Elizabeth's inappropriate mother who, at the end of the film, is seated on Lady Catherine's right in Rosing Park's reception room, and inquires whether the lady's eye patch is "function or fashion" (1:36:19).

Unlike Grahame-Smith's novel, Steers's film suggests that women can come together through mutual admiration and respect, rather than being divided by their pursuits of eligible gentlemen. Indeed, in this film perhaps there is no Final Girl, because multiple female figures of various ages, skill-sets, and marital statuses survive the film. Additionally, the suggestion that Lady Catherine is the epitome of English defense and the final scene of her sitting in the throne room presiding over, and implicitly blessing the unions of the two couples, posits a possible matriarchal society rather than the patriarchal nation that characterized much of England's history. And yet doubts remain, not least because in order for the women in the film to unite in a mutually supportive female-centered society, they must unite *against* an Other. Lady Catherine, it must be noted, is the most dismissive of the idea of a peace between humans and sentient zombies, suggesting her extreme xenophobia is what allows her to finally accept Elizabeth and the Bennets more generally (1:00:10). While Rosings Park might be presided over by a woman, this remains a patriarchal society governed by a sovereign state. There can be no peaceful interaction because, in order for the women to be recognized as agency-filled subjects and not bare-life in themselves, they must relegate zombies — or individuals of certain economic status — to the role of bare life.

Additionally and worrisomely, Elizabeth and Darcy *do* marry and although their wedding night is interrupted by zombie hoards, there remains the question of reproduction and specifically the reproduction of the state. Even Wickham mentions this earlier in the film and its inferiority to the speed of zombie reproduction (1:01:03). By rejecting an alliance with those downtrodden and alienated from the state and throwing in with its strongest supporters, there are indications that Elizabeth will now become both defender and propagator of this sovereign state, reproducing only the right kind of individuals and slaughtering those that threaten the sovereign state. *PP+Z* thus makes clear the fact that the patriarchy and the state collude to perpetuate cycles of violence between class-zombies-bare life and gender-zombies-bare life, which are distinct and yet continuously blurred into one another. Perhaps films like *PP + Z*, even if intellectually interesting box-office

Twice Dead: Gender, Class, and Crisis

failures, allow us a glimpse of such systems existing in synchronicity. As we leave the theater, audiences are left asking, can we have marriage without patriarchy? Can we have politics without biopolitics? The perverse liminality of the monster, presenting more questions than answers, prevents it from being compressed into the neat and simple categories by which we assess our world and ourselves.

Bibliography

Agamben, Giorgio. *Homo Sacer: Sovereign Power and Bare Life*. Trans. by Daniel Heller-Roazen. Stanford: Stanford UP, 1998.

_____. *State of Exception*. Trans. by Kevin Attell. Chicago: U of Chicago P, 2005.

Atterbury, Paul. "Steam and Speed: Industry, Transport, and Communications." *The Victorian Vision: Inventing New Britain*. Ed. John M. MacKenzie. London: Victoria and Albert Museum, 2001.

Austen, Jane and Seth Grahame-Smith. *Pride and Prejudice and Zombies*. Philadelphia: Quirk Books, 2009.

Beard, Pauline. "Pride and Prejudice and Zombies [Review]." *Interface: The Journal of Education, Community and Values* 9.4 (2009): 1-5. Web.

Bishop, Kyle William. *American Zombie Gothic: The Rise and Fall (and Rise) of the Walking dead in Popular Culture*. Jefferson, NC: McFarland, 2010.

_____. "Raising the Dead." *JPF&T: Journal of Popular Film and Television* 33.4 (2006): 196-205.

Castillo, David R. "Monsters for the Age of the Post-Human." *HIOL: Hispanic Issues On Line* 15 (2014): 161-178.

Crane, Jonathan Lake. *Terror and Everyday Life: Singular Moments in the History of the Horror Film*. Thousand Oaks, CA: Sage, 1994.

Carroll, Noel. *The Philosophy of Horror: Or, Paradoxes of the Heart*. London: Routledge, 1990.

Clover, Carol J. *Men, Women, and Chainsaws: Gender in the Modern Horror Film*. 1992. Princeton, NJ: Princeton U P, 2015.

Cohen, Jeffery Jerome. "Monster Culture (Seven Theses)." *Monster Theory: Reading Culture*. Ed. Jeffery Jerome Cohen. Minneapolis: U of Minnesota P, 1996. 3-25.

Creed, Barbara. *The Monstrous-Feminine: Film, Feminism, Psychoanalysis*. New York: Routledge, 1993.

Davis, Wade. *The Serpent and the Rainbow*. New York: Simon and Schuster, 1985.

_____. *Passage of Darkness: the Ethnobiology of the Haitian Zombie*. Chapel Hill, NC: U of North Carolina P, 1988.

Dendle, Peter. "The Zombie as Barometer of Cultural Anxiety." *Monsters and the Monstrous: Myths and Metaphors of Enduring Evil*. Ed. Niall Scott, Amsterdam: Rodopi, 2007, 45-57.

Dessens, Nathalie. *From Saint-Domingue to New Orleans: Migration and Influences*. Gainesville, FL: UP of Florida, 2007.

Eagleton, Terry. *Ideology: An Introduction*. London: Verso, 1991.

Evans, Eric J. *Britain before the Reform Act: Politics and Society 1815-1832*. 2nd ed. London: Routldge, 2014.

Favret, Mary A. "Reading Jane Austen in Wartime." *Romantic Circles*. August 2008. Web. 15 July 2016.

Fick, Carolyn E. *The Making of Haiti: The Saint Domingue Revolution from Below*. Knoxville, TN: U of Tennessee P, 2007.

Floud, Roderick and D.N. McClosky. *The Economic History of Britain since 1700*. Vol. 1. 2nd ed. Cambridge: Cambridge UP, 1994.

Foucault, Michel. *"Society Must Be Defended": Lectures at the Collège de France, 1975-1976*. 1997. Ed. Mauro Bertani and Alessandro Fontana. Trans. David Macey. 2003. New York: Picador, 2003.

Freeland, Cynthia A. *The Naked and the Undead: Evil and the Appeal of Horror*. Boulder, CO: Westview, 2000.

Grodal, Torben. *Moving Pictures: A New Theory of Film, Genres, Feelings, and Cognition*. Oxford: Clarendon, 1999.

Hesse, Monica. "Seth Grahame-Smith Repurposes Jane Austen in *Pride and Prejudice + Zombies*." *The Washington Post*. 17 April 2009. Web. 15 July 2016.

Heyck, Thomas William. *Peoples of the British Isles: A New History, from 1688 to 1870*. 3rd ed. Chicago: Lyceum Books, 2008.

Hurbon, Laennec. "American Fantasy and Haitian Vodou." *Sacred Arts of Haitian Vodou*. Ed. Donald J. Cosentino. Hong Kong: South Sea International Press, Ltd., 1988.

Kadish, Doris Y. ed. *Slavery in the Caribbean Francophone World: Distant Voices, Forgotten Acts, Forged Identities*. Athens, GA: U of Georgia P, 2000.

King, Stewart. *Blue Coat or Powdered Wig: Free People of Color in Pre-revolutionary Saint Domingue*. Athens, GA: U of Georgia P, 2001.

Mather, Ruth. "The Impact of the Napoleonic Wars in Britain." *Georgian Britain*. The British Library. n.d. Web. 30 June 2016.

McCarty, John. *The Official Splatter Movie Guide*. New York, NY: St. Martin's, 1989.

Miller, Sarah Alison. "Monstrous Sexuality: Variations on the *Vagina Dentata*." *The Ashgate Companion to Monsters and the Monstrous*. Ed. Asa Simon Mittman, Peter J. Dendle. Farnham, Surrey: Ashgate, 2012.

Twice Dead: Gender, Class, and Crisis

Nelson, Camilla. "Jane Austen...Now with Ultraviolent Zombie Mayhem." *Adaptation* 6.3 (2013): 338-354.

Paterson, Orlando. *Slavery and Social Death: A Comparative Study.* Cambridge, MA: Harvard UP, 1982.

Paul, William. *Laughing Screaming: Modern Hollywood Horror and Comedy.* New York: Columbia UP, 1994.

Pearce, Edward. *Reform!: The Fight for the 1832 Reform Act.* New York: Random House, 2010.

Russell, Gillian. "The Army, the Navy, and the Napoleonic Wars." *A Companion to Jane Austen.* Ed. Claudia L. Johnson. and Clara Tuite. Malden, NJ: Blackwell Publishing, 2009.

Seabrook, William. *The Magic Island.* New York, NY: Harcourt, Brace & Co., 1929.

Sheehan, Lucy. "Historical Context for Pride and Prejudice by Jane Austen." *The Core Curriculum.* Columbia College. n.d. Web. 15 July 2016.

Stratton, Jon. "Zombie Trouble: Zombie Texts, Bare Life, and Displaced People." *European Journal of Cultural Studies* 14.3 (2011): 265-281.

Sutherland, Kathryn. "Jane Austen: Social Realism and the Novel." *Georgian Britain.* The British Library. n.d. Web. 30 June 2016.

Trimble, Sarah. "(White) Rage: Affect, Neoliberalism, and the Family in *28 Days Later* and *28 Weeks Later.*" *The Review of Education, Pedagogy, and Cultural Studies* 32 (2010): 295-322.

Tudor, Andrew. *Monsters and Mad Scientists: A Cultural History of the Horror Movie.* Oxford: Wiley-Blackwell, 1989.

Walton, Kendall. *Mimesis as Make-Believe: On the Foundation of the Representational Arts.* Cambridge, MA: Harvard U P, 1993.

White, Matthew. "Popular Politics in the Eighteenth Century." *Georgian Britain.* The British Library. n.d. Web. 30 June 2016.

_____. "The Rise of Cities in the Eighteenth Century." *Georgian Britain.* The British Library. n.d. Web. 30 June 2016.

Wilentz, Amy. "A Zombie is a Slave Forever." *The New York Times.* 30 Oct. 2012. Web. 21 June 2016.

Woolf, Virginia. "The Leaning Tower." *The Moment and Other Essays.* San Diego and New York: Harcourt Brace & Co., 1975.

Ziarek, Ewa Plonowska. "Bare Life on Strike: Notes of the Biopolitics of Race and Gender." *SAQ* 107.1 (2008): 89–105.

_____. "Bare Life." *Impasses of the Post-Global: Theory in the Era of Climate Change.* Ed. Henry Sussman. Ann Arbor: Open Humanities Press of Michigan Publishing. 2012. Web. 15 July 2016.

Filmography

28 Days Later. Dir. Danny Boyle. Perf. Cillian Murphy, Naomie Harris, Christopher Eccleston. Fox Searchlight, 2002.

Birth of the Living Dead. Dir. Rob Kuhns. Perf. George A. Romero, Fred Rogers, H. Rap Brown, Mark Harris, Elvis Mitchell. Gravitas Ventures, 2013.

Creature from the Black Lagoon. Dir. Jack Arnold. Perf. Richard Carlson, Julie Adams, Richard Denning. NBC Universal, 1954.

Nosferatu. Dir. F.W. Murnau. Perf. Max Schreck, Gustav von Wagenheim, Greta Schroder. Kino Lorber, 1922.

Pride and Prejudice + Zombies. Dir. Burr Steers. Perf. Lily James, Sam Riley, Jack Huston. Lionsgate, 2016.

Romero, George, dir. *Dawn of the Dead.* Perf. David Emge, Jen Foree, Scott H. Reiniger, Gaylen Ross. Laurel Group, 1978.

_____. *Night of the Living Dead.* Perf. Duane Jones, Judith O'Dea, Karl Hardman, Marilyn Eastman. Image 10, 1968.

The Walking Dead. Perf. Andrew Lincoln, Chandler Riggs, Norman Reedus, Steven Yeun, Melissa McBride. AMC, 2010-2016. TV series.

White Zombie. Dir. Victor Halperin. Perf. Bela Lugosi, Madge Bellamy, Joseph Cawthorn, Robert Frazer. Viacom Media Networks, 1932.

World War Z. Dir. Marc Forster. Perf. Brad Pitt, Mireille Enos, Daniella Kertesz. Paramount, 2013.

Wright, Edgar, dir. *Shaun of the Dead.* Perf. Simon Pegg, Kate Ashfield, Nick Frost, Lucy Davis. NBC Universal, 2004.

Zombieland. Dir. Ruben Fleisher. Perf. Jesse Eisenberg, Woody Harrelson, Emma Stone, Abigail Breslin, Amber Head. Columbia, 2009.

Monstrous Parasites, Monstrous Selves

Kristine Larsen

1. Violating the Boundary of the Body

In her seminal work *The Monstrous Feminine*, Barbara Creed (drawing upon Julia Kristeva's influential concept of abjection) argues that "the concept of a border is central to the construction of the monstrous in the horror film; that which crosses or threatens to cross the 'border' is abject" (11). In Kristeva's words, the abject "disturbs identity, system, order" (4), including the all-important (yet permeable) border between "I/Other, Inside/Outside" (7). Anthropologist Mary Douglas adds that, since the "body is a model which can stand for any bounded system," its very personal "boundaries can represent any boundaries which are threatened or precarious" (142). It is no wonder, then, that a fear of, and feeling of revulsion toward, parasites, is nearly universal across individuals and cultures. Not only do these creatures violate the boundary of the body (most often against our wishes and frequently without our knowledge), but, as Frédéric Thomas argues, the "idea that something is *eating you* is rather unpleasant" (1). Indeed, so primal is our fear of parasites that it has spawned not only a well-defined psychological phobia (parasitophobia), but a condition — delusional parasitosis — in which individuals will injure and scar themselves trying to dig out parasites they believe to reside within their bodies (Fellner and Majeed 135). So reviled are these invaders that the terms *parasite* and *leech* (an example of a parasitic creature) are used metaphorically as terms of derision when applied to individuals, companies, or entire groups of people (for example, bankers, welfare-recipients or lawyers). Understanding well the public's interest in, and fear of, deadly parasitic diseases, the media is quick to report cases of unfortunate individuals (often children) who contract the rare (and nearly always fatal) disease Primary Amebic Meningoencephalitis (PAM) each summer while engaging in seemingly harmless water sports. Reporters graphically explain how the insidious and now-infamous "brain-eating amoeba" *Naegleria fowleri* invades the brain through the nose and literally devours the victim's brain over an agonizing one to two weeks (Rettner). Surely this is a monster worthy of starring in a Hollywood blockbuster, despite its microscopic size.

Parasites have, indeed, become a familiar trope in the horror and science fiction screenwriter's toolkit. While the example that most often comes to mind is the bloody and grotesque "chestbuster" of *Alien* (1979), parasites became a Hollywood staple long before this film, and have not only endured, but thrived, until today. Indeed, the cinematic depiction of the horrific parasite has literally wormed its way onto screens both large and small since the 1950s, a fact not lost on both media experts and parasitologists. For example, Julien Fielding asserts that screenwriters need only "couple our natural aversion to foreign invaders with our fear of the unknown and *voila* — you get a winning formula" (189), while Carl Zimmer adds that the "blockbuster can rest its plot on parasites without anyone worrying that it will seem too esoteric" (112). It is therefore no surprise that the parasitic monster is legion in both film and television — it speaks to what horrifies and simultaneously fascinates us, the same double-edged sword of successful horror media that is reflected in the current fascination with the zombie. Indeed, parasitic organisms are often tapped as the source of a supposed zombie infection in literature, film, and television (Larsen, "Monsters Inside Me"). Our simultaneous fascination with, and disgust at, parasitic infections of the human body is perhaps nowhere more vividly on display (and willingly fed) than in the Animal Planet Channel hit series *Monsters Inside Me* (2009-present). The series' website boasts of retelling "the real-life, harrowing dramas of people infected by deadly parasites as doctors and scientists try to unravel each case before it's too late," graphically depicting "what happens to unsuspecting victims when the smallest creatures turn out to be the biggest monsters" ("About Monsters Inside Me").

This essay does not intend to be an all-inclusive survey of all parasite-based media,[1] nor even a complete review of 21st-century parasite film and television. Rather, the intent is to demonstrate how specific examples of 21st-century parasite-based horror and science fiction film and television series not only draw upon our fear of parasites, but also demonstrate a cognizance of the science behind such fear (as well as the fascinating biology of the creatures themselves). It

---

1 For a survey of the use of parasites in film and television, see Julien R. Fielding, "Inside/Out: The Body Under Attack in American Popular Culture."

Monstrous Parasites, Monstrous Selves

will be demonstrated that parasite media capitalizes on a, if not clearly parasitic, at least symbiotic, relationship with both real-world parasites and our very real fears and fascinations with these organisms in order to effectively entertain and simultaneously horrify the audiences. In addition, the question of why parasites are the repulsive darlings of 21st-century horror and science fiction media will be considered in light of post-9/11 anxieties.

2. It's All Relative: Parasites, Symbionts, and Other Inter-species Relationships

Categorizing the wide variety of "intimate relationships between animals of different species" — sometimes grouped under the etymological umbrella of _symbiosis_ — has not proven an easy task for scientists, as the terms that have come to be utilized "possess subtle nuances of meaning," leading to sometimes "arbitrary distinctions" between them (Chappell 1). For the sake of this paper, the admittedly simplified triumvirate of _mutualism, commensalism,_ and _parasitism_ will be adopted, under the broader umbrella of symbiosis. As defined by Kaplan (3), mutualism (confusingly sometimes simply called symbiosis) is a relationship in which both members of the relationship benefit, while commensalism involves a one-sided relationship in which one member benefits and the other (called the host) is not harmed; parasitism is defined as a relationship in which the host is harmed. Perhaps the most well-known example of mutualism is that between clownfish (made famous in _Finding Nemo_) and the sea anemone. The fish — protected from the sting of the anemone by a mucous coating — is itself protected from predators through the same sting, while simultaneously guarding the anemone from predators. An example from science fiction is the "joined Trill" of _Star Trek: The Next Generation_ and _Star Trek: Deep Space Nine,_ specifically as reflected in the character of Jadzia Dax. Rather than physical protection, the sentient symbiotic worm that is surgically implanted into a humanoid body enhances the knowledge and experience of the humanoid through a melding of their consciousnesses. Being a host to a symbiont is not only voluntary, but is considered a much sought-after honor. An example of commensalism can be found in the Galapagos Islands, where crabs remove ticks from the skin of iguanas (Matthews 8).

_61_

Parasites come in a variety of subcategories. For example, ectoparasites reside on the surface of the host yet withdraw body fluids (usually blood) from the host (Matthews 6). In the process, diseases can be transmitted to the host (as in the case of the mosquito and the protozoan that causes malaria, or the deer tick and the bacteria responsible for causing Lyme disease). Endoparasites live inside their hosts (e.g. a tapeworm). Parasitoids, a particularly brutal form of parasitism, are organisms that spend a portion of their life cycle — often a juvenile or larval stage — living within the host (frequently feeding upon it), and in most cases killing said host when the juveniles mature to a point that they can exist safely outside the host (Matthews 6-7). The infamous chestburster of *Alien* is a particularly vivid example, its horror perhaps magnified a thousand fold from the unfortunate life of a caterpillar hijacked by a parasitoid wasp. There are also neuroparasites, parasitic organisms that hijack the nervous system of the host and cause changes in behavior that simultaneously benefit the parasite (often by helping to ensure it is spread to new hosts) while causing behavior that harms (or even kills) the host. These latter three categories will be explored in greater detail in later sections of this work.

Fictional ectoparasites can elicit an especially visceral reaction from an audience, as the invader is boldly situated in plain sight. These can include artificially enhanced versions of real-world ectoparasites, such as the titular characters of *Ticks* (1993) and *Leeches!* (2003), which achieved their nightmarish size due to the ingestion of steroids (a clear play on the evils of performance enhancing drugs). More recent examples of effectively creepy ectoparasites are the Time Beetle and Kantrofarri of *Doctor Who*. The former (featured in the Series 4 episode "Turn Left" [2008]) is a large (approximately 2 feet long) beetle that attaches to the back of Donna Noble and feeds off the changes in time resulting from the parallel universe it creates around her. As Donna and the Doctor have never met in this alternative timeline, she is not present to save him from the Racnoss. The parasitic beetle feeds off the cascading ripples in time created by this seminal change in events. Although the beetle is largely invisible, it can be sensed, and even viewed for brief periods of time, by particularly sensitive individuals. Each fleeting glimpse of the beetle evokes a palpable response of disgust in the character who spies it, with Donna herself ultimately willing to throw herself in front of a large box truck to rid herself of the creature and the consequences of this Doctor-less universe.

Perhaps even more unnerving are the Kantrofarri or Dream Crabs of the 2014 *Doctor Who* Christmas Special "Last Christmas." These

Monstrous Parasites, Monstrous Selves

ectoparasites also depend on a parallel universe of sorts, namely that found in dreams. In an admitted homage to the iconic "facehugger" of *Alien* (Anders), these creatures encase the face and much of the head of their victims and, similar to leeches, inject their victims with anesthesia (here a dreamworld that offers them what they desire most) to dull the pain of their bite. But unlike blood, these parasites desire the same delicacy as Hannibal Lecter, as they devour the brain tissue of their victims, leading to their deaths. The Doctor describes the process to Clara using quite graphic imagery:

> You have a pain right here [the temple]. It's like an ice cream pain, but gentle. Do you know what that is? The skin and bone have been parted, probably half an inch, and something has pushed right into the soft tissue of your brain and is very slowly dissolving it. I want you to picture it this way. Somebody has put a straw right through your skull and is drinking you. You should be screaming with agony, but there's anesthetic. Everything around you right now, even Danny, especially Danny, that's the anesthetic. ("Last Christmas")

Not only does the anatomy of the Dream Crabs resemble the *Alien* facehuggers, but the episode is replete with references to the film series. For example, one of the characters compares the Dream Crabs to *Alien*'s facehuggers, while *Alien* appears on the list of films another character plans to watch on Christmas Day. It is no wonder that one reviewer called the episode "a rather scary one for Christmas day, too (well, not just for Christmas day)" (Brew).

Parasites are inherently frightening because they are ubiquitous in nature and can infect virtually every known type of lifeform, including humans. Parasites can invade nearly any organ of the human body, and at least 179 species of multicellular parasites attack humans (Thomas 1).[2] Parasitic worms alone are estimated to infect one-third of the world's human population (Curtis, "Why Disgust Matters" 3479). Overall, more than half of all species on earth may qualify as parasites, and since these species evolved in concert with their hosts, biologist Donald Windsor

---

2 There is also a rare condition known as a parasitic twin, a type of conjoined twin in which one of the members does not fully develop and is not viable as an independent organism. An example from science fiction media is the rebel leader Kuato from the original *Total Recall* (1990). A survey of other important examples can be found in Gordon Jackson, "A Field Guide to Science Fiction's Greatest Parasitic Twins."

argues that "it might even be conjectured that life without parasites is not possible" (2). Hollywood has even exploited the pervasive nature of parasites for its own benefit: while the gargantuan alien monster of *Cloverfield* certainly invokes awe in the audience, it is the dog-sized, insectoid creatures that are shed from the monster's body that directly cause the most gruesome deaths in the film—those bitten by these creatures literally explode, an apparent side effect of contact with their venom. Director Matt Reeves refers to these unnamed creatures as "parasites" and explains of the *Cloverfield* monster's designer, Neville Page, that

> Everything had to be grounded in reality, and he drew on biology and evolution, even though this creature never existed, to try to understand it. We wanted to have an intimate terror that went beyond something huge stomping around. . .. In our minds, [these little monsters] were an evolutionary development, a protection that had developed over thousands of years. The same way we have bacteria on our skin, this thing has parasites. (Carroll)

It is also important to acknowledge that the common definition of parasite in the late 20th century has tended to exclude prokaryotic organisms such as bacteria and archaea, as well as viruses, instead reserving the term for eukaryotes (organisms whose DNA is contained within a cellular nucleus), despite the fact that infectious viruses and bacteria certainly act parasitic (Chappell 1; Zimmer 125-6). Some authors (Despommier xiv) additionally exclude particular eukaryotes such as fungi from discussions of parasites. Such narrow definitions are not only scientifically dubious, but rather ironic. In the first instance, this is because scientific evidence supports an endosymbiotic model for the development of the eukaryotic cell (Martin, Garg, and Zimorski) in which, billions of years ago, various organelles found within eukaryotic cells (most particularly the nucleus, mitochondria, and chloroplasts) originated through a symbiotic relationship between single-celled organisms. In a very real sense, we are all symbiotic creatures at the fundamental cellular level. In the second instance, as will be explored later, some of the most fascinating (and most-often appropriated by Hollywood) parasitic behaviors involve fungi, viruses, and bacteria.

The sometimes fuzzy line between mutualism, commensalism, and parasitism has been effectively (and occasionally ineffectively) explored

Monstrous Parasites, Monstrous Selves

by screenwriters. An example of the former is the Goa'uld and Tok'ra of *Stargate SG-1* (1997-2007), while among the latter we find the Souls of *The Host* (2013). Largely panned by critics, the film adaptation of Stephanie Meyer's book of the same name focuses on the hostile hijacking of human bodies by sentient aliens called Souls. A romantic adventure aimed at a tween population, *The Host* eschews the grotesque physiological changes associated with parasites in many films. Instead, the main physiological change precipitated by the possession of a human body by a Soul is merely a modification of the appearance of the eyes. While the human population has been converted without their permission (indeed, the struggle of the few remaining independent humans to remain so is a central theme in the film), these extraterrestrials have brought peace and prosperity to our planet. Indeed, the increasingly ambiguous nature of this relationship is highlighted as the film progresses, with the human host Melanie and the Soul within her, Wanderer, coming to a rather mutualistic understanding by the end of the film. Indeed, reviewer Todd McCarthy refers to this relationship as a "dual-personality" rather than parasitic in his review of the film.

A more sophisticated exploration of the thin line between mutualism and parasitism is found in *Stargate SG-1*. Both the Goa'uld and Tok'ra represent biologically identical symbiotic beings, a humanoid host and an intelligent, snake-like endoparasite that co-opts both the actions and speech of the humanoid host. The difference is one of philosophy: whereas the Goa'uld hijack the host's body without permission, and completely control it without regard for the host's wishes, the Tok'ra enter into a more mutualistic relationship with a humanoid. Not only does the humanoid benefit from the knowledge and experience of the Tok'ra (as in the case of the Trill), but receives improved health and increased lifespan. Fans of the series have found the juxtaposition of these two relationships fascinating, and have tried to situate them within the scientific taxonomy of real-world inter-species relationships, as seen in the thread entitled "Is a Goa'uld technically a parasite/parasitic creature??" on the GateWorld Forum. Along with debating the relationship between the humanoid and snake-like creature (including issues of free will), respondents to this thread (similar to ecologists and even parasitologists today) struggle with the seemingly imprecise and insufficient scientific definitions of parasitism, symbiosis, and mutualism. But regardless of the exact categorization of these cinematic symbionts, one thing is clear: the viewing public is fascinated by the concept of one organism living inside another, especially if it involves our own species.

3. Mind Control: Neuroparasites

Julien Fielding argues that the fears of "the unknown and the 'other,' . . . communism, McCarthyism, and totalitarian political systems" are well-reflected in the science fiction and horror media of the 1950s (189). In particular, the "lost identity" film plays to the audience's anxieties of losing control of their own individual thoughts and actions to an alien invader (Fielding 191). Some of these films, most notably *Invasion of the Body Snatchers* (1956) and *It Came from Outer Space* (1953), deal with clones or doppelgangers, while others, such as *The Brain Eaters* (1958), feature true parasites. Such fears of being possessed by a parasitic consciousness and reduced to merely a shell or a puppet continue to be fed by Hollywood through the Cold War and beyond. Two 1967 episodes of the original *Star Trek* fall into this trope, "Operation: Annihilate!" and "Wolf in the Fold." In the former, a macroscopic, single-celled ectoparasite that is part of a collective hive consciousness attaches to the nervous system of its victims and controls their behavior. In the latter, an aggressive alien parasite moves from humanoid host to humanoid host throughout history (including Jack the Ripper), inciting murderous behavior. In one of the most (in)famous scenes of the 1982 franchise film *Star Trek II: The Wrath of Khan* a leechlike parasite called a Ceti eel larva slithers into Pavel Chekov's ear, resulting in both excruciating pain and susceptibility to mind control (in this case, not by the eel itself, but the film's titular villain). This scene lingers, like a parasite, in the visceral memories of viewers decades later. The author of the web article "10 Parasitic Horror Movies" offers the seemingly rhetorical question "Can you honestly tell me that you didn't squirm in your seat when Ricardo Montlebon [sic] . . . put those slimy brain worms in Chekov's ear?" (Casey). Likewise Joe Reid ponders of the classic scene (featuring what he describes as "a disgusting slug with giant pinchers") that it "couldn't possibly be as harrowing as 6-year-old-me remembered it. . . . OH BUT IT COULD."

The films *The Puppet Masters* (1994) and *The Faculty* (1998) also focus on alien parasites controlling the minds and bodies of their human hosts. Ironically, in the second film, it is the most individualistic of the students at the infected high school, the misfits who do not conform to standard social pressures, who are able to remain independent and ultimately vanquish the parasitic alien queen. Similarly, the 2009 episode of *Doctor Who* entitled "The Waters of Mars" focuses on an intelligent colony of parasitic waterborne alien microbes called The Flood that controls the minds of

Monstrous Parasites, Monstrous Selves

several human astronauts living on Mars. The unaffected astronauts destroy the colony rather than allow the infection to spread to Earth.

Over the last several decades, parasitologists have greatly increased their understanding of a particularly fascinating subclass of parasites, those that actually control the behavior of their hosts, termed neuroparasites. Kathryn Knight, News and Views Editor of the *Journal of Experimental Biology*, refers to these organisms as "particularly pernicious" in their ability to "hijack their host's nervous system, turning their victims into zombies" (i). Michael Dickinson opines that the study of such organisms—termed neuroparasitology—is where "science meets science fiction" (qtd. in Knight i). Such organisms are both biologically and philosophically fascinating—and disturbing—in their ability to subvert the free will of the host, yet in an evolutionary sense it makes perfect sense that parasites migrate to the brain, where they are largely protected from the "full fury of the host's immune system" (Adamo and Webster 1).

Neuroparasites not only modify the host's behavior, but often fatally so, subverting the deeply ingrained survival instinct of the host. For example, there are several species of ants that are susceptible to infection by the parasitic fungus *Ophiocordyceps unilateralis*. The parasite manipulates the infected ant to leave the safety of its colony and bite into a leaf, locking its jaw so it hangs there, helpless, as the fungus eventually takes over its entire body and kills it; afterwards, the spores are released to the environment, where they can infect more ants. More specifically, the fungus manipulates the ant to position itself relative to the sun and ground in such a way as to provide the necessary temperature and humidity for the growth of the fungus (Simon, "The Zombie Ant"). A nod to this real-world zombie parasite is found in *Splinter* (2008), in which a parasitic fungus attacks and incorporates into itself warm-blooded creatures (including humans), turning them into grotesquely deformed zombies.

While the reduction of ants to zombies is certainly perversely fascinating, the possibility of the human brain being influenced by a microscopic parasite is truly the stuff of horror movies. Such is the case of the protozoa *Toxoplasma gondii* (Toxo for short). This particular parasite has the potential to influence the behavior of mice and rat hosts in such a way as to make them more likely to be killed by cats; rodents infected with Toxo lose their fear response to the scent of cat urine (Zimmer 93). After being passed from the rat to the cat, Toxo is excreted in the cat feces, where it passes back to the environment and can infect a new rat host. However, human hosts can be infected via cleaning a pet's litterbox. Toxo infection is normally only life-threatening for fetuses and individuals with compromised immune systems, such as those with AIDS (Zimmer 69). However, over the past few decades there has accumulated considerable evidence of correlations between Toxo infection and a variety of changes in human behavior, including prolonged reaction times, increased suspicion, lower altruism, and lower sociability (Flegr 129). Correlations have also been found between Toxo infection and enhanced risk-taking behaviors, suicidal behavior, and schizophrenia (Webster et al. 101). Therefore the possibility of a parasite hijacking human behavior has moved from the realm of science fiction and horror to that of horrific science.

A particularly interesting permutation in popular media of the mind-controlling parasite that blurs the line between biology and theology is disembodied parasites (a twist on the trope of possession by malevolent spirits such as in *The Exorcist* [1973]) that hijack the bodies (and minds) of the living, and create zombies by reanimating the dead. Examples include the 2001 John Carpenter film *Ghosts of Mars* and the 2005 *Doctor Who* episode "The Unquiet Dead." In the first, human miners on Mars are possessed by the spirits — the titular ghosts — of an extinct Martian civilization. In response, the miners descend into murderous madness and mayhem. In the second example, the Gelth, an endangered species reduced to gaseous form in the disastrous Time War, pass through a rift in space-time to 1869 Wales, and reanimate the bodies of the human dead in order to achieve corporeal form once more. While one of the human characters believes the Gelth to be angels, the Doctor discovers their true intention — to inhabit every human corpse and kill as many living humans as necessary in order to provide bodies for the remainder of their kind.

The parasitic possession of both living and dead bodies by angels and demons is central to three recent television series, *Supernatural* (2005-present), *Dominion* (2014-15), and *Ash vs. Evil Dead* (2015-present). These series are striking in their emphasis of the clearly horrific neuroparasitic nature of the possession, and at times juxtapose this with a more benevolent mutualism (similar to the division between the two symbiotic relationships of *Stargate: SG1*). In the world of *Supernatural*, both angels and demons can possess human bodies; the main difference lies in the exercise of free will in these relationships. Unlike demons, angels (including the fallen archangel Lucifer) cannot enter a host without his or her express permission, and prefer to use so-called true vessels that can withstand the symbiotic relationship without causing irreparable damage to the host. Angelic possession can

Monstrous Parasites, Monstrous Selves

also be reversed if the host desires it. In contrast, demonic possession in *Supernatural* is clearly parasitic; it benefits the demon alone and causes harm (and even death) to the host. The host's free will is completely subsumed by this demonic neuroparasite, and reversing this type of possession is extremely difficult. The universe of the *Evil Dead* franchise (1981-present), comprised of four films and the television series *Ash vs. Evil Dead* (2015-present) contains only demonic possession, by the so-called Kandarian Demon who is invoked by the ancient book the *Necronomicon*. The Demon can possess both the living and the dead (as well as other aspects of the natural world such as trees), not only causing those possessed (zombies known as Deadites) to act completely out of character (i.e. as depraved murderers) but also mutating and perverting their bodies, which are kept animated even after suffering horrific wounds that would kill an unpossessed form. Only decapitation (preferably with cremation) can dispatch a Deadite.

Conversely, in the world of *Dominion* (loosely based on the 2010 film *Legion*) only possession by angels is possible, although in the peculiar theology of this universe angels can, indeed, act rather demonic. The series follows the struggles of human survivors of a 25-year-long war against the Archangel Gabriel and his army of "eight balls" — humans possessed by a lower order of incorporeal angels (the pejorative term deriving from the blackening of a possessed human's eyes). Eight balls seize their host bodies without permission and completely overwhelm the host's personality, although they can access the host's memories and can be influenced by the strong emotions of the host. For example, the angel who possesses Clementine falls in love with Clementine's husband Edward Riesen, who in turn keeps the eight ball as his hidden "mistress" for two decades. As in the case of *Supernatural*, this parasitic, involuntary possession is extremely difficult to reverse, and the prowess to "evict" angels is one of the developing powers of the series' savior archetype, Alex Lannon. While masquerading as a human, the higher angel Noma (who, like the archangels, has an innate corporeal form) almost falls victim to possession herself, but is able to repel the parasitic spirit of a lower angel. Her later description of the process not only draws on parasitic imagery, but voices the disgust commonly attached to physical parasites: "I could hear that angel whispering at me while she tried to slither inside me and take my body. What she tried to do was vile. I've never felt so contaminated" ("A Bitter Truth").

The sometimes thin line between mutualism and parasitism is reflected in another type of symbiotic relationship in the series, the rare "dyad." Touted by Julian, the human (corporeal) half of a dyad with the disembodied higher angel Lyrae, as a mutualistic relationship in which both personalities are equal partners — "Symbiosis, not destruction" — the truth is shown to be far more complex ("The Longest Mile Home"). In the case of Julian the differences between human and higher angel are difficult to discern (possibly due to the aggressive and vengeful personalities of both members of this relationship), and both members of the partnership clearly do benefit (Lyrae by becoming corporeal and Julian by attaining — except in the case of extreme physical injury — an immortal body), although it is suggested that the angelic side of the personality is dominant. However, despite the fact that Julian convinces the dying Edward Riesen that in willingly joining with the higher angel Duma and eschewing his mortality he will remain in other regards himself "in every way," this is quickly demonstrated to be a bald-faced lie ("The Longest Mile Home"). The spirit of Edward Riesen is instead quickly devoured by the parasitic Duma, and during an altercation with Riesen's beloved daughter, Claire, one of the leaders of the human resistance, Riesen is only able to control his body for a brief period of time before Duma asserts his dominance by shooting and mortally wounding his host's only child.

An especially creative series that shifts between theology and biology is *[Rec]*, a Spanish quartet of zombie films (2007-14). In the original film, an apparently viral zombie outbreak in a Madrid apartment building (filmed live by a local television crew trapped inside) is revealed in the end to have some unknown connection to demonic possession and illicit scientific experiments conducted by a Vatican-sanctioned scientist in the attic of the tenement. The first sequel *[Rec]²* furthers this theological explanation, with a priest leading a security team into the quarantined building to retrieve a sample of the virus-infected blood of the demonically possessed girl who started the outbreak, in the hopes of creating a cure. Ángela Vidal, the television reporter presumed to have been killed by the possessed child at the end of the original film, returns, but with a dark secret. She is also possessed, and secures her escape from the building as the sole survivor at the end of the film, the clear intention of the demonic presence to further the infection well beyond this single building. The coda to the film takes the series in a decidedly parasitic, although perhaps not well-motivated, direction. In a flashback to the end of the first film, it is revealed that the possessed child has passed a rather large, leach-like parasite to the reporter. This scene is particularly graphic, meant to maximize the "ick" factor. As Ángela struggles, the girl uses her fingers to pry the reporter's mouth open, and then bends over the supine woman and vomits the moist, wriggling worm into her

Monstrous Parasites, Monstrous Selves

mouth. As if to further clarify this event as being a sexual assault, the girl clamps her mouth against Ángela's, forcing her into a grotesque kiss. As the girl pulls away, the widest part of the parasite slithers from her lips and into the reporter's mouth, and finally the tail leaves the original host and disappears into its new victim. As the camera lingers on Ángela gasping for breath, the woman's throat and chest ripple as the parasite worms its way into her flesh.

As noted by critic Remy Carreiro, the connection between the virus/possession and the parasite is nowhere explained (or even presaged) in the film. An explanation is, however, found in the final film of the series, *[Rec]⁴ Apocalypse*. Picking up the storyline with Ángela's escape from the tenement, she and the special operations members who rescue her are whisked away to a quarantine ship where it is revealed that she is surprisingly not infected with the virus. Neither is she hosting the parasite, the creature having passed from her to one of the special ops members. As scientists on the ship attempt to create a cure for the virus from a purposefully infected monkey (who becomes loose on the ship and starts a new infection among the crew), a more scientific than theological explanation for the virus/parasite relationship is stressed. For example, when a crew member becomes ill, it is initially blamed on an infection of the Anisakis worm, a parasite that infects humans through eating raw fish ("Parasites - Anisakiasis"). It is revealed that the parasite is able to camouflage itself and initially escapes detection on the ship because, despite the fact that it transmits the virus, it does not necessarily infect the intermediate host that houses the parasitic worm. The parasitic worm therefore acts as a vector, similar to the malaria-carrying mosquito, except that the worm can avoid passing on the virus to an intermediate host if it chooses. The closest scientific analogue is the concept of the "competent vector" species, in which not all members will become infected with the virus in question (Gray and Banerjee 128).

4. Parasitoids and Grotesque Childbirth

As illustrated in the *[Rec]* series, there are obvious overtones of sexual assault in the violation of the host's body by the (often phallic) assailing parasite. Indeed, the archetype of the orally passed-on macroscopic parasitic infection by a science fiction monster, the larval stage (facehugger) of the titular character of the *Alien* series, is widely viewed as a clear rape motif (Creed 19; Dietle; Hughes). Likewise, the infamous chestburster scene in which the infant monster rips apart its host—its male "mother" Kane—in a bloody and deadly travesty of normal childbirth, has been interpreted as a reflection of wider fears of childbirth, abortion, and the violation of reproductive freedom (Cobbs 198; Doherty 183). While these aspects of the primal horror of *Alien* are certainly important, as they have been successfully dealt with by other authors, they will not be elaborated upon here. Instead, parallels will be drawn between the chestburster scene and similar monstrous gestations and births in other works of science fiction/horror and perhaps the most horrific yet fascinating form of parasitic manipulation of the host, the parasitoid.

A parasitoid is a species that utilizes a host in order to facilitate the development and success of the former's offspring, at the expense of the host (Knight ii). The host can play the role of reluctant nursery (with the larval stage developing within and often consuming the host's flesh), the young emerging in a scene eerily reminiscent of the chestburster scene of *Alien*, and/or nursemaid, with the host's behavior manipulated by the invader to actively serve as a bodyguard for the vulnerable young. In this sense, the parasite acts as both a parasitoid and a neuroparasite, with the host, in turn, robbed of its body, its free will, and, in the end, often its very life. While Charles Darwin found the habits of parasitic wasp larvae so repugnant that he wrote "I cannot persuade myself that a beneficent and omnipotent God would have designedly created the Ichneumonidae with the express intention of their feeding within the living bodies of Caterpillars" (qtd. in Zimmer 15), the public's fascination with this behavior is reflected in myriad YouTube videos and website articles featuring hapless hosts and the monstrous progeny that burst forth from their flesh. For example, Matt Simon (author of the Wired.com column "Absurd Creature of the Week") crows:

> Few parasitoids are more bizarre or disturbing than the wasps of the genus *Glyptapanteles*, whose females inject their eggs into living caterpillars. There, the larvae mature, feeding on the caterpillar's fluids before gnawing through its skin en masse and emerging into the light of day. Despite the trauma, not only does the caterpillar survive—initially at least—but the larvae mind-control it, turning their host into a bodyguard that protects them as they spin their cocoons and finish maturing. ("The Wasp")

Although the eating habits of the parasitoid larva are perhaps the most gruesome (and hence fascinating) component of the relationship in the

Monstrous Parasites, Monstrous Selves

eyes of the public, it is the mechanism behind the neurological control — the absolute subverting of the host's free will — that makes these creatures a subject of intense interest and research by parasitologists. In a plotline seemingly ripped from the screenplay of *[Rec]*[4], in 2015 researchers discovered that a virus carried by the parasitoid wasp and passed from its larva to the nervous system of the ladybird beetle (ladybug) host is responsible for the bodyguard behavior of the host towards the larva that emerge from its flesh (Dheilly et al.).

While *Alien* is certainly the best-known example of a parasitoid alien infecting a human host, it is not the first work to incorporate this trope, and numerous clones continue to be produced to this day. It is often a male who initially plays the role of host to the parasitoid, again playing with the conceptual incongruity of male pregnancy and childbirth. An early example is the 1958 B-movie *Night of the Blood Beast*, which combines the trope of the parasite animating a corpse as its host with the visceral horror of the parasitoid. In this case, astronaut John Corcoran's test rocket crashes back to earth, killing him. But in the vein of a familiar Monty Python sketch, he "got better," with the exception that he is "pregnant" with lizard-like embryos in his abdominal cavity, and his behavior is controlled via a telepathic link with a large parasitoid alien. As Corcoran nobly commits suicide to protect the Earth from the alien before the embryos mature, the thorny issue of how such young are to actually be "born" is avoided. A similar scenario occurs in the 1975 *Doctor Who* episode "The Ark in Space," featuring the human-sized parasitoid insects the Wirrn. The Wirrn queen lays an egg in an alien or human host; the larva subsequently devours the host's flesh while simultaneously absorbing its knowledge and experiences. More recently, the aggressive alien species the Magog of the television series *Andromeda* (2000-2005) provides an effective example of the inherent horror of parasitoids. Comprised of a single gender, the Magog parent lays eggs in paralyzed sentient hosts, who provide both food and the mutating DNA necessary to assure the continuation of the species in a Darwinian sense. Likewise the first season episode "Unleashed" of the series *Fringe* (2008-13) features as its "monster-of-the-week" a genetically engineered parasitoid that — like the wasp whose DNA is one of the components in the creation of this chimera — injects its young into Agent Charlie Francis. The characters engage in a race against time to find a way to kill the larvae before they burst out of their host's visibly undulating abdomen.

Particularly gruesome parasitoid aliens are featured in the *Alien* clone *Xtro* (1983) and the sequel *Xtro 2: The Second Encounter* (1990),

73

as well as the cult classic *Night of the Creeps* (1986). In the first film, Sam returns to his family three years after having been abducted by aliens in order to reclaim his son, Tony. Unfortunately, Sam has been physiologically modified by the aliens in order to survive on their world, and must first be reborn into human form. This entails a phallic tentacle shooting from Alien Sam's mouth and orally impregnating an innocent woman, who is soon after ripped apart vaginally giving birth to a full-sized, adult human Sam. A curious side plot to the storyline (which is never fully motivated or explained) involves Sam preparing an invasion of parasitic aliens. After greedily slurping down the contents of the eggs of his son's pet snake, Sam orally implants slithering embryonic aliens into his son's shoulder. Tony, in turn, later orally implants slightly larger snake-like creatures into his nanny's abdomen, and the young woman is turned into a parasitoid host. Her modified, unconscious body is strung up in a cocoon in a corner of the apartment, and large eggs (the size of ostrich eggs but having the gelatinous appearance of frog eggs) are delivered from a large, tubelike opening in her lower body. After Tony and Sam are retrieved by an alien spacecraft, Tony's mother returns to the apartment, and, in an obvious homage to the infection of Kane in *Alien*, the egg she picks up shoots out a phallic appendage and she becomes the next host in the cycle. In the sequel (which has little to do with the original film), the alien creature is a clear ripoff of the *Alien* monster, right down to the parasitoid chestbursting juvenile. The most original addition to the parasite behavior is that the "infection" can be passed on through a bite or scratch, playing upon a classic fear of the routine spread of disease.

Sluglike alien parasitoids burst forth from the head, not the abdomen, of their victims in *Night of the Creeps*. After entering the host through the mouth, the creature lays its eggs in the brain, which drives the host to madness while killing them (turning them into zombies). Eventually the next generation of slugs are grotesquely birthed as the host's head explodes, releasing numerous young who instinctively seek new hosts to infect. A single slug can also emerge from the host's mouth, shoot through the air and into the mouth of a new host. Although it can be argued that the parasitoid monster and the explosive birth of its young is derivative of *Alien* (Darnton), *Night of the Creeps* is a more direct offspring of the classic 1975 David Cronenberg film *Shivers*. The plotline centers on a mad scientist, Dr. Hobbs, who develops a neuroparasitic creature that infects humans through sexual contact (or bites) and guarantees its reproductive success by turning the hosts to violence

Monstrous Parasites, Monstrous Selves

and exaggerated sexual promiscuity. Another of *Shivers'* monstrous progeny is the similarly named *Slither* (2006). After a meteorite falls to earth, Grant Grant, the sexually frustrated older husband of lovely local school teacher Starla, is stung by an alien pupa and begins to mutate into a mind-controlled, horrific creature that craves raw meat (including the bodies of local pets) and shoots tentacles from his chest. After sexually violating his would-be mistress, Brenda, with one of said tentacles, Grant holds her captive in a barn, where in a scene called one of the "Greatest Scariest Movie Moments" by Tim Dirks, she balloons into a behemoth spherical mass of raw flesh. She subsequently explodes as she gives birth to untold numbers of leech-like parasites that immediately begin to infect the locals — turning them into zombielike creatures — by invading their mouths (and possibly other orifices). In a scene clearly derivative of a similar one in *Shivers* (and featured in the official artwork for *Slither*), the parasites menace a young woman in her bathtub. While in the earlier film the parasites sexually assault the young woman by entering her vagina and infecting her, in *Slither* the teenager is instead orally violated by the leeches but is able to pull the creatures from her mouth and escape.

Perhaps the most infamous perversion of human reproduction by a cinematic parasite occurs in the *Alien* prequel *Prometheus* (2012). Infertile astronaut Elizabeth Shaw is impregnated with the chimeric embryo of an equally monstrous predecessor of the *Alien* xenomorphs after her partner is intentionally contaminated. Realizing that she is carrying a horrific parasite, in one of the most controversial and iconic scenes in the film she programs a robotic surgery machine to perform a caesarean section and forcibly removes the creature.[3] This grotesque parody of pregnancy/birth is particularly effective in provoking horror, for as Barbara Almond argues, the "horrifying idea of giving birth to a monster seems to be ubiquitous" (53). Even in the case of a "normal" pregnancy, there is much of the process that fits the definition of a parasitic relationship. Firstly, the embryo or fetus is a distinct organism from the mother. Secondly, the growing organism is in danger of being recognized as foreign tissue by the mother's immune system and attacked. In order to prevent this from occurring, a very young embryo will first establish a barrier around itself made of specialized

---

3 A detailed analysis of the reproductive issues reflected in this film is beyond the scope of this work. See Huleatt, "*Alien*, *Prometheus*, Giger, and Rape" and Rosenberg, "*Prometheus*, Pregnancy, and the Persistence of Patriarchy," for further discussion.

cells that emit chemical signals that make the mother's immune system "sluggish" (Zimmer 136). Thirdly, the child in the womb only grows through feeding off the mother, receiving oxygen and nutrients through the blood vessels of the placenta, tissue that exists only to sustain the growing organism. Once born, the baby continues to feed off its mother's tissues, in the form of breast milk, symbolically — if not literally — devouring the mother.[4]

Thus in all these parasitoid films there is reference to the horrors of sexual assault, resulting in aberrant conception and the birthing of monstrous progeny through decidedly unnatural means. While much of this is certainly true (at least in a metaphoric way) of the parasitoids of nature, when applied to a human host there is a far deeper pool from which to dredge up the horrific, monstrous, and plainly disgusting.

5. Parasites: Feeding Upon the Perfect Storm of Disgust and Delight

Mark Hughes summarizes the inherent horror of the *Alien* series as follows:

> Rape, forced deadly birth, and then consumption. All by an alien with lots of S&M and phallic imagery, a series of violent disturbing attacks of different varieties that play upon some of our worst fears and views about some of the most repugnant, inhumane and unacceptable behaviors — particularly rape and consuming human flesh. On top of all of that, add the use of dripping spit, sweat, and blood — lots of bodily secretions that we find gross and disturbing — all in copious quantities. And we witness the face-rape, the chest-"birth," and the mouth-tongued head-bursting consumption of human flesh, in vivid detail at times. That's a combination of styles, themes, metaphors, and actual images that will terrify and disgust just about anyone.

The concept of the universality of disgust as a human emotion slithers its way through the scholarly literature of the past several centuries, starting with the work of Charles Darwin (Curtis, de Barra, and Aunger

---

4 In the horror film *Grace* this feeding of the baby upon its mother's breast is literal indeed. See Larsen, "When Procreation Becomes Perversion: Zombie Babies," for further analysis.

Monstrous Parasites, Monstrous Selves

390). What has been debated among anthropologists, biologists, and experts in other fields is the ultimate source of this primal reaction. Anthropologist Mary Douglas argues for a culturally relevant definition of what is considered "dirt" and against appealing to "abstract pathogenicity and hygiene" (based in part on the relatively late date of the scientific understanding of germs); dirt is simply "matter out of place," and can only considered as such in relation to some accepted standard of order (44). In Douglas's framework, an organism that enters the human body uninvited is undeniably worthy of being called dirty.

Julia Kristeva explains the connection between horror and abjection most viscerally in terms of bodily fluids and the corpse. While we live, we continually expel the filth of feces (and less often pus) as part of the process of remaining alive. One of the conditions of death is the loss of this ability to define a boundary between ourselves and filth. Kristeva defines the corpse as "death infecting life" (4). While such a definition is certainly relevant to a discussion of zombies, as Barbara Creed argues, horror media more generally reflects abjection, in three aspects: a heavy reliance by the filmmaker on (and on the side of the audience, a vicarious, perverse delight in) images of the corpse and bodily fluids; the centrality of the monstrous (that which transgresses the established border); and the "construction of the maternal figure as abject" (10-11). While this third aspect is well beyond the scope of this work, it is relevant to note that one of Creed's primary illustrations of this concept is the depiction of the monstrous feminine in *Alien*. Parasites can feed off and/or live within various bodily fluids as well as feces, and sometimes, as in the case of the previously described *Naugleria fowleri*, can lead to death. Alexandra French additionally points out that parasites are "remarkably abject figures. Without a host, a 'stolen body,' they fail to grow and soon die; in a sense, they have no body of their own" (49).

In contrast to Douglas's cultural hypothesis of disgust, work by Nesse and Williams (1995) and Pinker (1998) suggests that disgust has an evolutionary component; by refraining from contact with infectious agents, we improve our health and thereby increase the likelihood that we will survive to reproduce and pass down our genes. Valerie Curtis and collaborators discovered that universal causes of disgust reactions (found in cultures from across the globe) include bodily fluids, spoiled food, rodents, flies, and worms (Curtis and Biran 24). Not coincidentally, these can all harbor parasites as well as provide the method by which they are passed to the next victim. Curtis later broadened this concept into the "parasite avoidance theory of disgust (or PAT for short)" (*Don't*

Look 5). In this theoretical framework, disgust is explained as "a voice in our heads, it is the voice of our ancestors telling us to avoid infectious disease and social parasites" (Curtis "Why Disgust Matters" 3486). Work by Prokop, Fančovičová, and Fedor (237) supports this proposal; high school students in Western Slovakia demonstrate higher levels of disgust when shown pictures of organisms that are related to disease transmission (e.g., mosquitoes and ticks) as opposed to those that are not (e.g., earthworms and rhinoceros beetles). Such findings should come as no surprise, as numerous animals have evolved instinctive behaviors to avoid pathogens, including grooming to remove parasites, avoiding prospective mating partners who appear in ill health, and segregating feces within an individual's or community's territory (Curtis, de Barra, and Aunger 389). It should also be noted that not only will cancer patients sometimes consider their tumors to be parasites eating away at them, but controversial research also suggests that cancer cells may, indeed, act as a new parasite species invading its host (Sanders).

While disgust—and with it, a feeling of revulsion towards and fear of parasites—is apparently an innate human response, that which is disgusting simultaneously mesmerizes us. In the cinematic world, the *Alien* franchise is a particularly vivid example of the public's love-hate relationship with human-infecting parasites. We may view the chestburster through widely spaced fingers thinly veiling our eyes, but we *do* watch it—again, and again, and again. As Curtis explains,

> Freak shows at fairs have always been a draw, as have been body parts in jars. The news industry thrives on our desire for gory and ghastly details, and bloodsucking vampires, slimy aliens, and deformed monsters fuel the horror fiction and film industries. . . . It seems that we like to take our emotions out for a spin; we can't help taking a second look at something that makes us squirm. (*Don't Look* viii).

In addition to stories concerning the "brain-eating amoeba" *Naegleria fowleri*, the media also terrorizes and intrigues us with tales of individuals who lose chunks of flesh, including entire limbs, to infections of so-called "flesh-eating bacteria" (necrotizing fasciitis). The mental image of a microscopic invader actually consuming one's flesh invokes the iconic figure of the zombie, or other horrific monsters.

However sensational the language, the media is merely feeding the public what it has clearly demonstrated it wants to read and view in

Monstrous Parasites, Monstrous Selves

order to satiate its fascination with parasites. For example, the blogger Baronmind admits that

> Parasites fascinate me. The idea of creatures that have evolved in such a way that they're wholly dependent on other creatures is extremely bizarre, and more than a bit creepy. It's also exceptionally gross, in most cases; reading about parasites is one of the few things that causes me to have train-wreck syndrome. It's foul and disturbing, and I can't look away.

Columnist Renee Watson likewise admits "Maybe I am a bit strange, but I seriously love the gross side of the human body. I particularly love the beautiful and beastly creatures that like to invade us." In response, websites frequently feature lists of particularly sensational parasites and their unappetizing eating habits, such as "The 7 Most Horrifying Parasites on the Planet" (Hayden), "10 Parasites That Do Horrifying Things to People and Animals" (Plaue), and "Nature's Most Delightfully Depraved Parasites" (Bittel). The more savvy articles draw direct connections to monsters found in film and television series, such as the titular character of *Alien* and the brain infecting Ceti eel of *Star Trek* (Pappas). Scientists who study parasites have likewise capitalized on this public fascination with their objects of research, serving up blogs such as "Parasite of the Day" (Perkins and Leung) and "Creepy Dreadful Wonderful Parasites" (Pritt) that feature the riveting yet horrifying lifestyles of real-world parasites.

The seminal example of the successful capitalization by Hollywood on our perverse passion for parasites is Animal Planet's *Monsters Inside Me*, a series that *The New York Times* media critic Neil Genzlinger names "the scariest show on television." In his 2009 review of the premiere episode, Mike Hale of *The New York Times* explains that the series "with its shadowy re-creations of agonizing illness and horror-movie animations . . . reinforces a trend on Animal Planet and its sister channel Discovery: the depiction of the natural world in terms of violence, threat, warfare and paranoia." *Boston Herald* writer Mark Perigard (2009) warns that the premier episode is sure to "unsettle the hardiest couch potato" and that "After viewing this, you may never want to venture outside again." It is no accident that episode titles of *Monsters Inside Me* often sound openly zombie-ish, such as "Flesh Eaters," "The Eyeball Eater," "My Face Eating Parasite," and "The Flesh-eating Monster."[5]

5 A list of episode titles can be found at http://www.tv.com/shows/monsters-inside-me/episodes/

Other episodes name specific classes of parasites, such as "Worms are Eating My Lungs" and "Maggots are Eating Me," adding to the visceral response. Viewers apparently eat up this clear pandering to the horror genre, as the series is now in its 7th season. A statistical analysis of the parasites featured over the first six seasons (three case studies in each of 56 episodes) suggests that besides fearing contracting necrotizing fasciitis (featured in 5 episodes) and PAM (4 episodes), we have a deep-seated fear and fascination with maggots (6 episodes) and tapeworms (8 episodes). Indeed, in the first-season episodes, worms and flukes are featured in 44% of the case studies, insects (including maggots) in 39%, and protozoa in 44%.[6] While the statistics are similar in Season 2 (57%, 25%, and 33% respectively), in successive seasons the series broadens its definition of "parasite" to include viruses and bacteria (such as those that cause necrotizing fasciitis), fungi, and, surprisingly, foreign objects such as button batteries swallowed by children and survival implements left inside patients. Public anxieties, rather than scientific definitions, have, like a neuroparasite, apparently co-opted the minds of the series writers.

6. *The Strain*: The Ultimate Work of Parasitic Horror?

In an interview with *TV Guide*, Executive Producer Carleton Cuse explains of his FX horror/science fiction series *The Strain* (2014 —), "What really excited me about this project was the possibility of re-staking the claim — no pun intended — that vampires are scary-ass creatures" (Abrams). Central to the success of Cuse (and the authors of the source novels Guillermo Del Toro and Chuck Hogan) in achieving this is "a lot of emphasis placed on the biology of the vampires" (Abrams). As in the case of the *[Rec]* series of films (and the previously mentioned real-world case of the parasitic wasp and the ladybug), the infection is two-fold: a parasitic worm is transferred to a new host through the same six-foot-long stinger that the vampire (here termed a *strigoi*) uses to drink the blood of its victim. Interestingly, the stinger is reminiscent of the horrifically and exaggerated phallic appendages of the creatures in *Xtro* and *Slither*, which, themselves, draw inspiration from the iconic piston-like inner jaw of the *Alien* monster. The worm, in turn, passes on

6 The total is over 100% due to case studies that feature both an insect vector and the microscopic parasite transferred by the vector.

Monstrous Parasites, Monstrous Selves

a virus that changes the anatomy and physiology of the victim, hijacking its organs and converting them into grotesque caricatures that simply support feeding on victims and transmitting the virus-carrying worms (which can be done through a simple bite or scratch). Simultaneously the virus reduces the victim's mind to a zombie-like state that is not only obsessed with "turning" its loved ones, but is also easily controlled by the mind of the supreme vampire who started the infection in New York City, the Master.

Clearly the combination of a parasitic worm and a virus provoke a deep-seated disgust response consistent with the previously described PAT model. The apparent need of the Master to rest within the worm-infested dirt of his homeland (as well as the monstrous "birth" of the "feelers" — blind strigoi children — as they emerge from a mound of dirt after their parasitic conversion has been completed) designate the strigoi as examples of Douglas's dirt as matter out of place. The harmful effects of ultraviolet light on strigoi also strengthens their connection with infection and the "dirty," as ultraviolet radiation is used in medical and laboratory settings as a disinfectant (specifically killing and/or destroying the reproductive capabilities of bacteria, viruses and protozoa).

Blood is not the only bodily fluid that is highlighted in the series. As noted by CDC scientist Ephraim "Eph" Goodweather during an autopsy of an infected host, the "excreting organs have been fused into a cloaca," explaining for the benefit of the other characters (and the audience) that in "reptiles, birds, other lower animals, their urine and feces are all expelled through the same opening" ("It's Not For Everyone"). It is therefore appropriate when strigoi hunter Abraham Setrakian rebukes the former Nazi officer turned strigoi Thomas Eichorst by calling him "a creature of filth" ("Night Train"). Areas in which the strigoi have congregated (or individuals have lingered for any length of time) can easily be determined by the massive amount of ammonia-rich liquid excretions (similar to the guano of birds and bats) left behind, which shows up under ultraviolet light. As Setrakian notes in the novel, "The creatures will shit while they eat," to which rat exterminator Vasiliy Fet jokes "I guess a vampire doesn't have much need for good hygiene" (Del Toro and Hogan, *The Strain* 346).

This emphasis on the filth of bodily fluids obviously aligns well with both Kristeva's abjection hypothesis and the PAT model of disgust, however there are other important parallels as well. The strigoi/worm/virus combination plays the role of both neuroparasite (the mind-control

81

aspect) and parasitoid, as a single worm infects the victim, turning him or her into a host for the exponential reproduction of myriad worms that can burst forth from the body at a later time. Most notably, when the Master's human host body is damaged beyond repair, he selects another and transfers his consciousness by first smearing some of his worm-infested home soil into the new host's mouth, and then vomiting all of the parasitic worms from his old body into the mouth of his new one. Shown once in a flashback and once in the current day of the series, the ceremonial preparation of a new body (the manner by which the Master essentially reproduces himself) is undoubtedly one of the most grotesque aspects of strigoi behavior. In addition, in the pilot episode "Night Zero" Eph and fellow CDC scientist Nora Martinez discover some of the parasitic worms wriggling in the dirt and compare them to horsehair worms. Like the strigoi-creating worms of *The Strain*, horsehair worms are both neuroparasites and parasitoids, infecting crickets. A larva will bore into a cricket and grow to a foot in length within the host, stealing nutrition from the host (feeding like a vampire off the food in the cricket's gut). When the worm is fully developed, it exerts its mind control, forcing the cricket to commit suicide by jumping into a body of water, where the worm leaves the host and promptly breeds with another of its kind, continuing the cycle (Simon, "The Parasitic Worm").

There is a particular type of parasitoid behavior that is relevant to *The Strain*: those who become strigoi lose their ability for human procreation. Like in the 2007 film *Days of Darkness*, the external sexual organs of infected men shrivel up and fall off, and both these desexualized men and women conceive and give birth to the parasitic young (i.e., gestate worms in their bodies and then "give birth" to them to infect human victims). The process by which real-life parasites neuter, change the gender of, or otherwise prevent the normal reproduction of their hosts is termed parasitic castration (Lafferty and Kuris). For example, the parasitic bacteria *Wolbachia* can turn male wasps into females, kill male embryos, cause infected females to give birth to other infected females without fertilization by a male wasp, or make the sperm of males unable to fertilize the eggs of infected females. These strategies ensure the most effective reproduction and passage of the parasite to new hosts, as the bacteria can only infect mature eggs and not mature sperm ("Sequencing Wasp Genome"). Another example, mentioned in the second novel in the *Strain* series (Del Toro and Hogan, *The Fall* 134), is the *Sacculina carcina* barnacle. A female larva enters and infects a crab, retaining a small entrance to the crab's shell. A male joins with

Monstrous Parasites, Monstrous Selves

her through this entrance, and together they continually produce eggs within the host. To add insult to injury, the barnacle forms an egg sac exactly where the crab's own brood pouch would be, and chemically manipulates the crab into tending the invader's young as it would its own, until the crab spurts out the parasites from its infected body in a mockery of its own reproductive cycle (Zimmer 81-2).

The clearly abject nature of the parasite in general, especially the parasitoid, also brings to mind Kristeva's model for the nature of horror. It is therefore surprising to learn that, under the right conditions, it is actually beneficial to humans for usually malevolent monsters to violate the sanctity of the "I." In such cases, humans actually welcome the parasite inside themselves as willing hosts, achieving a temporary form of mutualism. The practice is actually millennia-old, dating back to ancient uses of leeches in the medical practice of blood-letting. While most people consider this practice to be medieval (literally and figuratively), an updated form of this therapy is embraced by the medical establishment, in the form of specially raised leeches and maggots that are used to prevent blood clots from forming in reattached limbs and aid in the healing of wounds and skin ulcers (Sherman 336; Singh 213). There is also evidence that the recent rise in industrialized countries of immune-mediated diseases such as multiple sclerosis and inflammatory bowel disease (IBD) is related to our reduced exposure to parasitic worms (Elliott and Weinstock 2012). In other words, there is such a thing as being too clean. According to the so-called "hygiene hypothesis," infections (including parasitic infections) occupy the attention of the immune system and dissuade it from turning it on itself (Stachowiak). Clinical trials of this "helminth therapy" (the intentional infection of humans with specific parasitic worms in order to produce specific immune responses) have shown promising results in the treatment of Crohn disease, IBD, and ulcerative colitis (Maizels 483). There are also stories of people using parasitic worms without a doctor's prescription, buying tapeworms on the Internet and intentionally ingesting them in an extreme effort to lose weight (Dahl 2013). These patients soon discover that having a 30-foot-long monster inside them leads to more severe effects than weight loss, such as malnutrition, severe abdominal pain, and even convulsions.

Given the apparent universality of feelings of disgust towards parasites, one concern of physicians has been whether or not patients would refuse helminth, leech, or larval (maggot) therapy, perhaps especially the last one, due to the obvious connection between maggots and rotting flesh/corpses. Surprisingly, studies have demonstrated that patients who are well informed about such treatments overwhelmingly agree to take part; perhaps this is because the innate desire for self-preservation (both in terms of our overall lives as well as individual limbs) overrides the so-called "'Yuk' factor" (Steenvoorde et al. 351). Interestingly, a significant number of patients in a study of maggot therapy reported "adverse reactions from social interactions," most commonly that others around them found the "idea of maggots eerie" (351).

Helminth therapy plays an important role in *The Strain*. Full-blown infection by the Master's worms leads to immortality for the host, albeit as a strigoi. However, significantly enhanced health (or, in the case of gunshot victim Coco, recovery from a mortal wound) without conversion into a strigoi can be temporarily granted to a human if the Master pierces his flesh and allows a few drops of his white bodily fluid (akin to blood) to be consumed by the human. This is how the critically ill and elderly Eldritch Palmer regains the health and vigor of a much younger man, and Eph's young son Zack's acute asthma is controlled. Setrakian likewise periodically distills the essence of the worms and injects it through eye drops in order to rejuvenate his 94-year-old body. Like many of the patients in the aforementioned maggot therapy study, Setrakian is on the receiving end of "adverse reactions"—a palpable sense of disgust—from those around him when his secret is revealed.

For these reasons, *The Strain* appears to be perhaps the ultimate work of parasitic horror, masterfully drawing upon cutting-edge science, a distinguished history of fictional works of parasitic horrors, and research on human disgust responses. In the words of MTV's Shaunna Murphy, the series is notable for "Effectively using body horror unlike anything we've ever seen before." A final question remains: why is the early 21st century unique as a suitable host for a series such as *The Strain*?

7. Conclusion: Parasites and Post-9/11 Paranoia

Parasites continue to manipulate human behavior to this day, not only in the literal neuroparasitic behavior of Toxo infection, but in our well-founded fear of parasitic infections. A number of world-class athletes pulled out of the 2016 Summer Olympics over fears of the Zika virus (spread by parasitic mosquitoes), while others took the precautionary

Monstrous Parasites, Monstrous Selves

step of freezing their sperm in order to guarantee that they will not pass on a potential infection to their future children (Branch). Parasites have also clearly been used in popular culture as metaphors for the issues infecting the society of any given decade. As Kirk Combe reminds us, "the fictional beasts a culture creates provide insights into that culture: its fears, its anxieties, its hatreds, its prejudices, its most troublesome problems (934). For example, as Zimmer reflects, Cronenberg uses parasites "to expose the sexual tension buried under the blandness of modern life" in *Shivers*, while in *The Faculty* they "represent the stupefying conformity of high school, which only outsiders can fight," and in *The Puppetmasters* the parasite infection is a reflection of the threat of Communism (115). Given the continued success of the cinematic and televisual parasite to horrify and entertain us, it is necessary to ask to which aspect(s) of 21st-century culture they most clearly speak.

John Cobbs reflects that the central theme of *Alien* is "the 'horror within,' the terrible threat that is more terrible because it invades the ostensibly safe confines of the self" (201). Similarly, as Bruce Kawin argues, due to the nightmare-infecting image of the sluglike parasites of *Shivers*, the film moves from merely drawing upon our fear of "diseased people" to the larger horror of "powerful, active monsters" who "not only symbolize but also effect the damage that can be done by a foreign organism that can bond with us and change our nature, making us over for its own purposes and killing us as we were" (88). In the post-9/11 world, the parasite metaphor — the outsider who invades and destroys the intimate body — takes on heightened meaning. In a culture of enhanced suspicion and fear of those who are different or who come from the outside, the parasitic invader feeds upon rampant xenophobia, racism, and religious intolerance. Indeed, as Adam Wadenius argues, not only is the "sudden and unprovoked attack carried out by a monstrous other" central to much of post-9/11 media, but "particular attention is paid to accentuate the foreign, or outside nature of the threat to normality." An Internet search demonstrates that the term "terrorist parasite" is often applied to individuals, groups, and even entire countries (such as Israel and Pakistan), while undocumented workers are also often negatively referred to as parasites. It is not coincidental that in Nazi propaganda Jews and other minority populations were referred to as "*parasites* on the German people's *body*," more specifically "*bacteria, viruses, bacilli, elements of decomposition, maggots, bloodsuckers, vipers, vermin*, which cause or spread *deadly illnesses*" (Musolff 220; emphasis his). The analogy is not only universally understood, but feeds upon universal fears.

85

It is therefore no surprise that, as Kevin Wetmore explains, the "post-9/11 world—fraught with terrorism, war, disease, financial meltdowns, and global climate change—proves an extremely fertile ground for vampire films" (5-6). Similar arguments have been made to explain the popularity of zombie media (Bishop). *The Strain* openly references a number of political hot-button issues, from euthanasia and the right to die (in the case of the infected), to a mistrust of mega-corporations and their links to government conspiracies (as in the case of the fictional Stoneheart Corporation). The dangers of a loss of civil liberties in the name of local or national security in the age of the Patriot Act has also been highlighted in the series, reflected in the so-called "Enabling Act" creating the office of Special Director of Security in New York City in the series. Indeed, in a post-9/11 world, the setting of the novels and of the series in New York City is itself an intentional creative decision meant to play on deep-seated fears of destruction perpetrated by the Other. The novels go even further, exploiting other widespread 21st-century anxieties such as the safety of nuclear power plants and nuclear weapons stockpiles and global climate change.

Parasitologist Thomas Cameron wrote in 1958 that "No organism is an entity unto itself" (vii). This is not only true in terms of the myriad inter-species relationships that include mutualism and parasitism, but of human culture as a whole. Just as the outer boundary of our skin and the defense mechanisms of our immune system can be hijacked by parasites, regardless of our personal hygiene, similarly in a global economy there is no fool-proof method that guarantees that those who would do us harm are prevented from penetrating our borders or escaping the defense system of our intelligence agencies and law enforcement. Such a realization can understandably lead to anxiety and even to a political form of delusional parasitosis (similar to the McCarthyism of the 1950s) where every itch or blemish of the skin represents a parasite (in the form of a terrorist) that has invaded our body, our neighborhood, our country. It is therefore ironic that our innate fear of parasitism may have actually aided in the creation of deep-rooted fears of those whose origins lie outside our cultural or religious groups as a way of avoiding infection by parasites (Fincher and Thornhill). In the end, it seems that our visceral fear of the xenomorph of *Alien* and xenophobia apparently have much in common.

Works Cited

"About Monsters Inside Me." *Animal Planet*. 31 October 2012. Web. 5 June 2016.

Abrams, Natalie. "*The Strain*: Is FX's Vampire Drama Too Graphic?" *TV Guide*. 11 July 2014. Web. 7 June 2016.

Adamo, Shelley A., and Joanne P. Webster. "Neural Parasitology: How Parasites Manipulate Host Behaviour." *Journal of Experimental Biology* 216 (2013): 1-2.

Almond, Barbara. *The Monster Within: The Hidden Side of Motherhood*. Berkeley: University of California Press, 2010.

Anders, Charlie Jane. "This Concept Art of Doctor Who's Facehuggers is Wonderfully Repulsive." *Io9*. Gizmodo. 6 January 2015. Web. 30 June 2016.

Baronmind. "De Vermis Mysteriis." *We're All Mad Here*. Baronmind. Livejournal. 23 Aug. 2006. Web. 23 June 2016.

Bishop, Kyle. "Dead Man Still Walking: Explaining the Zombie Renaissance." *Journal of Popular Film and Television* 37.1 (2009): 16-25.

Bittel, Jason. "Nature's Most Delightfully Depraved Parasites." *Wild Things*. Slate.com, 12 Aug. 2015. Web. 16 June 2016.

"A Bitter Truth." *Dominion*. SyFy. 30 July 2015.

Branch, John. "Among Olympians' Zika Precautions: Fewer Guests, Frozen Sperm." *New York Times* 15 June 2016.

Brew, Simon. "*Doctor Who* Christmas Special: 'Last Christmas' Review." *Den of Geek*. 25 Dec. 2014. Web. 15 June 2016.

Cameron, Thomas W.M. *Parasites and Parasitism*. London: Methuen, 1958.

Carreiro, Remy. "From REC to REC 3: Best to Worst Trilogy I've Ever Experienced." *Unreality Magazine*. 12 September 2012. Web. 18 June 2016.

Carroll, Larry. "'Cloverfield' Secrets Revealed." *MTV*. 23 Apr. 2008. Web. 23 June 2016.

Casey, "10 Parasitic Horror Movies." *Bloody Good Horror*. 24 June 2011. Web. 17 June 2016.

Chappell, L.H. *Physiology of Parasites*. New York: John Wiley, 1980.

Cobbs, John L. "*Alien* as an Abortion Parable." *Literature Film Quarterly* 18.3 (1990): 198-201.

Combe, Kirk. "Spielberg's Tale of Two Americas: Postmodern Monsters in *War of the Worlds*." *The Journal of Popular Culture* 44.5 (2011): 934-53.

Creed, Barbara. *The Monstrous-Feminine*. London: Routledge, 1993.

Curtis, Valerie. *Don't Look, Don't Touch, Don't Eat: The Science Behind Revulsion*. Chicago: University of Chicago Press, 2013.

_____. "Why Disgust Matters." *Philosophical Transactions of the Royal Society B* 366 (2011): 3478-3490.

Curtis, Valerie, and Adam Biran. "Dirt, Disgust, and Disease: Is Hygiene in Our Genes?" *Perspectives in Biology and Medicine* 44.1 (2001): 17-31.

Curtis, Valerie, Micheál de Barra, and Robert Aunger. "Disgust as an Adaptive System for Disease Avoidance Behaviour." *Philosophical Transactions of the Royal Society B* 366 (2011): 389-401.

Dahl, Melissa. "Iowa Woman Tries 'Tapeworm Diet', Prompts Doctor Warning." *Canada MSN News*. 16 Aug. 2013. Web. 22 June 2016.

Kristine Larsen

Darnton, Nina. "'Creeps,' Horror Tale." *New York Times* 23 Aug. 1986. Web. 20 June 2016.

Del Toro, Guillermo, and Chuck Hogan. *The Fall.* New York: William Morrow, 2012.

————. *The Strain.* New York: Harper, 2011.

Despommier, Dickson D. *People, Parasites, and Plowshares.* New York: Columbia University Press, 2013.

Dheilly, Nolwenn M., et al. "Who is the Puppet Master? Replication of a Parasitic Wasp-associated Virus Correlates with Host Behaviour Manipulation." *Philosophical Proceedings of the Royal Society B* 282 (2015): 2014-2773.

Dietle, David. "Alien: A Film Franchise Based Entirely on Rape." *Cracked.* 2 Jan. 2011. Web. 2 June 2016.

Dirks, Tim. "Greatest Scariest Movie Moments and Scenes." *AMC Filmsite.* n.d. Web. 19 June 2016.

Doherty, Thomas. "Genre, Gender, and the *Aliens* Trilogy." *Dread of Difference.* Ed. Barry Keith Grant. Austin: U of Texas P, 1996. 181-99.

Douglas. Mary. *Purity and Danger.* London: Routledge, 2002.

Elliott, David E., and Joel V. Weinstock. "Where Are We on Worms?" *Current Opinions in Gastroenterology* 28.6 (2012): 551-556.

Fellner, Michael J., and Muhammad Hassan Majeed. "Tales of Bugs, Delusions of Parasitosis, and What to do." *Clinics in Dermatology* 27 (2009): 135-38.

Fielding, Julien R. "Inside/Out: The Body Under Attack in American Popular Culture." *Parasites, Worms, and the Human Body in Religion and Culture.* Ed. Brenda Gardenour and Misha Todd. New York: Peter Lang, 2012. 189-213.

Fincher, C.L., and R. Thornhill. "Parasite-stress Promotes In-group Assortative Sociality: The Cases of Strong Family Ties and Heightened Religiosity." *Behavioral and Brain Sciences* 35.2 (2012): 61-79.

Flegr, Jaroslav. "Influence of Latent *Toxoplasma* infection on Human Personality, Physiology and Morphology." *Journal of Experimental Biology* 216 (2013): 127-33.

French, Alexandra. "Human Gardens: Grotesque Love and Abject Terror in a World of Parasitic Infection." Honors Thesis. U. of Colorado, 2013.

GateWorld Forum. "Thread: Is a Goa'uld Technically a Parasite/Parasitic Creature?" Forum.gateworld.net. 12 Aug. 2012. Web. 21 June 2016.

Genzlinger, Neil. "10 Unconventional Halloween Diversions." *New York Times* 22 Oct. 2015. Web. 28 June 2016.

Gray, Stewart M., and Banerjee, Nanditta. "Mechanisms of Arthropod Transmission of Plant and Animal Viruses." *Microbiology and Molecular Biology Reviews* 80.3 (1999): 128-48.

Hale, Mike. "The Enemy Within: Wrigglies From Hell." *New York Times* 30 June 2009. Web. 21 June 2016.

Hayden, Matthew. "The 7 Most Horrifying Parasites on the Planet." *Cracked.* 30 Mar. 2009. Web. 24 June 2016.

Hughes, Mark. "Why Are the Aliens in the *Aliens* Series of Films SO Gross and Scary?" *Quora.* 3 Nov. 2011. Web. 2 June 2016.

Huleatt, Richard. "*Alien, Prometheus*, Giger, and Rape." *Real/Reel Journal.* 24 July 2012. Web. 7 June 2016.

88

"It's Not For Everyone." *The Strain*. FX. 3 Aug. 2014.

Jackson, Gordon. "A Field Guide to Science Fiction's Greatest Parasitic Twins." *Io9*. Gizmodo, 21 Mar. 2015. Web. 30 June 2016.

Kaplan. Eugene. *What's Eating You? People and Parasites*. Princeton: Princeton University Press, 2010.

Kawin, Bruce F. *Horror and the Horror Film*. London: Anthem, 2012.

Knight, Kathryn (2013). "How Pernicious Parasites Turn Victims Into Zombies." *Journal of Experimental Biology* 216 (2013): i-iv.

Kristeva, Julia. *Powers of Horror*. Trans. Leon S. Roudiez. New York: Columbia University Press, 1982.

Lafferty, Kevin D., and Armand M. Kuris. "Parasitic Castration: The Evolution and Ecology of Body Snatchers." *Trends in Parisitology* 25.12 (2009): 564-72.

Larsen, Kristine. "'Monsters Inside Me': Zombification as Parasitism." Mid-Atlantic Popular/American Culture Association. Atlantic City. 8 Nov. 2013. Presentation.

_____. "When Procreation becomes Perversion: Zombie Babies." *Monstrous Children and Childish Monsters*. Ed. Markus P.J. Bohlmann and Sean Moreland. Jefferson: McFarland, 2015. 61-77.

"Last Christmas." *Doctor Who*. BBC America. 25 Dec. 2014.

"The Longest Mile Home." *Dominion*. SyFy. 27 Aug. 2015.

Maizels, R,M, "Parasitic Helminth Infections and the Control of Human Allergic and Autoimmune Disorders." *Clinical Microbiology and Infection* 22 (2016): 481-86.

Martin, William F., Sriram Garg, and Verena Zimorski. "Endosymbotic Theories for Eukaryote Origin." *Philosophical Transactions of the Royal Society B* 370: 1678 (September 2015): 20140330.

Matthews, Bernard E. *Introduction to Parasitology*. Cambridge: Cambridge University Press, 1998.

McCarthy, Todd. "The Host: Film Review." *The Hollywood Reporter* 28 Mar. 2013. Web. 30 June 2016.

Murphy, Shaunna. "The 11 Grossest GIFS From 'The Strain' Will Make You Lose Your Lunch." *MTV*. 13 July 2014. Web. 7 June 2016.

Musolff, Andreas. "Metaphorical *Parasites* and 'Parasitic' Metaphors: Semantic Exchanges Between Political and Scientific Vocabularies." *Journal of Language and Politics* 13.2 (2014): 218-33.

Nesse, Randolph M., and George C. Williams. Evolution and Healing. London: Weidenfield and Nicolson, 1995.

"Night Train." *The Strain*. FX. 4 Oct. 2015.

"Night Zero." *The Strain*. FX. 13 July 2014.

Pappas, Stephanie. "5 Alien Parasites and Their Real-world Counterparts." *LiveScience*. 29 May 2012. Web. 20 June 2016.

"Parasites—Anisakiasis." Centers for Disease Control. 18 Mar. 2015. Web. 20 July 2016.

Perigard, Mark. "Buggin' out: Animal Planet's horrifying 'Monsters' worms its way into your brain." *Boston Herald* 1 July 2009. Web. 27 June 2016.

Perkins, Susan, and Tommy Leung. *Parasite of the Day*. Daily Parasite. Web. 11 June 2016.

Pinker, Steven. *How the Mind Works*. Harmondsworth: Penguin, 1998.

Plaue, Noah. "10 Parasites That Do Horrifying Things to People and Animals." *Business Insider* 27 June 2012. Web. 23 June 2016.

Pritt, Bobbi. *Creepy Dreadful Wonderful Parasites*. A Parasitologist's View of the World. Web. 11 June 2016.

Prokop, Pavol, Jana Fančovičová, and Peter Fedor. "Health is Associated with Antiparasite Behavior and Fear of Disease-relevant Animals in Humans." *Ecological Psychology* 22.3 (2010): 222-37.

Reid, Joe. "My First Time… Watching 'Star Trek: The Wrath of Khan' and My Ears Still Hurt." *Decider*. 1 Mar. 2016. Web. 22 June 2016.

Rettner, Rachael. "5 Key Facts About Brain-eating Amoebas." *Livescience*. 22 June 2016. Web. 25 June 2016.

Rosenberg, Alyssa. "*Prometheus*, Pregnancy, and the Persistence of Patriarchy." *Think Progress*. 11 June 2012. Web. 2 June 2016.

Sanders, Robert. "Are Cancers Newly Evolved Species?" *Berkeley Newscenter*. 26 July 2011. Web. 19 June 2016.

"Sequencing Wasp Genome Sheds New Light on Sexual Parasite." *ScienceDaily*. Vanderbilt University. 16 Jan. 2010. Web. 16 June 2016.

Sherman, Ronald A. "Maggot Therapy Takes Us Back to the Future of Wound Care: New and Improved Maggot Therapy for the 21st Century." *Journal of Diabetes Science and Technology* 3.2 (2009): 336-44.

Simon, Matt. "Absurd Creature of the Week: The Parasitic Worm That Turns Crickets Into Suicidal Maniacs." *Wired*. 30 May 2014. Web. 7 July 2016.

_____. "Absurd Creature of the Week: The Wasp That Lays Its Eggs Inside Caterpillars and Turns Them Into Slaves." *Wired*. 17 Oct. 2014. Web. 5 July 2016.

_____. "Absurd Creature of the Week: The Zombie Ant and the Fungus That Controls its Mind." *Wired*. 13 Sept. 2013. Web. 27 June 2016.

Singh, Amrit Pal. "Medicinal Leech Therapy (Hirudotherapy): A Brief Overview." *Complementary Therapies in Clinical Practice* 16 (2010): 213-15.

Stachowiak, Julie. "Parasites and MS: an Emerging Treatment?" *National MS Society*. 19 Oct. 2011. Web. 7 June 2016.

Steenvoorde, Pascal, et al. "Maggot Therapy and the 'Yuk' factor: An Issue for the Patient?" *Wound Repair and Regeneration* 13.3 (2005): 350-52.

Thomas, Frédéric. "The Alarming Proximity of Parasites." Review of Eugene H. Kaplan, *What's Eating You? People and Parasites*. PLoSBiology 8.11 (2010): 1. Web. 18 June 2016.

Wadenius, Adam. "In Violation of the Balance: Foreignness and the Post 9/11 Horror Film." *Global Cinema*. n.d. Web. 7 June 2016.

Watson, Renee. "Foul Fascination of World's Worst Human Parasites." *Oxfordmail.co.uk*. 6 Sept. 2013. Web. 10 June 2016.

Webster, Joanne, et. al. "*Toxoplasma Gondii* Infection, From Predation to Schizophrenia: Can Animal Behaviour Help Us Understand Human Behaviour?." *Journal of Experimental Biology* 216 (2013): 99-112.

Wetmore, Kevin J. *Post-9/11 Horror in American Cinema*. London: Continuum, 2012.

Windsor, Donald A. "Equal Rights for Parasites." *Conservation Biology* 9.1 (1995): 1-2.

Zimmer, Carl. *Parasite Rex*. New York: The Free Press, 2000.

Spot the Monster: Pack, Identity, and Humanity in MTV's *Teen Wolf*

TRACEY THOMAS

"Not all monsters do monstrous things," Lydia Martin tells Meredith in season 4 of MTV's *Teen Wolf*. Lydia is referring to Scott McCall and his lycanthropy in response to Meredith's unintentional aiding of a hit list on all of Beacon Hills' supernatural community; a list that she, Scott, and his pack attempt to locate and remove without lethal force. The quote emphasizes the dual nature of Scott and his lycanthropy — how can he be a hero and a monster all at once? Is Lydia's assertion of Scott as a "monster" not a misnomer since he tries so hard to save everyone without killing? This chapter explores the connotation of "monster" as used by Lydia in MTV's *Teen Wolf* in relation to Scott. It relies on examples of his personality and ethics as seen in his decisions throughout the show, arguing that Scott's dualism is a demonstration of the complexities of *Teen Wolf* lycanthropy. Furthermore, the dual identity of human/werewolf and human/other, as explored in the television show, complicates not only Scott's role as student and crime fighter but also the self-identity of other supernatural creatures.

This chapter will not explore the *Teen Wolf* seasons chronologically, but rather in reverse chronological order before returning to the most recently aired season. I begin with season 4, as season 4 focuses more on the idea of monsters and their definition, here used as a reference point for how show runner and executive producer, Jeff Davis, develops his supernatural creatures. The events in season 3 influence the problematic conception of "monsters" due to the insecurities of Scott and his friends, and outside events which make them question their decisions. As such, I aim to use examples from 3A and 3B to develop the conflicting idea of monstrosity in *Teen Wolf* through Scott's rise into a True Alpha and the characteristics it requires, using the villains of 3A and 3B to act as a foil to the True Alpha. This chapter ends with season 5 and the conflict between

91

a True Alpha and a Demon Wolf,[1] and the inconspicuous actions of the Demon Wolf. These actions led to the unaddressed revelation of Scott and Liam's lycanthropy by their fellow high school classmates and Scott and Liam addressing their dual identities as human/other towards the end of season 5.

The evolution of werewolves in film and television is extensive, especially when one considers the period, starting with the filmic origins of Stuart Walker's *A Werewolf in London* (1935),[2] to the contemporary representations found in *Teen Wolf* (2011-2017).[3] Often, representations of werewolves are those of savage, lust- and carnage-driven beasts; however, contemporary representations are at odds with the idea that a werewolf must *only* be a savage beast. As one commentator writes, "a werewolf is certainly 'at the mercy of his flesh,' but is not in himself inherently evil" (Huckvale 138). After all, is that not what viewers have expected and seen over the years? Historically, werewolves were seen as a multiple threat spanning class, race, gender, sexuality, and human identity, since they "embodied a composite Otherness which gave expression to anxieties about working-class degeneracy, aristocratic decadence, racial atavism, women's corporeality and sexuality, and the human relationship to the animal world" (Du Coudray 50). More recently, however, and particularly in *Teen Wolf*, werewolves are not always consumed by rage, fear, self-loathing or the desire for revenge (151), but rather they are a metaphor for thinking about selfhood (3). When one is a werewolf like Scott McCall, the search for self and identity becomes problematic: is he man, or wolf? Is he both, or neither? Ultimately, as Huckvale notes, "all monsters are outsiders, persecuted by the norm, terrified most of all by themselves" (145), which may suggest that werewolves (and the man inside) are more frightened of what they are capable of and of the monster they can become. This fear of the internal monster becomes apparent in season 4 of *Teen Wolf*, with its catchphrase of "can't go back." The catchphrase indicates the main characters' inability to return to the way of life they experienced in season 3 and earlier. It relates in particular to the death of Allison

1 The "Demon Wolf," also known as "la Bête" or the Beast of Gévaudan, was first mentioned in season 1 of *Teen Wolf* and later explored as the main villain alongside the Dread Doctors in season 5.

2 See Hawkins for more information..

3 During the writing of this chapter, San Diego Comic Con occurred, and Jeff Davis announced that season 6 would be the final season for the television show *Teen Wolf*, ending its 6-season run in (potentially) winter 2017 with its 20 episodes split between November 2016 for the first ten, and the remainder in early 2017.

Spot the Monster: Pack, Identity, and Humanity

Argent, Scott's first love, as well as his rise to a True Alpha, in addition to the many changes and growths that many characters experience as they navigate the supernatural world. With Kate Argent returning as a villain, her storyline continues as a corrupt human werewolf hunter[4] and the physical changes she undergoes turns her from human to werejaguar. These changes in season 4 draw attention to the question: what does it mean to be a "monster," and ultimately, who is the monster in *Teen Wolf?*

The word "monster" appears in the season during several episodes: beginning in 4.01[5] with reference to Scott and his fears of losing control, then in 4.04 when Scott bites and turns Liam into his beta. The word appears in 4.08 when Scott is worried about his lycanthropy physically changing further as a reference to losing control, in 4.10 when Lydia and Meredith discuss what it means to be a monster, and in the finale (4.12) when Scott accuses Peter of being a monster because of his actions. The continuous message of the question "who is the monster?" plays through the characters and their interactions with others as they attempt to uncover how the word plays into their own ethics and morals. The OED defines *monster* as "a mythical creature which is part animal and part human, or combines elements of two or more animal forms, and is frequently of great size and ferocious appearance. Later, more generally: any imaginary creature that is large, ugly, and frightening;" *monstrous* appears as "having the appearance or nature of a monster, esp. in being hideous or frightening" and "like or befitting a monster; inhumanly wicked or depraved; atrocious, horrible" (the latter, frequently hyperbolical). While the two definitions are true, if not simplistic, when referencing the characters in *Teen Wolf*, the final definition of *monstrous* is far more applicable to the duality human/ other, as Scott and his fellow werewolves demonstrate. The werewolves in Jeff Davis' world are fast, strong, and have heightened senses which addresses the "combines elements of two or more animal forms" and their abilities. Scott's own fears of losing control during the first moon lead to Stiles chaining him in his bedroom (1.01), as well as fears of him

---

4 Kate previously revealed that she courted a young Derek Hale in high school to gain his trust and love, only to use it against him. She then burned his family home while his family was still inside. Many characters note that not all of the Hale family were werewolves and that her actions were against the Argent family code, leading viewers to wonder who the true monsters are: the supernatural or the humans.

5 Unless specifically relevant for quoting purposes, all future episodes will be referenced by their season and episode number.

violently attacking a bus driver but having no memory of the event (1.03), thus fulfilling the "inhumanly wicked or depraved, atrocious, and horrible" part of the definition, as well. However, the same definition of *monstrous* explains the difference between Scott McCall as a werewolf, and the many other characters who are werewolves: very rarely, and under only the most human and teenage-angst ridden moments of the show, does Scott McCall ever act cruelly. In fact, Scott spends his time as a werewolf constantly in fear of letting his friends down, not making the right choices, or hurting someone. He is the antithesis of someone who is "inhumanly wicked or depraved, atrocious, and horrible." Yet, much of *Teen Wolf* places Scott as worried about his humanity. From season 1 onward, Scott is either worried about managing his lycanthropy and participating in a human world, managing his lycanthropy along with his love life while understanding his position in a pack, to the life-changing events of season 3 where his—as well as his friends'—humanity is called into question.

The third season of *Teen Wolf* split the series into two sections; each had twelve episodes, and explored two sets of villains and plotlines that were not immediately discernible as interrelated. While Scott worried about defeating an Alpha Pack and Derek Hale watched as his pack disbanded before his eyes, season 3A established the importance of a "True Alpha" and their rarity. In 3.07, Dr. Alan Deaton, Scott's veterinarian boss, is kidnapped and left to die;[6] Scott is the one who saves him in a scene that is pivotal not only for the season, but also for the mythos of *Teen Wolf*. Deaton, once safely returned to his clinic, tells Scott:

> Deaton: Your eyes, they were red! Bright red!
> Scott: How is that possible?
> Deaton: It's rare, something that doesn't happen within a hundred years. But, every once in a while, a beta can become an alpha without having to steal or take their power. They call it a True Alpha. It's one that rises purely on the strength of character, virtue, by sheer force of will. ("Currents" 3.07)

---

6 Scott locates and saves him, but must cross mountain ash to do so (mountain ash is used as a magical barrier against supernatural creatures and the show has previously established that werewolves cannot cross that boundary). However, Scott pushes against the barrier, and his emotional state and the desire to save Deaton has him nearly breaking the barrier through sheer willpower. His eyes change from "beta-yellow" to "alpha-red" on their own; however, they do not remain red and Sheriff Stilinski inadvertently breaks the mountain ash barrier to help Scott save Deaton.

Spot the Monster: Pack, Identity, and Humanity

This scene highlights the importance of Scott's character, not only as the titular teen wolf, but also as a human being with defined morals and ethics. As regular Alphas in the Davis universe steal or take their powers, the importance of Scott's rise to True Alpha based on merit and strength of character is unquestionably important. Additionally, Scott demonstrates that he is unique as a True Alpha, able to transcend the human/other binary by maintaining his morals and ethics, whereas other were-creatures fall into the generalized belief of lycanthropes as vicious and savage. Thus, while many movies, television shows, and novels focus on the savagery of the werewolf, *Teen Wolf* attempts to deconstruct and eliminate the brutality of lycanthropes through the point of view of Scott and his rise to becoming a True Alpha.

Deaton notes that, to become a True Alpha, one must demonstrate "strength of character [and] virtue, by sheer force of will." *Virtue*, in itself, can encompass a large umbrella of terms: the OED describes it especially as any of several "morally good qualities regarded . . . as of particular worth or importance."[7] Yet, the first few episodes of *Teen Wolf* provide a picture of Scott McCall that does not correspond with the qualities required of a True Alpha; initially, Scott is a terrible student failing some of his high school classes, is second-string on the lacrosse team, is not in physical shape and has asthma, and has little to no self-confidence. Despite a good relationship with his single-parent mother, Scott rarely speaks of or acknowledges his absentee father; his mother struggles with bill payments and drives a beat-up car but works long hours at the hospital to provide for her family, which results in Scott's part-time positions as a vet assistant for Deaton. Scott even attempts to run (figuratively and literally) from his lycanthropy; however, by embracing it, and thanks to his new relationship with Allison Argent, he is able to begin the process of becoming an adult and a True Alpha. Speaking of the protagonist of *Teen Wolf*, McMahon-Coleman and Weaver note that "adolescence is a period of transition when an individual's sense of self is established" (17), thus suggesting that Scott's junior year of high school is the beginning of his sense of self, which is also the period of firming his virtue and ethics.

However, his high school career and the subsequent seasons demonstrate that his ethics and morals are not yet firm. As viewers learn more about Scott and his personality, viewers also learn more about

---

7 Many of these virtuous qualities relate to cardinal virtues of justice, prudence, temperance, and fortitude, often accompanied by theological virtues of faith, hope, and charity.

Tracey Thomas

the mythos of Davis' universe and how the inclusion of Scott's morals and ethics work against villains, situations, and his own insecurities. Leading into the two-part episodes of 3.05 ("Frayed") and 3.06 ("Motel California"), a discussion between Deaton and Scott about his friends dying leads Scott to confess in a flashback during 3.05, "I don't know what else to do. Do I keep trying to get them to listen to me? Do I tell Derek that he's gonna get them all killed? How do you save someone who doesn't wanna be saved? How do I stop them?" Later in the same episode, Scott stops Isaac from beating up Ethan by yelling his name — it is Scott's process of becoming an Alpha that has Isaac listen and immediately stop.[8] In 3.06, Scott's heightened insecurities and fears are due to his drugged, wolfsbane-induced state that results in him attempting suicide. Plaintively, he tells Lydia, Stiles, and Allison:

> Scott: Every time I try to fight back, it just gets worse. People keep getting hurt. People keep getting killed.
> Stiles: Scott, listen to me, okay? This isn't you, alright? This is someone inside your head telling you to do this. Okay? Now–
> Scott: What if it isn't? What if it is just me? What if doing this is actually the best thing that I could do for everyone else? It all started that night, the night I got bitten. You remember the way it was before that? You and me, we were– we were– we were nothing. We weren't popular. We weren't good at lacrosse. We weren't important. We were *no one*. Maybe I should just be no one again. No one at all. ("Motel California" 3.06)

Scott's fears, his concerns about his health, popularity and status has him questioning not only his place amongst his friends, but also his place as a werewolf. When Deucalion attempts to goad Scott into fighting him in 3.07 ("Currents"), Scott angrily replies, "I'm not like you. I don't have to kill people [to become an Alpha]." At this point in the television show, Scott is beginning to exhibit the necessary qualities of virtue and those of a True Alpha: he is moral, demonstrating power that is not conflicting in moral nature through the capacity to act, and he is no longer in a physical relationship with Allison, leaning towards chastity.

Furthermore, those Scott fights against in seasons 3A and 3B also help shape and determine the necessary qualities of a True Alpha by what these villains *lack*. In 3A, the Alpha Pack is dangerous, strong,

---

8 All Betas obey Alphas in *Teen Wolf*, and Peter makes a point to Derek that Derek is losing control of his pack due to Scott's evolution to True Alpha. Isaac loses faith in Derek's ability to lead and looks for a new Alpha to pledge his allegiance to.

96

Spot the Monster: Pack, Identity, and Humanity

and vicious. Deucalion's back-story provides information on not only the Hale family and their lycanthropy, but also the involvement of the Argents as werewolf hunters in America. A man who once had "great vision" ("Visionary" 3.08; "Lunar Eclipse" 3.12), Deucalion let revenge and the need for strength overtake him when his beta attempted to kill him; he instead absorbed his beta's power (3.04). This led to him seeking other packs and telling a single pack member to kill their Alphas and the entire pack in order to gain strength through murder. Almost every scene the Alpha Pack appears in—from hunting Braeden and eventually slashing her throat, manipulating Marin Morrell in order to aid the Alpha Pack, stabbing Derek through the stomach with a pipe, capturing and confining Erica and Boyd until they go insane during an eclipse—results in mayhem, chaos, or death. Here, the previously mentioned definitions of *monster* and *monstrous* are apt: the Alpha Pack cannot be controlled; they cause many problems, and even employ acts of wickedness and cruelty on a constant basis.

Du Coudray writes that "the werewolf has been thoroughly constructed as an alien 'other' threatening the social body; the negative of a normalized social identity" (44)—the person who is outside of societal norms, the one who is stigmatized. However, while the werewolf is a common shapeshifter, *Teen Wolf* mythos also explores other were-animals (werejaguars and werecoyotes, for example), and the physical manifestation of humans shifting—or changing—into something other than werewolf. The "other" being becomes someone who "hide[s] those aspects from [their] selves which would rather not have anyone else know about. Sometimes [they] hide them from [them]selves" (Huckvale 141). Those who become "other" in *Teen Wolf* are not the werewolves anymore. No longer the savage monsters everyone is afraid of, the "others" are the ones who fall under the monster definition; for example, season 2 focuses on Jackson Whittemore becoming a kamina,[9] and season 3A explores Jennifer Blake, a Dark Druid.[10] The dual nature of Jennifer as schoolteacher/Dark Druid, as well as Jackson/kamina, conflates the idea that being a "monster" no longer equates to werewolves and the supernatural—monsters can come from within.

---

9 A "kamina" is the result of the inner personality and character of a human emerging from one who has been bitten by a werewolf and does not take to the bite. In *Teen Wolf*, Derek Hale bites Jackson at the end of season 1, but instead of turning into a werewolf, Jackson becomes a kamina.

10 Jennifer is a "Darach" in *Teen Wolf* mythology. She previously was an Emissary, like Deaton. Kali, a pack member, killed her, as well as her entire pack to gain power and join Deucalion as part of an Alpha Pack.

97

The monster coming from within plays an important role in season 3B.[11] Deaton tells Stiles in 3.13, "When the three of you went under the water, when you crossed from unconsciousness to a kind of super-consciousness, you essentially opened a door in your minds." The result of opening a path into their super-consciousness appears in the beginning of 3B: Scott cannot transform into a werewolf or tap into any of its benefits, including having dreams of the werewolf side turning into a rampaging beast. Furthermore, Allison sees her dead aunt, Kate Argent, haunting her to the point of excessive paranoia; and Stiles, who is constantly valued for his knowledge, begins to lose the ability to read or make logical deductions. For 3B, the three protagonists spend much of their time coming to grips with their abilities and questioning their morals; this carries over into season 4 and the opening line to this chapter: "Not all monsters do monstrous things." Of course, this line only reaffirms the belief that werewolves are synonymous with monster, when the actions of the werewolf suggest that they are more human than monster. It is no surprise that it is Meredith who feels threatened by the supernatural in Beacon Hills, as her own fledgling banshee abilities are manipulated and used by Peter Hale, Eichen House, and the Benefactor. Who is Meredith supposed to trust — the human orderlies in Eichen House who abuse her, or the supernatural creatures who use her? She represents the human element in werewolf narratives of instinctively fearing the other — the wolf — as she arranges Scott McCall and his friends to be executed through the Dead Pool. In Meredith's mind, equating Scott, a werewolf, to a monster is simplistic and obvious, despite Lydia's belief that he is a good person. For du Coudray, the (contemporary) werewolf unites in a single body the elements of the hero and the villain (85), as exhibited in *Teen Wolf*'s Scott McCall. Much like in comic books, heroes who come from non-traditional families — that is, families with a single parent, domestic abuse issues, and others — form other communities to support themselves mentally and physically (Coughlan 235). Scott, once bitten, creates his own community based on his werewolf needs by establishing his own pack; furthermore, his pack is comprised of those who also come from non-traditional backgrounds. Scott, Stiles, Isaac,

---

11 Season 3A concluded with Scott, Stiles, and Allison's parents learning the truth of the supernatural in Beacon Hill, as well as their children's involvement as either a werewolf or part of his pack due to Jennifer Blake kidnapping and attempting to kill them for her final sacrifice. In order to find and save their parents, Scott, Stiles, and Allison underwent a dangerous procedure of drowning themselves to discover Jennifer's plan, as well as learning that everything from Scott's bite, to Allison's move to Beacon Hill, was preordained.

Spot the Monster: Pack, Identity, and Humanity

and Malia all come from single-parent households (with Isaac coming from an abusive one, in addition); and Lydia's parents are divorced and more focused on gaining an advantage over one another than paying attention to her. Although both Kira and Allison came from families with both parents, Allison's family disliked Scott and lied about the Argent family heritage, just as Kira's mother lied about her past. While much of this article focuses on Scott McCall and his abilities as a True Alpha, one should note that a werewolf is nothing without his pack: the pack plays an important role in *Teen Wolf*, not just on the werewolf aspect of the supernatural and the Davis mythos, but also because Scott McCall is a sixteen-year-old teenager when Peter Hale bites him and infects him with lycanthropy.

"The . . . werewolf genre allows for distinctions between self and other, life and death . . . framed against distinctions between childhood and adult responsibilities, and as such, teens often attempt to locate themselves in terms of social groups to which they belong, in order to find ways to express their identities," write McMahon-Coleman and Weaver (17). Jeff Davis suggests this idea when he states that season 5 is "very much about our teenagers becoming adults and heading into their senior year" (Bernardino) and learning who they are as people and supernatural creatures. McMahon-Coleman and Weaver's exploration into teen supernatural literature and film/television documents much of what du Coudray calls "subject- and identity-formation in Western discourse" (4) in the werewolf genre. Scott's pre-lycanthropy identity remains very different to the person he becomes after being bitten; furthermore, his relationships with his friends—Stiles, Allison, Lydia, even Jackson, Isaac, Derek, and others, to varying degrees of interaction—ultimately change as the series progresses and Scott experiences character growth. The question here, however, is: how does Scott McCall, as a werewolf, manage his pack while maintaining his abilities as a True Alpha and without compromise?

McMahon-Coleman and Weaver note that there is a divide between human and supernatural socialization in contemporary TV shows, suggesting that there is "a feeling of dislocation or not adhering to the social norms and prevalent ideologies in the adolescents' mortal lives, even before they enter into the complexities of supernatural politics" (31). Pre-lycanthropy Scott emulates this with his social pecking order at the bottom, alongside Stiles; both are passed over by the opposite sex and other lacrosse players. Neither teenager feels fully comfortable with himself or his position, yet once Scott is bitten, Stiles' popularity

99

rises with him through association. Of course, it is important to note that, although bitten, Scott's rise in popularity is due to the abilities his lycanthropy provides him with, but that he still works to improve himself instead of treating his lycanthropy as a "cure-all." The feeling of dislocation does not leave Scott throughout the earlier seasons of *Teen Wolf*, because he navigates the politics of the supernatural world clumsily and is often left scrambling for answers that neither Derek nor Deaton feel comfortable providing. Furthermore, Scott's "dual identity," so to speak, that of werewolf and teenage high school student, complicates his human/other identity — leading back to the question of whether he is man or beast, and to the problematic way in which his friends, his pack, ultimately view him.

In each season of *Teen Wolf*, Scott's lycanthropy is revealed, usually due to a high-intensity situation unfolding in front of those who are unaware of the supernatural presence in Beacon Hills. Allison is unaware of her family's werewolf-hunting past until the final episodes of season 1 reveal Scott's secret and, in season 2, Scott is forced to reveal himself to his mother in order to save her life, only for her to feel afraid and scared of her son for several episodes. Derek bites outcast teenagers in season 3, risking their secrecy in order to build himself a ragtag pack, but spends the majority of his time as Alpha chasing after them; also in season 3, Stiles' father, Sheriff Stilinski, finally learns of the supernatural in Beacon Hills. Finally, season 4 provides new adult helpers in the form of Kira Yukimura's 900-year-old kitsune mother. Slowly, as the *Teen Wolf* seasons progress, the number of people in Beacon Hills remaining unaware of the supernatural is dwindling. However, it is not until the climax of season 5 that the citizens of Beacon Hills are provided with irrefutable proof.

In 5.18, when attempting to learn the identity of the Demon Wolf, the Beast of Gévaudan, Scott and his supernatural friends fight the Beast in wolf form while inside the school, during an attack in the middle of a lacrosse game. Not only does Scott fight the Demon Wolf, but so do Malia Tate and Liam Dunbar, two other were-creatures in Scott's pack. When Malia leaves Scott and Liam, the two young men ultimately make a stand in the library, where several students have hidden. When Scott and Liam transform to fight the Demon Wolf, they do so in front of those students trapped in the library, revealing their werewolf forms, their strength and abilities, and the fact that the supernatural exists.

In her 2014 article, "'I was hoping it would pass you by': dis/ability and difference in *Teen Wolf*," Kimberly McMahon-Coleman writes that

Spot the Monster: Pack, Identity, and Humanity

"all werewolves texts at some point deal implicitly or explicitly with the concept of 'passing' or hiding one's difference; the werewolf, after all, is only a monster under certain circumstances . . . and is human most of the time" (147). This concept of hiding one's self identity plays an obviously important role in *Teen Wolf* because of Scott's dual identity as werewolf and high school student. In fact, it is a common werewolf genre trope, on which even actress Arden Cho, who played Kira, casts doubt: "Can we just become superheroes and just go save the world and be teens by day and superheroes by night?" (Saclao). *Teen Wolf* explores this trope thoroughly throughout the seasons, but season 5 pushes friendships and relationships to a breaking point—it becomes a question of why they have to hide who they are, and if their pack can survive Scott's leadership decisions when he is focused on his high school student identity? An important aspect of season 5 is the external complication in teen television shows of the leads growing up. Jeff Davis indicated that season 5 would take place during senior year— the last year of high school—and that Scott, Stiles, Lydia, and Malia would have to make decisions of where to go after graduation.[12] Thus, not only is Scott struggling with his high school identity and "normal" human complications of college and careers, he is also struggling with maintaining the supernatural side of himself and his pack and managing threats against them. Hiding a part of their selves—whether human or wolf—causes Scott to lose control of his pack and, according to Jeff Davis, "Stiles loses faith in Scott" and that "much of the previous seasons were about Scott finding and building a pack . . . this is going to see him possibly losing it—possibly ending up on his own without his friends by his side, wondering how he's going to face life without them" (Saclao). In Davis's mythology, an Alpha without a pack is nothing.

The second half of season 5 attempts to ask what happens when the monsters take over, when the pack is divided. Where can Scott go from here? How does his identity as wolf, as a potential monster, complement his human side? And can the two exist together? Much of what it means to be a True Alpha is due to morals and ethics, and identity construct, as well as to Scott defining himself against those who seek to harm others and Beacon Hills. The loss of Scott's pack drives the question of identity

---

12 Davis said in an interview before season 5 began, "One of our big themes this season is, how do high school friends stay together, after graduation? And are the friends you make, as a teenager, the friends you keep for the rest of your life, or do you find other people? For characters like Scott and Stiles, that's a tragedy. They want to keep their friends and their Pack together. That's why our tagline this season is, 'Watch your Pack,' and I think it's brilliant" (Radish).

101

and duality; even more so, it continues to demonstrate that although Scott is considered a "monster," not all monsters do monstrous things. Even when Liam attempts to fight Scott due to a super moon in episode 5.10, "Status Asthmaticus," Scott allows Liam to engage with him, continues to tell him that it is the moon speaking, not truly Liam, and his anger in order for his pack to communicate with him. It is only when Theo's plan to use Liam to kill Scott fails that Scott continues to point out the differences between him as a True Alpha and his pack, and that of Theo and his attempts to recreate a pack with the same abilities as Scott's:

> Theo: I should've stayed. I should've made sure.
> Scott: Because now you have to kill me yourself. They're still mine.
> Theo: Maybe not yet, but they'll come around.
> Scott: Not for you. They're not like you. They never will be.
> Theo: Because I'm a chimera? Because I'm not a real werewolf?
> Scott: Because you're barely even *human*. ("Status Asthmaticus" 5.10)

This scene reinforces the idea that despite Scott being conflicted with his dual identity of high school student and werewolf (as well as the troubles it creates for his graduating friends), Scott continues to maintain his True Alpha virtues *despite* being what others traditionally call a "monster." Even when in werewolf form, Scott displays such a disparity in comparison to the other creatures and monsters on the television show, that it is difficult to see him as the "monster." His final words to Theo ("Because you're barely even human") further emphasize the difference between monsters who do monstrous things, and those who do not.

Referencing the break in the pack for season 5, Davis notes that it is "a long road to recovery for Scott and Stiles' friendship — it's not going to be easy . . . it's all going to be on Scott's shoulders. He's got to learn from his failures — it's up to him to give them hope again, as Melissa tells him" (Gajewski). In her 2007 article, "The Big Bad Wolf: Masculinity and Genetics in Popular Culture," Heather Schell notes that the term *Alpha* was originally used in early twentieth-century studies of animal behavior to refer to the dominant individuals in rigidly hierarchical animal societies like primates and wolves (113). Furthermore, sustaining this hierarchy is possible through one's ability to control one's true inner nature at the price of physical and psychological agony (117). In

Spot the Monster: Pack, Identity, and Humanity

terms of Scott's abilities as a True Alpha, not only must he re-establish the hierarchical society required by wolves and regain his pack, but he must also overcome the physical and psychological agony experienced by losing his pack to begin with, in season 5A. After the fight with Liam and Theo in 5.10, Davis calls the remainder of season 5 (season 5B), "[a] classic hero's journey – the midseason finale is the death and resurrection. Now that [Scott's] basically resurrected, he's going to carry a loss of innocence with him, and he's got to do what his mother says, which is give them hope. You got to get them back" (Gajewski) with Scott reaffirming his identity and position as Alpha.

On July 21, 2016, at San Diego Comic Con, the *Teen Wolf* panel (with show runner and executive producer Jeff Davis, stars Tyler Posey, Holland Roden, Dylan Sprayberry, and others) announced that season 6 of *Teen Wolf* would be the last season of the MTV television show. Originally devised as a "teen" comedy/horror show, based on the Michael J. Fox film of the same name, *Teen Wolf* built an entirely new mythology based on Davis's imagination and some real-world historical fact.[13] As some of Kimberley McMahon-Coleman and Chantal Bourgault du Coudray's assertions about contemporary supernatural narratives make clear, werewolves and puberty go hand-in-hand in terms of a process of becoming and identity formation; furthermore, as several commentators cited in this article suggest, in the duality of the werewolf as a human/other, complications arise from the fact of the "other" being outside societal norms. These are all important points; however, *Teen Wolf* attempts to deconstruct the complications of Othering within the supernatural world of the television show in ways that differ from the original *Teen Wolf* movie (1985). While the movie may not have lent as much material to its television adaptation, it did bring awareness to the fact that it was a product of its time and generation; the contemporary adaptation explores multiple avenues of lycanthropy and the supernatural, but also deals with rarely explored issues of mundane teenage issues (homework! driving lessons!), and focuses on the eventuality of growing up and outgrowing one's friends. Furthermore, by complementing these issues with the supernatural, Davis was able to explore deeper issues of Othering amongst teenagers and family dynamics when related to the "pack."

Over the six years the television show has aired, *Teen Wolf* has explored the character of Scott McCall in numerous facets and situations,

---

13 See Smith for further information on the Beast of Gévaudan, an actual wolf that terrorized the French countryside of Massif Central in 1764-5.

constantly surrounded by the idea of "monster" and "monstrosity" in his dual identity as a teen wolf. From an unwilling recipient of the bite, to discovering what it means to be a werewolf, especially one primed by emotion, Scott—and the television show—has demonstrated that the misnomer of "monster" is outdated and ill-used. Furthermore, unlike other werewolf films or television shows, *Teen Wolf* explores the role of the "pack" and the dynamics of family and friends in relation with the lycanthrope. Where Scott and his friends struggle against their inner "monsters," they overcome and persevere against the traditional connotations of the word. To continue to do so, Scott must maintain the virtues of a True Alpha without straying; he must exhibit virtues of justice, prudence, temperance, and fortitude, as well as demonstrate faith, hope, and charity. Yet, when he does begin to feel monstrous— when he feels the darker nature of the werewolf pull at him—he relies on community in the process of identity formation; as he explains to Deaton in 3.12: "I look for my friends."

Works Cited

"Anchors." *Teen Wolf*. Dir. Russell Mulcahy. Perf. Tyler Posey, Dylan O'Brien, Crystal Reed. Season 3, Episode 13, MTV, 6 January 2014.

"Currents." *Teen Wolf*. Dir. Russell Mulcahy. Perf. Tyler Posey, Dylan O'Brien, Crystal Reed. Season 3, Episode 7, MTV, 15 July 2013.

"Frayed." *Teen Wolf*. Dir. Robert Hall. Perf. Tyler Posey, Dylan O'Brien, Crystal Reed. Season 3, Episode 5, MTV, 1 July 2013.

"Lunar Eclipse." *Teen Wolf*. Dir. Russell Mulcahy. Perf. Tyler Posey, Dylan O'Brien, Crystal Reed. Season 3, Episode 12, MTV, 19 August 2013.

"Motel California." *Teen Wolf*. Dir. Christian Taylor. Perf. Tyler Posey, Dylan O'Brien, Crystal Reed. Season 3, Episode 6, MTV, 8 July 2013.

"Status Asthmaticus." *Teen Wolf*. Dir. Russell Mulcahy. Perf. Tyler Posey, Dylan O'Brien, Holland Roden. Season 5, Episode 10, MTV, August 24 2015.

"Unleashed." *Teen Wolf*. Dir. Tim Andrew. Perf. Tyler Posey, Dylan O'Brien, Crystal Reed. Season 3, Episode 4, MTV, June 24 2013.

"Visionary." *Teen Wolf*. Dir. Russell Mulcahy. Perf. Tyler Posey, Dylan O'Brien, Crystal Reed. Season 3, Episode 8, MTV, 22 July 2013.

Bernardino, Shiena. "'Teen Wolf' Season 5 Spoilers, Latest Update: New Villains and Challenges Expected." *Christian Today*. Christian Media Corporation, 9 May 2015. Web. 21 June 2016.

Coughlan, David. "The Naked Hero and Model Man: Costumed Identity in Comic Book Narratives." *Heroes of Film, Comics and American Culture: Essays on Real and Fictional Defenders of Home*. Ed. Lisa M. Detora. Jefferson, NC: McFarland, 2009. 234-252.

Spot the Monster: Pack, Identity, and Humanity

Du Coudray, Chantal Bourgault. *Curse of the Werewolf: Fantasy, Horror and the Beast Within.* London: I.B. Tauris, 2006.

Gajewski, Ryan. "*Teen Wolf* Creator on Finale's 'Death and Resurrection,' New 'Epic' Storyline." *The Hollywood Reporter* 24 August 2015. Web. 23 June 2016.

Hawkins, David. "Late Night Howl—The History Of Werewolf Movies." *WhatCulture.com.* 6 October 2011. Web. 21 June 2016.

Huckvale, David. "Interlude: Werewolves." *Touchstones of Gothic Horror: A Film Genealogy of Eleven Motifs and Images.* Jefferson NC: McFarland, 2010. 134-145.

McMahon-Coleman, Kimberley and Roslyn Weaver. *Werewolves and Other Shapeshifters in Popular Culture: A Thematic Analysis of Recent Depictions.* Jefferson, NC: McFarland, 2012.

McMahon-Coleman, Kimberley. "'I was hoping it would pass you by': dis/ability and difference in *Teen Wolf.*" *Remake Television: Reboot, Re-use, Recycle.* Ed. Carlen Lavigne. Lanham, MD: Lexington, 2014. 141-153.

Radish, Christina. "'Teen Wolf' Showrunner Jeff Davis Talks Senior Year, Breaking Points, and More." *Collider.* 29 June 2015. Web. 23 June 2016.

Saclao, Christian. "'Teen Wolf' Season 5 Spoilers: Scott And Stiles' Friendship Will Be Tested." *Design&Trend.* 13 March 2015. Web. 23 June 2016.

Saclao, Christian. "'Teen Wolf' Was Supposed To End After Season 5, Reveals Showrunner Jeff Davis." *Design&Trend.* 17 August 2015. Web. 23 June 2016.

Schell, Heather. "The Big Bad Wolf: Masculinity and Genetics in Popular Culture." *Literature and Medicine* 26.1 (Spring 2007): 109-25.

Smith, Jay M. *Monsters of the Gévaudan: The Making of a Beast.* Cambridge, MA: Harvard University Press, 2011.

Stitching Together a Soul: Plato, St. Gregory of Nyssa, and *I, Frankenstein*[1]

HEATHER L. DUDA

While the monster narrative has long been a staple of western culture, the end of the twentieth century saw the monster grow and change into a myriad of incarnations. The monsters' popularity can be seen from their presence in places as diverse as the big and small screens to dorm-room posters of Josh Harnett's Ethan Chandler from *Penny Dreadful* and the zombie family decals on minivans. The monster has long represented that which a society fears but the end of the twentieth century and beginning of the twenty-first also saw monsters being championed by society. Among these visual representations of society's angst and morality emerged the monstrous monster hunter, a creature who, by society's standards, is a monster but who has chosen to protect humankind. Some of the more notable examples are Nick Knight (Geraint Wyn Davies) from the television show *Forever Knight* (1992-96), Blade (Wesley Snipes) from the film trilogy of the same name (1998, 2002, 2004), and both Angel (David Boreanaz) and Spike (James Marsters) from the television shows *Buffy the Vampire Slayer* (1997-2003) and its spin-off *Angel* (1999-2004). This monster-turned-monster-hunter is typically a badass "monster" (or "other") with easily identifiable human emotions like love and remorse.

Although a community of fellow monster hunters and possibly a love interest are predominant in motivating a monster's change, the soul often receives mention in the monster's transformation to monster hunter. In Western Christian thought, the soul is a vital element of one's humanity. The connection between the soul and humanity emerges in Plato's writings when Socrates explains how the soul helps a person overcome negative emotions and desires. The church leader St. Gregory

---

1 My thanks to Jeremy Hollingshead for all his help in the initial brainstorming and revision process and Erin Gyomber for all her help in the editing process. I greatly appreciate the time and attention both have given to this essay.

Stitching Together a Soul

of Nyssa applied this Platonic ideal of the soul to early Christian thought and intertwined Christianity's concept of humanity with the soul, a connection that informs much of western Christian thought to this day. Over time, this connection between the soul and humanity also came to include the body. In her work on resurrection in Western Christianity, Caroline Walker Bynum comments that by the early fourteenth century,

> hundreds of years of insistence on bodily resurrection had come to locate in "soul" much of our common sense understanding of "body." Souls were gendered and ranked, bearing with them the marks of occupation, status, religious vocation, even martyrdom. . . . Although soul now seemed to carry not only the particularity of self but also the pattern of body, it needed body as a place to express that particularity and pattern. (10-11)

Over the centuries, western thought has come to link the soul, the body, and humanity and this link emerges as an important connection when a monster shifts from hunting humans to hunting his/her own kind.

Unfortunately, the soul is a challenging thing to represent visually and the presence of a soul usually takes a backseat to the other elements, like love and redemption, in the monster's transformation, which are much easier to represent visually. However, Stuart Beattie's 2014 film *I, Frankenstein* focuses on the soul's importance in transforming a monster into a monster hunter. This essay seeks to examine the transformation of The Monster (Aaron Eckhart) as he moves from a self-proclaimed "living corpse without a soul. Stitched. Jolted. Bludgeoned back to life by a madman" to a defender of humankind. While many monster-hunting narratives skirt around the edges of the importance of the soul to humanity, Beattie delves head-first into that importance and gives twenty-first-century viewers their first in-depth and provocative look at the transformative power of the soul on a monster. In doing so, Beattie emphasizes the importance we still attach to the soul in differentiating between human and monster, a differentiation that is more and more blurred in modern society as we continue to praise the monstrous in popular culture. That said, even when Eckhart's title character possesses that which makes him most human, his soul, the film ends by emphasizing his difference, thus proving that contemporary society is still not entirely ready to fully dismantle that line between "human" and "monster."

In his 2004 book *Alien Chic: Posthumanism and the Other Within*, Neil Badmington uses the theoretical lens of posthumanism to analyze America's interest in alien invasion texts and how this interest reflects twenty-first-century society's anxiety over the difference between human and inhuman.[2] Badmington examines what he calls "alien love," a cultural phenomenon that, at first glance, seems to embrace aliens: "If the human and inhuman no longer stand in binary opposition to each other, aliens might well be expected to find themselves welcomed, *loved*, displayed and celebrated as precious treasures" (3). In this way, aliens appear to take a significant step closer to being like "us," humans, and therefore wholeheartedly accepted into modern society. Badmington goes back to the ideas of humanism as a basis for his critique of this alien love. The old signifiers of humanity, Badmington argues, are external signifiers. In the twenty-first century, these external signifiers are becoming more and more difficult to see as aliens look more and act more like humans. At first glance, then, this appears to be a good evolution because it seems to signify a larger societal change toward openness of others. However, Badmington argues that the opposite is actually occurring. Where do we, as humans, turn for that difference, that "thing" which gives humanity its collective identity, when the other looks and acts like us? Badmington says that although the line between human and inhuman is difficult to determine, it still exists but instead of looking outward, we, as a society, now look inward. The line exists because humans are conditioned to become "human":

> Humans, that is to say, *become* human with time and a little encouragement. Left entirely to their own devices, they would probably never make the leap, never take up their places within the symbolic order.... "We" need to be kept in check, kept human. The inhuman is never too far away. Through its institutions, its apparatuses—education, law, religion, morality, ethics, common sense—culture ceaselessly (re)makes humans (why else would "we" need such entities in our adult lives?). (126)

Society and culture seek to humanize us and those who are not acculturated in this way are still alien, either literally or figuratively. For Badmington, although American society may love and embrace aliens,

---

2 When talking about posthumanism in general, I use the binary human/inhuman because "inhuman" means a wide variety of entities in posthuman theory. When referring to the horror genre specifically, I change "inhuman" to "monster" because "monster" is often the label used for the "other" when dealing with horror texts.

Stitching Together a Soul

society still recognizes the aliens as being different, thus continuing to maintain the "us versus them" mentality of humanism.

Badmington published his book over a decade ago but as we move through the first two decades of the twenty-first century, we can see that the binary he critiques gets more and more blurred and, to combat this blurring, the humanizing agents seek to uphold that binary, continuing to use popular culture as a humanizing apparatus. Posthumanists analyze this blurring, not necessarily to tear down the boundary — posthumanists recognize that the boundary will always exist in every society — but to understand where the boundary is and how society constructs and reconstructs that boundary because that boundary is always in flux. As Christopher Peterson argues, "All forms of belonging — no matter how open and hospitable they are toward others — inevitably produce 'beasts' (both human and nonhuman) whose exclusions function at cross purposes with our apparent desire for inclusivity and nonviolence" (133). Society seems to need the human/inhuman difference because it maintains the hierarchical binary and enforces an always present tenuous feeling of security in humanity's "superiority." According to Myra Seaman, when determining a "human" ideal,

> Ideologically shaped distinctions have determined inclusion and exclusion, so that features with cultural significance, such as race and gender, have been misinterpreted as biologically significant and used as markers of supposed superiority or inferiority within the "species." Posthumanism rejects the assumed universalism and exceptional *being* of Enlightenment humanism and in its place substitutes mutation, variation, and *becoming.* (247)

Seaman's statement illustrates why contemporary society is interested in the monster-hunting narrative: the monster hunter is always already in a state of becoming less monstrous and more human. However, we must also recognize that while posthumanists criticize Enlightenment humanism, society as a whole does not. In other words, fans of monstrous characters can hang pictures of those characters on their walls and people can put zombie family decals on their cars but those fans still recognize that the monsters they celebrate are "other" and certainly different from themselves.

The ultimate humanizing apparatus in much of western thought is the soul because the soul is that which clearly differentiates us from "not-us." According to Badmington, "In the Cartesian model, the essence of

109

the human lies in the rational mind, or soul, which is entirely distinct from the body" (7).[3] In the monster-hunting subgenre, the soul is less equated with the rational mind and more equated with compassion and remorse. If a being can experience compassion for others and remorse for its own actions, that being is considered "humane" and recognizably more like us than them/monster. The monster-hunting texts that delve most deeply into the humanizing power of the soul are *Buffy the Vampire Slayer* and *Angel*.[4] In the Buffyverse, humans lose their souls upon becoming a vampire, a mythology explored through the storylines of both Angel and Spike. Angel's soul is returned to him when his vampire self is cursed by a Gypsy and Spike's soul is returned to him when he asks another supernatural being to help him get back at Buffy.[5] It is important to note that, in both cases, the vampires do not request the return of their souls, although future story arcs will deal with the second loss and desired reclamation of Angel's soul. Without their souls, both vampires care nothing for human life and seek only to terrorize, torture, and kill; with their souls, both vampires regret their years as monsters and seek to make up for past evildoing by protecting the very beings they once exploited and destroyed. Angel and Spike both recognize that they can never make up for their past actions, but their reclaimed souls propel them to try and, as Badmington says, "take up their places within the symbolic order" (126), even though they know, and we as viewers know, their place is never truly within the order but always just outside of it.

While The Monster in *I, Frankenstein* follows his predecessors' similar paths to monster hunting, Stuart Beattie significantly complicates the us/them binary while, at the same time, upholding the importance of the soul as humanizing apparatus. In explaining how the human/inhuman binary is always ultimately upheld in science fiction texts, Badmington argues,

---

3 This quote may seem at odds with the earlier quote from Bynum that equates the soul with the body. As will be shown in my discussion of Plato and St. Gregory of Nyssa, the body and the soul are both needed for a living person but the soul itself can exist without the body, a separation that forms the basis of some resurrection beliefs.

4 In my book *The Monster Hunter in Modern Popular Culture*, I more fully examine the evolution of Angel and Spike from monsters to monster hunters. What follows is a very brief summary of one aspect of that evolution: the soul.

5 Spike words his request in such a way that he thinks he is asking to be made a more powerful vampire but the supernatural being chooses to interpret the request as Spike wanting to be more "human." This interpretation would imply that human emotions are more powerful than monstrous strength, thus further upholding the privileging of human in the human/monster binary.

Stitching Together a Soul

> In the complete absence of "bug-eyed monsters," the essential distinction between the human and the inhuman moves from the physical to the metaphysical: humans have feelings, but aliens do not. This binary opposition supports the film's [*Invasion of the Body Snatchers* (1956)] humanism in four principle ways. First there is a belief in an absolute difference between the human and the inhuman. Second, this difference is hierarchical. Third, there is an appeal to the uniquely human essence that cannot be replicated. Fourth, there are clearly identifiable rules according to which a simple versus — human versus aliens — may be maintained. (137)

Beattie's film complicates the hierarchical binary by creating a character whose soul is not restored but developed and developed by choice. Beattie's film presents that "uniquely human essence" as something which can be developed by a monster, thus indicating that said monster can choose to enter into the symbolic order and chip away at the humanizing ideology society holds so dear.

I, Frankenstein picks up where Mary Shelley's novel ends: Dr. Frankenstein has died pursuing his Monster into the frozen wilderness. The movie opens with the Monster bringing Victor's body back to the Frankenstein family gravesite. While burying his maker, the Monster is attacked by demons and manages to descend (send back to Hell) a couple of them before being knocked unconscious. Gargoyles — an order created by the Archangel Michael to protect humanity from demons — take the Monster to their cathedral and their queen, Leonore (Miranda Otto). Instead of killing what her first in command, Gideon (Jai Courtney), refuses to acknowledge is anything more than a soulless monstrosity, Leonore allows the Monster, whom she names Adam, to live. Adam spends the next two hundred years avoiding humanity but returns to the city — which seems to be both the demon and gargoyle headquarters — when demons begin searching for him once again. The demon/ gargoyle war comes to a head because the demon prince, Naberius (Bill Nighy), wants to use Dr. Frankenstein's creation to reanimate a demon army from millions of soulless corpses. Terra (Yvonne Strahovski), a scientist who is working for Naberius but does not know who he is or his ultimate plans for her work with tissue reanimation, connects with Adam. In the end, Adam becomes humanity's self-avowed protector thanks to his recognition and acceptance of his soul.

Plato's *Phaedo* is the work from which many of western civilization's beliefs about the soul emerge. Like many of Plato's texts, *Phaedo* is a dialogue; the dialogue takes place in 399 BC on the day before Plato's Socrates' death. In the text, Socrates is explaining the immortal nature of the soul as a way to comfort his students and followers. The *Phaedo* struck a nerve with western readers and scholars and set up many of Western civilization's dualities, including the immortal and mortal. Another useful text illustrating Plato's view of the soul is the *Phaedrus*, possibly written around the same time as the *Phaedo*. Although the main purpose of the *Phaedrus* is for Plato's Socrates to argue for the importance of proper discourse and condemn the use of writing, he uses a discussion of the soul to help prove his point. What begins as Socrates' rebuttal to Phaedrus' use of a written document becomes an in-depth metaphor of a charioteer and his two horses, a metaphor representing the immortal soul.

While Plato's dialogues and discussions of the soul were highly influential, it was St. Gregory of Nyssa who integrated the Platonic ideal of the soul into early Christian thought. Set in 379 AD, but most likely written in 380, *On the Soul and the Resurrection* clearly parallels Plato's ideas and dialogic format. In Gregory's work, his sister, St. Macrina the Younger, a devout and respected woman in the early Christian church, is facing a mortal illness at a time when both she and Gregory are mourning their dead brother, Basil, who was Bishop of Caesarea in Cappadocia. Gregory's text is an attempt to, as Catharine P. Roth writes in her introduction, "present the doctrine of bodily resurrection in terms of the Platonic philosophical tradition, but also in accord with the biblical revelation" (11). As a leader of the young Christian faith, Gregory is trying to merge a familiar concept for Christianity's followers — the Platonic ideal of the soul — with the theology of the early church. Gregory did not follow scripture with his merging of belief systems, but he did succeed in carrying Plato's ideas about the soul into early Christianity. Over the centuries, Gregory's views of the soul have become ingrained in western Christian thought. Whether we realize it or not, much of modern Christianity believes in a conception of the soul that has little, if any, basis in biblical passages but, rather, directly stems from Platonic teachings. It is this Platonic definition of the soul as retold by Gregory of Nyssa that *I, Frankenstein* conveys.

For both Plato and Gregory, the soul exists with or without the body and, therefore, is immortal. Plato believes that the soul is a "first principle" which can create movement but is not created or moved by something else. In *Phaedrus*, he claims, "Every soul is immortal, for that which moves itself is immortal" (27). In other words, the soul can

Stitching Together a Soul

animate the body, but the body is not necessary to animate the soul. And since the soul is not created by anything else, it also cannot die. Plato's understanding of the immortality of the soul permeates Gregory's belief as expressed by Macrina: "[I]f we desire to know ourselves . . . the soul itself teaches us well enough what we should understand about the soul, namely that it is immaterial and bodiless, working and moving in accord with its own nature, and revealing its motions by means of the bodily organs" (37). Again, the understanding is that the soul is separate from the body and immortal. The body is the outward appearance of the Platonic soul's movement but the soul is always in control of the body's actions, both physical and emotional. To help emphasize the immortality of the soul, Plato likens the soul to a charioteer with two winged horses; one of the horses is "good" while the other is "difficult." A truly divine being, like a god, can learn to master both horses and command both elements of the soul; however, humans predominantly cannot master the horses because they do not have the necessary emotional mastery of divine beings and often allow the difficult horse to be in control. In simpler terms, humans like to give in to their desires more often than they should. According to Plato, "when it [the soul] is perfect and fully winged, it soars on high and is responsible for all order in the universe; but if it loses its wings, it is carried down until it can fasten on something solid. It settles there, taking on an earthly body which seems to be self-moving because of the power of soul within it" (28). In Plato's view, humans are all fallen souls whose charioteer could not manage both horses.

In *I, Frankenstein*, the necessary vessel for the soul is created in a laboratory. When he sews together the various parts to create his Monster, Dr. Frankenstein creates a vessel into which a fallen — in Platonic rather than Christian understanding — soul can enter. However, Adam does not believe a soul ever did enter his re-animated body. The opening sequence of the film is accompanied by Adam's voiceover, given here in its entirety: "I was cast into being in the winter of 1795, a living corpse without a soul. Stitched. Jolted. Bludgeoned back to life by a madman. Horrified by his creation, he tried to destroy me, but I survived and found my way back to him." It is clear that neither Dr. Frankenstein nor Adam believe there is a soul in the re-animated vessel; however, neither Plato nor Gregory believed that a soulless, living corpse could exist. The very fact that Adam is a walking, talking, sentient being indicates that he must have a soul. Adam actually seems to be the ideal posthuman; as stated by Myra Seaman, "although all of these [bodily] features of

113

our person can be modified (except, it is maintained, the 'soul'), the experiences of the body—perceived through sensation and processed through emotion—remain the locus of individual identity" (249). As will be shown, Adam does experience sensation and emotion. Even though Adam may not believe he has a soul, both the Platonists and the posthumanists would argue otherwise.

As a hodgepodge of body parts from different corpses—each, presumably, with separate souls—the argument may be raised that Adam cannot have a soul. The belief that there is one soul for one body is actually the contemporary result of an evolution of cultural and spiritual beliefs. In fact, Gregory took into consideration a fractured vessel. Using the image of a sailor whose vessel is shipwrecked and broken, Macrina tells her brother that the sailor will latch on to the part of the ship near him. She continues, "[I]n the same manner, since the soul is naturally unable to be split up along with the separation of the elements [the vessel], if indeed it is firmly attached to the body, it will surely join itself to some one of the elements and be divided from the others" (47). Macrina continues,

> When the vessel is dissolved, the soul which has possessed it continues to recognize its own vessel just as well from the mere remains. The soul does not depart from its own elements either when the fragments are collected together or if they are mixed with the unworked part of the elemental matter. The soul always knows its own body as it is when it coheres in its shape: and it is not deceived concerning its own body after the dissolution, because of the signs which persist in the remnants. (69)

The impetus for St. Gregory's exploration of a "broken" vessel stems, in part, from the early Western Christian concern over the decomposing body and resurrection. Those who believed in a literal bodily resurrection would have serious concerns about the state of their bodies both in life and in death, concerns St. Gregory attempts to address. Therefore, if the soul does latch on to an element of the original vessel, it would certainly make sense that Adam would possess at least one soul and, in fact, perhaps more than one. Adam tells Terra that he is made up of eight corpses. Even if only half of those corpses retained their souls, as could happen in Macrina's analogy, Adam could be struggling with at least four different souls. Adam believes himself to be soulless, but the reality of his unique situation may be that his "true" soul is trying to emerge. As Platonic charioteer, perhaps Adam must determine which soul will be the one to give meaning to his life.

114

Stitching Together a Soul

Even though the film opens with Adam's soulless view of himself, an important scene just six minutes into the film indicates that Adam's situation is more complicated than he believes. When Adam wakes up after being brought to the gargoyles' cathedral, he looks like some kind of wildling. His hair is unkempt, dirty, and hanging over his face. Throughout this scene, the gargoyles refer to Adam as "it" and "the thing" because they believe he is not human and, by extension, lacking self-awareness or a soul. When he first awakens, Adam even tries to back away as if he is making choices based on animal instincts and not human rationale. When Leonore enters the chamber, her face is devoid of expression and the low-angle shot makes her tower over the scared and chained being. As Adam struggles with his chains, Gideon says, "No more than a wild beast, your majesty. Destroy it and be done with this." The shot cuts from Gideon, also shown in a low-angle shot so he stands above Adam, to an extreme close-up of Adam as he pulls the metal bracket holding his right-side chains up from the floor. The cinematography and editing choices in this scene indicate Adam's point of view. The use of a low-angle shot implies that the gargoyles have both a physical and moral superiority over Adam; because the gargoyles believe Adam to be a soulless monster or animal, they are looking down on him. By giving Adam the point of view in much of this scene, Beattie is actually manipulating the viewer into sympathizing with him, especially since the viewer already knows from the opening sequence that Adam is, indeed, self-aware. Beattie's manipulation illustrates a kind of crack in humanity's privileging of itself over what Christopher Peterson calls "animal" or what I call "monster": "The assertion of animal lack . . . presupposes an acknowledgement of transspecies similarity, no matter how minimal, that is nonetheless denied" (130). The gargoyles want to deny Adam his humanity because of his actions; however, Beattie forces the viewer to witness much of the scene through Adam's point of view so the viewer will sympathize with Adam by recognizing that he is experiencing fear at waking up a prisoner in an unfamiliar setting. The viewer can relate to Adam's response so the viewer immediately identifies with Adam, thus marking him as "human" and not entirely "other."

The next moment in this scene indicates to Leonore that Adam is not as monstrous as originally assumed. After the extreme close-up of the bracket holding Adam's chains, the shot cuts again and the two gargoyles who brought Adam to the cathedral—Keziah (Caitlin Stasey) and Ophir (Mahesh Jadu)—place their blades against Adam's

115

neck and he settles down. Lenore sees this reaction and says, "So. You understand reason." As Gideon moves in to kill him, Adam says "no" and Leonore stops Gideon. When Gideon steps away and out of the frame, Leonore becomes the scene's focus. Both her silvery-blue costume and the lighting emphasize Leonore but, more importantly, the lighting allows the viewer to see that her expression has changed. Where there was once an emotionless look on her face, now her face has softened and her brows are knit together in a questioning glance. As she moves toward Adam, the background music, which has been present throughout the scene, swells, implying that something important is about to happen. The shot cuts to a high-angle long shot which includes Adam in the top center of the frame facing the camera, Leonore in the bottom center of the frame with her back to the camera, and Keziah and Ophir in the middle on the left and right, respectively, of the frame. This change from Adam's first-person point of view to the omniscient third-person point of view further emphasizes the importance of the scene because now everyone is equally presented within the frame with no character privileged over another. The shot cuts back to Adam's point of view as Leonore stands within touching distance. Again, Leonore is the focus of the shot and the lighting illuminates her entire face with no shadow; she is clearly having a moment of realization. When she reaches out her hand, the shot cuts to a close-up of Adam's head as he tries to move away from her hand. Like her face in the previous shot, her hand is fully lit. The shot cuts back to Leonore's face and her look of concentration. Again, there is a quick shot-reverse shot and the viewer sees from Leonore's point of view as, in a delicate motion, she removes Adam's hair from his eyes. The extreme close-up focuses the viewer's attention on Adam's terrified eyes, which are looking at Leonore's hand. When she removes her hand, Adam's expression changes from one of terror to one of confusion. Leonore's touch was not what he expected. The shot-reverse shot format continues and viewers see a close-up of Leonore's face followed by an extreme close-up of Adam's eyes. This time the emotion within Adam's eyes seems to be confusion as well as desire. It is difficult to say what Adam desires in this moment but given his reaction to Leonore's touch, it is quite possible to assume that Adam desires kindness and compassion, even if he does not yet understand that desire. In the final two shots of the sequence, director Stuart Beattie returns to his familiar framing of Leonore and then Adam as she says, "Him. Not it" and Adam continues to look at her with confusion but also a sense of understanding the importance of the moment. The entire

Stitching Together a Soul

scene lasts about one minute but that one minute serves to move Adam more towards the human side of the human/monster divide.

When Leonore says that Adam is a "him" instead of an "it," she is acknowledging that he is not the monstrous being everyone, including himself, believes him to be. She sees something in him—what the viewer learns in a later scene is "Not a soul but the potential for one"—that allows Adam to live. Along with the potential of a soul, Leonore also puts her faith in God and Adam's presence on Earth. After letting Adam go, Gideon confronts her about her decision; Gideon believes that his queen should have killed Adam. Leonore responds, "I am not blind to the risks. Adam is alive and all life is sacred." Later in the film, Gideon again confronts Leonore about her choice to let Adam live. This time she responds, "God may not have put Adam on this Earth but He did allow him to live for over two hundred years against incredible odds. It is not for you or I to deny God's purpose." In both instances, Leonore acknowledges the importance of Adam's "movement." Adam is a sentient being who can walk, talk, and think and that, at least, gives him the chance to make his way in the world.

In some ways, Leonore's responses illustrate what Myra Seaman calls the "contemporary popular posthuman," a being who is a human/ science hybrid and "while features are adapted and weaknesses improved through scientific application, the self is not lost but enhanced, made not into another species but ultimately more like itself, yet better. Through the hybridization of human and supplement, what is supposedly best about the human remains—its supposedly open susceptibility, rooted in its unpredictable emotional responsiveness" (250-51). Leonore recognizes that Adam must be given the opportunity to discern his own purpose in life, or to become more like himself, yet better. This purpose is directly linked to his potential for a soul and his humanity not his monstrosity. After she has Adam unchained, Gideon reminds Leonore that the Creature killed Dr. Frankenstein's wife. Leonore responds both to Gideon and Adam, "All in the heat of passion, driven by emotions he was never taught to control. He may be more human than he realizes. I understand Frankenstein never offered you a name. I should like to call you Adam. I promise you this, Adam, each of us has a higher purpose. Yours has simply yet to reveal itself." Beattie returns to the shot-reverse shot format from the earlier scene but this time there is no low-angle shot because Adam is standing, equal with Leonore. There is, however, a third shot in the sequence this time, that of Gideon. As Leonore is explaining why Adam should not be killed, she

117

is once again in the right-hand third of the frame and fully lit. The shot cuts to Gideon, standing behind Leonore's left shoulder taking up the right-half of the frame. Gideon is lit from the left so that the right side of his face is in shadow thus implying that he is not convinced of Adam's "worth." His expression is one of contempt for Adam. The shot cuts again when Leonore says "he may be more human" and Adam takes up the majority of the frame, with only a small bit of Leonore's profile in the far right. Although Leonore is speaking directly to him, Adam's eyes are not on her but on Gideon. Adam is almost completely in shadow with the light behind him. His long dark hair, again covering much of his face, and his dark clothing contrast him with Leonore and Gideon. The meaning conveyed in this scene is that Adam is not fully convinced by what Leonore has been telling him. As Leonore uses the word "human," Adam's gaze abruptly shifts from Gideon to Leonore and she is once again the focus of the shot. As Leonore continues speaking, her look is one of pleading. When Adam is present in the frame, his look is once again questioning as he furrows his brow and cocks his head to the left in a pose of confusion. Although he sees himself as a monster, Leonore, and the viewer, sees him as living within the border between monster and human, able to move in either direction.

As was previously stated, in Plato's metaphor, the difficult horse can bring the chariot and charioteer down to earth. According to the *Phaedrus*, when this fall occurs, "the horse of evil nature weighs down their chariots, pulling heavily toward the earth any charioteer who has not trained him well. And here the extremity of toil and struggle awaits the soul" (29). For Plato, a chariot ruled by negative passion is doomed to fall to earth. Before he can become Plato's successful charioteer, Adam must first deal with the rage inside him and move beyond his isolationist tendencies. Two hundred years does little to calm that rage, and Adam spends most of that time seething in isolation. A life without purpose tends to be a life lived for the immediate gratification of wants and desires, the exact excesses warned against by both Plato and Gregory. Once the demons seek him out, however, Adam makes it his personal mission to descend as many demons as Naberius sends after him. When the film moves to the present day, Adam has followed the demons back to the city that they and the gargoyles inhabit. The Gargoyle Order once again captures Adam but this time Leonore has a very different reaction to him. In his second time as Queen Leonore's prisoner, the shot-reverse shot sequence among Leonore, Gideon, and Adam differs significantly

Stitching Together a Soul

from the earlier Adam-as-captive sequence. It is clear from this second visit that Leonore is fed up with Adam's refusal to find his purpose and acknowledge his soul.

The scene opens in much the same way as the first scene, with Adam chained in the cathedral; however, this time Adam has short hair and is chained to a chair instead of the floor, indicating that Adam is less of a "monster" now than in his early years. While her back is to the camera and the viewer is focused on Adam, Leonore says, "Ours is a war that must be fought in the shadows. It is not an open battlefield for you to do as you please." Halfway through this statement, the point of view shifts to Adam and the viewer sees Leonore. In the earlier scene, Leonore's face is completely lit; in this scene, she has a shadow over the right side of her face, like Gideon's facial lighting in the earlier scene, helping to emphasize her anger. Adam's lighting mirrors Leonore's but the shadow is on the left side of his face and much darker. This contrasting lighting indicates that Leonore's negative emotions are not nearly as strong as Adam's. Adam's deeper shadow indicates that his difficult horse, his rage, is still in control. When Gideon is finally shown, he has no shadow upon his face, indicating that there is no emotional turmoil going on within him; he still believes that Adam has no business living.

When Gideon tells Adam that he will remain in the cathedral, Adam tells Leonore that she cannot keep him there. It is the first time Adam's face registers anything but contempt. In a close-up, Adam says, "My life is my own. You will not take it from me." Neither Adam nor Leonore have moved at all during this scene, remaining stationary each time the camera cuts to one of them. Their positions are rigid and the lighting remains consistent: neither has any intention of changing his/ her mind. Both are being stubborn as Leonore is no longer willing to give Adam a chance to find his soul and Adam has no intention of ending his vendetta. For the first time, Leonore gets visibly angry as she raises her voice in response, "Your life was not granted to you by the grace of God. It was fabricated in a laboratory. And until you learn to use it wisely, I will do what I must." This statement is in direct contrast to what she said to Gideon in the earlier scene about God letting Adam live. Because he refuses to even attempt to tame his soul and embrace his human nature, Leonore has decided that Adam is no better than a demon; she is moving him from the border to the monstrous side of the binary. Leonore continues, "When I met you, my first thought was to

119

have you destroyed. But then I looked into your eyes and do you know what I saw there? Not a soul but the potential for one. Now all I see is darkness." The shots continue to cut back and forth between her and Adam during this explanation and although Leonore's expression does not change, the close-up on Adam allows the viewer to see the same expression he had when Leonore first called Adam "him." Adam's eyes are filled with confusion and possibly even conflict. In a very subtle way, Beattie has also moved to a low-angle shot and Adam is looking up at Leonore by the end of the scene, implying that Leonore has the higher position and the higher morality while Adam is beneath her because he still focuses on himself. As Leonore leaves the room, the shot cuts back to Adam who is not nearly as contemptuous and antagonistic as before; his face has softened and his eyes are wide. After Leonore leaves, Adam is left alone, chin trembling, a possible sign that he has begun to regret his previous actions.

Adam is, as yet, incapable of controlling his difficult horse. In some respects, he does not care about controlling his rage as he chooses to fight the demons for no outcome other than isolation. But, throughout the film so far, Adam at least has had a choice and has made his own decisions about his path, good or bad. Humankind's free will is vital to the development of the soul for both Plato and Gregory. Both men understand that humans must choose which path to follow: virtue or vice. As Macrina tells Gregory, "Instead, by the particular use of our free choice such impulses of the soul become instruments of virtue or wickedness, just as steel, forged according to the intention of the craftsman, is shaped towards whatever the smith desires, becoming either a sword or some agricultural implement" (57). It is the person who controls the emotional impulses, not the soul itself that is imbued with one nature or another. Just as every human must determine his/her fate, so too must every monster seeking a monster-hunting path. Once a monster hunter has a soul, s/he must decide whether to ignore that soul and hide in the shadows or stand up and fight for humankind. Just like the monster hunters who came before him, Adam is on this same path.

Ultimately, Adam needs a guide on his path to recognizing his soul. In the *Phaedo*, Socrates tells his listeners that the soul needs a guide to find its way from one world to the next because the path does not follow a simple, straight line: "Now the wise and well-ordered soul follows along, and is not unfamiliar with what befalls it; but the soul in a state of desire for the body, as I said earlier, flutters around it for a

Stitching Together a Soul

long time, and around the region of the seen, and after much resistance and many sufferings it goes along, brought by force and against its will by the appointed spirit" (67). Although Leonore attempts to set Adam on his path, it is the scientist, Terra, who eventually serves as Adam's guide. Socrates' guide helps the soul to move to judgment but Adam's guide helps him move from a world of anger and isolation to a world of acceptance and purpose.

Throughout much of the film, Adam does not think he has the free will or agency to change his path. He believes himself to be a monster, even after he experiences his first moment of human kindness. Soon after Adam and Terra meet, Adam is wounded in a battle with a demon and Terra tends to his injuries. When Terra first sees Adam without a shirt, she is shocked by, and Adam is embarrassed by, the many scars left from Dr. Frankenstein's work. Terra recovers herself and has Adam sit on the bed so she can sew up his new wounds. Adam remains standing, clearly uncertain as to what he should do. The scene parallels the scene when Adam first meets Leonore. However, it is clear from Beattie's direction that Terra has a better chance of guiding Adam to his soul. First, the music throughout this scene identifies it as an intimate moment, soft and melodic as opposed to the ominous music playing under the earlier Leonore-Adam scene. Second, as he did when Leonore was kind to him, Adam is once again uncertain how to react. The shot sequence begins with a close-up of Adam's head and shoulders prominently displayed in the middle of the frame. Adam is looking down and to his right, with a pained or confused look. There are shadows in this scene but, significantly, more on his shoulders and forehead than his face. In past scenes of importance to Adam's path, those characters whose faces have been without shadow have either had a moment of realization or been without doubt in their beliefs. The lack of shadows on his face indicates that Adam is about to have a significant self-realization. The shot then cuts to an extreme close-up of Terra grabbing Adam's arm to make him sit. Whereas Adam flinched earlier in the film when Leonore touched him, here he allows Terra's hand on his arm, again indicating that Terra will serve as an important guide. The prominent image in the frame is Adam's bare torso and his right arm with Terra's hand on it, the only part of her visible in the frame. The shot then cuts to Adam's head and shoulders and back to Terra holding his arm. This scene is only the second time in the film that someone has touched Adam in a way that is gentle and kind rather than violent and aggressive. It is unclear whether his acceptance of Terra's touch comes from two hundred years

121

of isolation, a subconscious desire to connect with humans, or some combination of both. What is clear is that Adam does not immediately reject Terra's assistance.

Given the intimacy of this scene, the viewer may expect that Adam's opinion of himself and humanity has changed, yet he continues to insist on his status as monster, as is demonstrated by Adam and Terra's exchange about the oncoming war between gargoyles and demons for what Adam calls "your world":

> Terra: "And what will you do?"
> Adam: "It has nothing to do with me."
> Terra: "Of course it does. You're as much a part of this world as anybody."
> Adam: "No. I'm different."
> Terra: "You're not that different."
> Adam: "I'm a dozen used parts from eight different corpses. I'm a monster."
> Terra: "You're only a monster if you behave like one."

As Terra says this, Adam is the prominent figure in the frame as the viewer sees his back and shoulders over Terra's left shoulder. All the colors around Adam are muted with Adam himself partially lit. Adam turns around to face Terra and the look in his eyes is one of thoughtfulness and perhaps surprise. The shot cuts to Terra and then back to Adam, who is no longer looking at her. This time his expression is that of someone questioning what has just been said. This moment may be the dawning of Adam's understanding of free will and it certainly indicates that Adam has a choice of whether he becomes human or not. If Terra is, indeed, Adam's guide, then she has just given him a very important insight into his soul. In the *Phaedo*, Socrates repeatedly says that the soul can achieve truth only through reason and when not distracted by bodily needs: "And it reasons best, presumably, whenever none of these things bothers it, neither hearing nor sight nor pain, nor any pleasure either, but whenever it comes to be alone by itself as far as possible, disregarding the body, and whenever, having the least possible communion and contact with it, it strives for reality" (11). Plato argues that the ideal soul is beyond human emotional frailty; this ideal is not that far afield of a truly posthuman creation as indicated by Myra Seaman: "[I]n the posthuman as imagined in popular culture, the bodily modifications are pursued because of the superior capabilities they can add to the already-established self" (248). Both emotion and

Stitching Together a Soul

reason mark a human despite what the body might look like. Adam has been ruled by his rage for so long that he has not been able to focus his attention on anything else, but in this moment with Terra, Adam's reason begins to break through his emotional turmoil and he is seen by the viewer as a bit closer to human.

Beattie never clearly states where Adam's rage comes from. Viewers are led to assume it is a combination of being abandoned by his maker, being called a monster, and being hunted by demons. Those viewers who also know the novel will remember Dr. Frankenstein's promise to his creation, a promise of a companion that remains unfulfilled and leads the Monster to kill Frankenstein's love, thus beginning the end of the story for both creature and creator. After the exchange between Adam and Terra, Terra asks Adam if he would like her to make him the companion Dr. Frankenstein promised. After she poses the question, the shot focuses on Adam's reaction. Adam is in the right half of the frame with Terra's back in the left half. As he looks at her with narrowed eyes and a furrowed brow, the left side of Adam's face is almost entirely in shadow, again indicating a conflict of emotion. It is clear to the viewer that Adam is giving Terra's offer some thought. In the last moment of the shot, his face softens and he opens his mouth just a bit as if to say something, but Terra's phone rings and the moment is gone. Although Adam does not answer Terra's question about a companion, Beattie's cinematic choices and Aaron Eckhart's acting indicate to the viewer that Adam needs to think and, possibly, re-assess what it is he wants.

Even if Adam spends the majority of the scene shirtless and Terra spends a lot of time looking at his chest, this intimate scene between Adam and Terra is not a scene of blossoming love. St. Gregory warns against giving in to the power of love if a Platonic soul is to seek truth. To illustrate his point, Gregory turns to a metaphor of a farmer who plants good seeds among useless weeds. As both plants grow together, the good seeds are in danger of being choked out by the weeds; in this metaphor, the good seeds are the soul and the weeds are human emotions. One weed is love: "Likewise the power of love has turned away from the intelligible, running riot in the immoderate enjoyment of the sensual. The other emotions in the same way have produced the worse plants instead of the better" (59). Love is an emotion that can negatively affect a person's path to an idealized soul; whether consciously or not, Beattie's treatment of Adam and Terra's relationship seems to indicate that sensual love is not their focus. For both Plato and Gregory, once the Platonic soul is cleansed of all negative emotions and desires, it attains the ideal of godliness. In *Phaedrus*, this end result is achieved through logic: "Consequently, when the soul has at long last beheld Reality, it rejoices, finding sustenance in its direct contemplation of the truth and in the immediate experience of it until, in the revolution of its orbit, it is brought round again to the point of departure. . . . [I]t is Real Knowledge whose object is the truly existent" (30). In *On the Soul and the Resurrection*, the end result is beauty. Macrina tells Gregory, "So you see, if our soul should become free of its attachment to the irrational emotions either by our effort in this life or by the purification hereafter, it will in no way be hindered from the contemplation of the beautiful. For beauty has in its own nature an attractiveness for everyone who looks at it. So if the soul becomes clean of all evil, it will exist entirely in beauty" (77). Whether reality or beauty, the end result of taming one's soul is a conquering of emotion-driven decision-making. Because Adam's goal is to recognize his soul, he must work through his emotions and not add other emotional baggage to his rage. Although emotional expression is an indication of human-ness, too much emotion, especially negative emotion, can work to distinguish a being as "other." The scene between Adam and Terra works as an interaction between a lost soul and his guide and not as a romantic subplot.

It is through Adam's connection to Terra that he finally recognizes his soul and willingly *becomes* "human." He is able to let his rage-filled past go and focus on the present. Part of this break with the past comes when Adam burns the journal Dr. Frankenstein kept. In destroying the journal, Adam destroys all hope of another reanimated vessel like himself. His action alleviates any fears that an army of monsters will be created in Adam's image; the only character who wants such an army is Naberius, who is definitely coded monstrous. Adam is palatable to the viewer because his soul makes him just human enough to be accepted despite the scars on his body that will always mark him as other and recognizably different. When Adam goes to save Terra from Naberius, he is aligning himself with humankind and, although he uses the gargoyles to help him save Terra, he does not align himself with either of the supernatural, and clearly not-human, beings. In case viewers have any doubt about Adam's newfound soul, Naberius confirms its existence during the battle scene between him and Adam. While they are fighting, Naberius makes a demonic sign on Adam's forehead so a demon can inhabit what Naberius believes to be a soulless vessel. A fiery demon spirit ascends from underground and encompasses Adam, seeming to consume him. Naberius says, "Welcome, my son. You have possessed a

Stitching Together a Soul

truly remarkable body." Adam responds, "I am not your son. And this body is mine" as he wipes off the symbol. While Adam says this, he is captured in a high-angle shot, looking up at Naberius. Adam's face is fully lit, one of the few times in the film that this occurs. His face, like his soul, is no longer in shadow. Naberius, shocked, exclaims, "No! It's not possible. You have a soul."

After Queen Leonore saves Adam and Terra from the lab's demise, one final exchange between them indicates that Adam has finally tamed his difficult horse. Adam asks why Leonore saved him and she responds, a smile on her face, "Because you finally found your higher purpose." The shot cuts to Adam, his face again half in shadow and wearing a quizzical look. This time, though, the shadowed lighting implies a dawning realization rather than angry confusion. The shot then cuts to Terra, sitting on the cathedral floor watching the exchange. The implication of this brief sequence further confirms that it was Terra who helped Adam find his higher purpose, his humanity, and his soul, both Plato's reality and Gregory's beauty.

When Leonore leaves, Adam squats down to talk to Terra. She asks him where the journal is. When Adam responds, he is taking up the right half of the frame and his face is bathed in a soft light with no shadow. As he responds, "I don't need it anymore," the look on his face is no longer one of anger or confusion — the looks he has worn throughout most of the film — but one of peace and possibly even happiness. The scene cuts to Terra and then back to Adam as he stands up and holds out his hand to help her up off the floor. This is the first and only time in the film that Adam initiates any type of intimacy by choosing to touch another being out of kindness and not rage. In *On the Soul and the Resurrection*, Gregory says,

> Thus we can say both that the constitution of the soul is from God and (since we do not conceive of any evil in connection with the Divine) that the soul is free from the necessity of evil. When it comes into existence in this manner it is led by its own inclination to what seems good to it. It may live in the darkness of deception, closing its eyes to the good by choice, or by a plot of the enemy which besets our life suffering an injury to its eyes; or else looking in purity towards the truth, it may move far away from the passions of darkness. (96)

When he takes Terra's hand at the end of the film — a significant moment given that the clasped hands are shot in extreme close-up and are in the center of the frame—Adam is choosing humankind and, in so doing, choosing his own humanity and moving away from the passions of darkness.

Adam spends two hundred years in darkness, filled with rage. When he discovers his humanity, he comes into the light, a Platonic reality of monster hunting. Such an evolution implies that the human/inhuman binary is far less secure than we might expect. If the soul is a predominant humanizing apparatus, and a monster can cultivate a soul, then surely a monster can be accepted as human. Such an ending would imply that contemporary society is overcoming its human/inhuman binary. But is the soul enough for acceptance? At the end of her essay, Myra Seaman states, "[T]he contemporary posthuman defends the beauty of the singular human by deliberately retaining, within its machinery or altered physical state, the weaknesses and vulnerabilities that result from the memories of its old, historical body, and hence, its all too affected and affective self" (270). This statement can be read in two ways. In a positive light, the posthuman has the best of both worlds: an improved physical vessel with the original soul. In a negative light, the posthuman is always distinguished as different through its physical transformation, no matter how much of the original personality or soul is retained. And herein lies the complication Stuart Beattie adds to the human/inhuman binary. Just as Seaman's statement can be interpreted in two ways, so too can the ending of *I, Frankenstein*. The film ends with a pan over the nighttime city. The pan ends on a long shot of Adam, holding his weapons and standing in the foreground of the frame atop a building. Adam and the gargoyle cathedral, which is to his left, take up almost equal space in the frame. Over the pan and final shot, the viewers hear Adam's voiceover: "We do not ask for the lives we are given. But each of us has the right to defend that life. I have fought to defend mine. And when the forces of darkness return, you should know that I am out there, fighting to defend yours. I, descender of the demon horde. I, my father's son. I, Frankenstein." In these last moments, Adam stands alone, powerful protector of mankind and claimant of his name, his identity, and his soul. For all intents and purposes, he is aligned with the human. But he stands *alone*, atop the human world, visually aligned in the frame with the supernatural creatures and not humanity. He is a monster hunter, always both recognizably human and recognizably other, existing in the space between the human/inhuman divide.

Stitching Together a Soul

Works Cited

Badmington, Neil. *Alien Chic: Posthumanism and the Other Within*. London and New York: Routledge, 2004.

Bynum, Caroline Walker. *The Resurrection of the Body in Western Christianity, 200-1336*. New York: Columbia UP, 1995.

I, Frankenstein. Dir. Stuart Beattie. Perf. Aaron Eckhart, Bill Nighy, and Miranda Otto. Lionsgate, 2013.

Peterson, Christopher. "The Posthumanism to Come." *Angelaki* 16.2 (June 2011): 127-141.

Plato. *Phaedo*. Ed. and trans. David Gallop. Oxford and New York: Oxford UP, 1993.

_____. *Phaedrus*. Trans. W. C. Helmbold and W. G. Rabinowitz. Upper Saddle River, NJ: Prentice Hall, 1956.

Roth, Catharine P. "Introduction." *On the Soul and the Resurrection*. By St. Gregory of Nyssa. Crestwood, NY: St. Vladimir's Seminary Press, 1993. 7-25.

Seaman, Myra. "Becoming More (Than) Human: Affective Posthumanisms, Past and Future." *Journal of Narrative Theory* 37.2 (Summer 2007): 246-275.

St. Gregory of Nyssa. *On the Soul and the Resurrection*. Trans. Catharine P. Roth. Crestwood, NY: St. Vladimir's Seminary Press, 1993.

"That's Not a Real Dinosaur": The Indominus Rex and Monstrosity in *Jurassic World*

BROOKE SOUTHGATE

The plot of Colin Trevorrow's *Jurassic World* (2015) picks up twenty years after the events of Steven Spielberg's *Jurassic Park* (1993), yet both films' depictions of technology and nature reverberate with similar themes of monstrosity, domination, corporate exploitation, and a broader cultural desire for that exploitation. The creation, in *Jurassic World*, of a hybrid dinosaur that escapes its confines to run amok on the island, terrorizing visitors and other dinosaurs alike, depicts monstrosity as something beyond nature, embodied in a cyborg creation that does not fit within even the artificial nature of the park, let alone as an example of prehistoric nature. The *Indominus rex* exists for profit, and in that quest for profit the visitors in the film who want to see something bigger and more spectacular are echoed by movie-goers who want to see the impressive special effects of a giant dinosaur on screen. To satisfy both audiences, a monster was created. Within the film, the CEO of the park, Simon Masrani, exclaims, "I never asked for a monster" (*Jurassic World*), but such a declaration ignores that the corporate-run theme park asked for the technological creation of a biological specimen. The company then attempted to utilize the resultant cyborg for profit. The *Indominus rex* serves as a warning against the creation and exploitation of monstrous attractions and questions the cultural desire for such attractions.

Dinosaur as Cyborg

A creation of living animal and advanced technology, the *Indominus rex* blends these binary concepts into a single entity; thus, she

"That's Not a Real Dinosaur": The Indominus Rex

is a cyborg. Although cyborg studies are largely focused on human and technology merging, the thematic concept of biology and technology fusing into a single entity is important in considering how humans view nature. Val Plumwood defines nature as passive and the "background" against which active reason and culture occur (4). Such a definition is common in Western society in which nature is considered a non-agent that is dominated by culture and society, usually through some form of technology. Nature is valued because of what it offers humans through its resources, which places it firmly in a submissive, passive role (Plumwood 147). This idea that nature is to be used to benefit humans is evident through the portrayal of the dinosaurs of Jurassic World, and particularly the *Indominus rex*, as part of a corporate endeavor aimed at profit. The dinosaurs are thus aligned with nature, but they are not completely natural creatures; they exist because of technology and are depicted as advanced technological creations. This places the dinosaurs between the binary of nature and technology without being fully categorized as either. Elaine Graham writes that through reconfiguring these classifications, new creatures emerge that further the discussion of the limits of such categories (12). By representing both an exploited resource of nature and the exploiting technology, the dinosaurs of *Jurassic World* are cyborg creations that problematize such binary distinctions.

The *Indominus rex* is a creature that questions what is biological and what is technological. Unlike the other dinosaurs in the park, she is a genetically engineered hybrid, and as such, she is presented as being more closely aligned with the technological than the biological. The raptors that hatch in *Jurassic Park* are shown in a nest with other eggs, and even have a mechanical egg turner tending to them; the dinosaurs are presented as cyborgs, but they remain linked to nature. This representation echoes something people are familiar with in nature, a bird roosting in its nest and tending its eggs. The tiny raptor struggles to break through the shell (*Jurassic Park*), an image that is familiar to viewers who may have seen chicks hatch. The cyborg elements of the *Jurassic Park* animal are overpowered by the seemingly natural, even endearing, hatching. In contrast, the *Indominus rex* is presented as a technological creation from the very beginning: the film opens with a stark white laboratory and a cracking egg on a metal pedestal (*Jurassic World*). A thumping heartbeat is heard to emphasize that the egg is alive within these stark surroundings, yet the egg, and the life within it, is presented as a technological achievement rather than a biological one.

129

The juxtaposition of the natural-looking egg shell against the sterile, plain walls and the lack of a nest accentuates the unnatural setting of the hatching. As the egg cracks, the first glimpse of the *Indominus rex* is her long, black claws breaking through the shell, and then a close up of her large, red eye (*Jurassic World*). Highlighting these specific characteristics of the *Indominus rex* amplifies how different she is from other animals since no other known species hatches with similar features. The contrived elements of the *Indominus rex*'s hatching links her firmly to her technological origins as a cyborg creation.

Her cyborg status is confirmed by the melding of technology and nature inherent in the unnatural creation of the *Indominus rex*. Dr. Wu tells a tour group that "Indominus wasn't bred; she was designed" (*Jurassic World*), and his emphasis on technological creation divorces the *Indominus rex* from natural concepts such as breeding animals, and it introduces a focus on unnatural reproduction. Reproduction was a primary focus in *Jurassic Park* both as the supposedly all-female dinosaur population began breeding and as a portrayal of cloning and bypassing natural forms of reproduction. Laura Briggs and Jodi I. Kelber-Kaye argue that genetic technology in *Jurassic Park* stands for science at large and is placed in conflict with nature and maternal reproduction (94). Donna J. Haraway notes, however, that integral components to the cyborg include the erosion of binaries and a divorce from concepts of natural reproduction (51). Technological creation "is a dangerous breach of the nature/technological boundary," and although Briggs and Kelber-Kaye are discussing an earlier generation of dinosaurs in *Jurassic Park* (96), this concept of scientists breaching the binary between nature and technology applies to the creation of the *Indominus rex*. Her creation is depicted as a technological achievement and positions her beyond both nature and science as a combination of both.

Cyborg as Monster

Because she is a cyborg, the *Indominus rex* is a monster that questions the cultural construction of a binary distinction between nature and technology. The blending of technology and nature into a seemingly seamless creation accentuates the instability of such a boundary, and the *Indominus rex* emphasizes the binary through transgressing it. She is a monster because she is neither natural nor technological, but a combination of both. Graham expresses this duality of monsters when

"That's Not a Real Dinosaur": The Indominus Rex

she writes, "Monsters have a double function, therefore, simultaneously marking the boundaries between the normal and the pathological but also exposing the fragility of the very taken-for-grantedness of such categories" (38). It is not simply that the binaries can be transgressed, but that doing so demonstrates that the binaries are actually fluid and not strictly defined. As the result of genetic engineering in a scientific laboratory, the *Indominus rex* violates expectations of realistic nature; the theme park Jurassic World took the technology of cloning dinosaurs a step further and created a monster. Her status as something beyond the park's usual cloned dinosaurs is demonstrated in the film when an image of the *Indominus rex* flashes on a computer screen and young Gray says, "That's not a real dinosaur" (*Jurassic World*). This recognition that the *Indominus rex* is not a dinosaur but rather a monster supports her position as a cyborg and as an allegory for the eroding boundaries between nature and technology. As such she calls them, and their social constructions, into question.

The cultural creation of monsters is evident in *Jurassic World* because of the film's emphasis on providing what the public desires: something bigger, scarier, with more teeth. Haraway includes the role of society in her definition of the cyborg as "a cybernetic organism, a hybrid of machine and organism, a creature of social reality as well as a creature of fiction" (50). The cyborg in science-fiction film complicates not only the binaries from which it is created but also the social construction of the binaries. The creation of a cyborg reworks nature and culture to create something new from the parts which is its own whole creation (Haraway 51). The idea that culture is an integral part of the cyborg, generally through the form of technology, also connects the cyborg to the monster. Slavoj Žižek writes that the monster exists between nature and culture as a type of "missing link" that bridges the two supposed binaries (136). The *Indominus rex* creates such a bridge because she incorporates culture, technology, and nature into a single being. The *Indominus rex* is a monster that exists beyond the culturally created binary viewpoints, and her position as such reveals the problematic view of nature and technology as distinct categories.

The *Indonimus rex* is additionally monstrous because of her representation as female. Her gender is particularly highlighted in the beginning of the film when Clair Dearing, the operations manager, refers to the *Indominus* as "it," later switching to "she" when Dearing describes how the *Indominus* ate her sibling. As *Indominus* is presented as more and more monstrous, the emphasis on her gender as female increases until

131

her escape, after which only feminine pronouns are used to describe her. *Jurassic World* does not directly state that all of the dinosaurs are female, but the representation of similar cloning technology as that used in *Jurassic Park*, where all the dinosaurs are female, supports that the dinosaurs are still female. The gender of the dinosaurs adds to their monstrosity as it depicts cultural concepts of the monstrous feminine that breaks free of accepted roles. Jeffrey Jerome Cohen writes that women have frequently been cast in the role of monster, and that it is because of their position as Other within cultural constructs (9). The monster serves as a warning, in this case against women who might risk cultural taboos by becoming active agents (Cohen 12). Thus it becomes significant that it is a female dinosaur that escapes masculine/technological confines and threatens male lives. *Indominus* breaks taboos by becoming an active, aggressive female. The *Indominus rex* escapes her enclosure through a thought-out plan in which she creates a diversion by clawing the wall to make it appear she climbed out and uses her abilities to shield her heat signature to hide from the tracking equipment (*Jurassic World*). *Indominus* is thus presented as intelligent, and she is an active agent in her escape. Barbara Creed notes that "the monstrous feminine challenges the view that femininity, by definition, constitutes passivity" (151), and the portrayal of the *Indominus rex* escaping her enclosure through the clever implementation of her own plan demonstrates that she is breaking free from a confining, patriarchal system. Through violating socially constructed expectations for females, the *Indominus* proves herself to be a monster.

Although they ultimately lead to the destruction of the park, initially these monstrous qualities of the *Indominus rex* are what make her a valuable zoological attraction. Despite the claim from Owen Grady, the raptor trainer, that, "It's a dinosaur, wow enough," Dearing recognizes that times have changed and people want to see bigger, more ferocious attractions. The predatory characteristics need to be increased in order to increase the thrill. Grady may seem to speak in favor of a more natural approach to the creation and care of the dinosaurs, but he is in a cultural minority. The park is responding to the audience's desire for ever more fantastic experiences, and a dinosaur isn't enough. In order to meet public demand, the scientists further blur the binary between nature and technology to create a monstrous cyborg. The monster inspires both fear and wonder, or, according to Cohen, it inspires desire because it inspires fear (17). Graham presents a similar concept when she writes that "The monster is both awful and aweful"

"That's Not a Real Dinosaur": The Indominus Rex

(53). The desire for the monstrous is apparent early in the film. When Masrani first sees the *Indominus rex*, he is in awe. Dearing asks, "Do you think it will scare the kids?" to which Masrani replies, "Kids? This will give the parents nightmares." Concerned, Dearing asks, "Is that good?" Masrani responds, "It's fantastic" (*Jurassic World*). This brief exchange highlights the importance of monstrosity in the exhibit as a means of thrilling audiences. The *Indominus rex* is captivating because of her size and teeth, impossibilities of nature, which allude to her cyborg construction and the cultural desire for such monsters.

The *Indominus rex* is the newest creature created for profit and consumption, but she is a part of a long history of needing to meet visitor expectations. Although this idea was not emphasized in the previous movies, it was evident in Crichton's novel. The geneticist Dr. Henry Wu talks to John Hammond, then the mastermind behind the park, about creating more docile, controllable dinosaurs. Hammond rejects the idea, insisting that people want "real" animals (Crichton 121). However, the animals that Hammond insisted were "real" were not even the accurate representations that he believed them to be. This is because there is no definitive way to know if recreated dinosaurs look or behave as the original animals did millions of years ago. In *Jurassic World*, Wu insists that the creatures in the park are not exact dinosaurs, and there is no way to know how much of the dinosaur's behavior is true to the prehistoric DNA donor and how much is influenced by other factors, like a dramatically different environment. The dinosaurs have always been modified, altered by the fragmented DNA. This is an important plot point in *Jurassic Park* which leads to female dinosaurs changing their sex due to frog DNA, and it resurfaces in *Jurassic World* when the *Indominus* exhibits characteristics not previously seen in a dinosaur, namely the abilities to hide her heat signature and trigger a cephalopod-type form of camouflage. Wu attributes these qualities to the genetic puzzle that is the *Indominus rex*, further demonstrating the cyborg character of the creature as she is a blend of dinosaur and modern animal, but framing it in terms of a cultural desire for such monstrous features.

Natural Animals and Technological Monsters

In comparison, the other dinosaurs, although still female cyborgs, are not presented as being monstrous but instead as a potential part of a prehistoric ecosystem. They are more closely aligned with nature

133

than they are to the technology that created them. The final scene of the movie shows the *Tyrannosaurus rex* standing on the helipad and roaring (*Jurassic World*). Having defeated the monstrous cyborg of the *Indominus rex* and caused the humans in the park to flee, *Tyrannosaurus* is dominant on the island, and her bellow confirms her place against any challengers. Although Richard Dyer claims that the *Tyrannosaurus rex* in *Jurassic World* is a male and that the final scene depicts a masculine mastery of nature (23), this ignores earlier portrayals of *Tyrannosaurus* being lured to food with a flare, a reference to the first film that suggests that it is the same female dinosaur in a new park enclosure. Thus her position at the end of the film is not one of masculine mastery but a return to feminine nature. The technology that restricted the dinosaurs is no longer active, and the park is already reverting to a more natural ecosystem. Nature and femininity have frequently been linked culturally, a connection that Stacy Alaimo argues positions both as passive resources for dominant male culture (104). By instead presenting an active, dominant female that destroys social constructs of technological mastery and breaks taboos of confinement, *Jurassic World* aligns its female dinosaurs with the monstrous. However, *Tyrannosaurus* at the end of film was released, she did not escape, so that while she is aligned with nature and is depicted reclaiming the island from masculinized technology, she is less monstrous than the *Indominus rex* that actively destroys technology and human-created structures. The *Tyrannosaurus rex* is therefore presented as being part of a more balanced nature.

The emphasis on natural animals goes back to the first film and even Michael Crichton's novel. These earlier representations of dinosaurs were more animal than monster. In the film *Jurassic Park*, realistic representations of dinosaurs based on current paleontological theories were used. The raptors may have been a good deal larger than known fossils at the time, but overall, the dinosaurs were presented as real animals. Spielberg is quoted as saying, "I wanted my dinosaurs to be animals. I wouldn't even let anyone call them monsters or creatures" (qtd. in Baird 91). In order to achieve the realism of a living animal, Spielberg implemented ground-breaking new technologies in robotics and digital scanning. Characteristics of contemporary animals, like the jiggle of loose skin on an elephant and the leg motions of ostriches, were incorporated into the digital models in order to create the most realistic dinosaurs possible (Baird 93). This adds a level of realism to the special effects, but it also supports that despite their technological creation, the dinosaurs are animals. They are presented as something natural and as

"That's Not a Real Dinosaur": The Indominus Rex

a part of a prehistoric landscape. The first shot of dinosaurs in the park further demonstrates this as several species are seen peacefully drinking from a pond together (*Jurassic Park*), an image mimicking that of African herbivores at a watering hole and emphasizing the naturalness of the scene. The dinosaurs are giant, prehistoric animals capable of making the ground shake when they walk, but they are animals and connected to the natural environment.

Jurassic World does not maintain this fidelity to animal realism because realistic animals are no longer thrilling to audiences. The *Indominus rex* is not a representation of a "real" dinosaur; she is a hybrid of at least two species — *Tyrannosaurus* and *Velociraptor* — and as such is not even an attempt at a paleontologically accurate dinosaur. This move away from dinosaurs to hybrids is acknowledged in the film when Dearing gives a tour to potential sponsors. She tells them, "No one's impressed by a dinosaur anymore. Twenty years ago, de-extinction was right up there with magic. These days, kids look at a *Stegosaurus* like an elephant from the city zoo" (*Jurassic World*). This need to escalate attractions is more than a plot point; it expresses the thematic issues at the heart of the movie: audiences want to see something bigger. The metafictional references within the film further support the blurring of binaries as they comment on the need to create larger attractions to entertain the masses while the film itself must implement increasingly complex special effects and action-packed plot lines in order to engage viewers. Twenty years ago, viewers were stunned by the special effects of the first *Jurassic Park* film. It was a blockbuster because it showed audiences dinosaurs on the screen. Now, people see the CGI — of which there is remarkably little — as dated, a product of its time. The realistic dinosaurs Spielberg painstakingly created do not excite audiences like they once did.

In order to renew audience's interest in dinosaurs in films, something new, never before seen, must be promised. *Jurassic World* achieves this with the *Indominus rex*. Presented in IMAX 3D, she is a whole new way to see dinosaurs on the screen. Michele Pierson writes about how special effects in science fiction are themselves the spectacle even above what they depict, and that it is the technological achievement that the display represents that awes the audience (165, 169). Hobart Baird concurs that a successful blockbuster must provide something new in order to become an *event* that draws in crowds, and that it typically relies on special effects to do so (88). *Jurassic World* broke box office records to become one of the top-grossing films of all

135

time ("All Time Highest"), proving itself to have been a summer event. This success is tied to many elements of the film, but the presentation of a new dinosaur in a new—for the franchise—format contributed to the film's blockbuster status. The magic of seeing a *Stegosaurus* on the big screen became commonplace in the explosion of effects-driven and CGI-dominated films that followed *Jurassic Park*. In order to keep people returning to the franchise, something new had to be offered, and the *Indominus rex* in IMAX 3D provides that new thrill because the technology has been updated to present something audiences have never seen before.

Within the film, the *Indominus rex* is also a new attraction and a money-making opportunity. Dearing gives a tour at the beginning of the film to promote corporate sponsorship of the exhibit: "Verizon Wireless Presents the *Indominus Rex*" (*Jurassic World*). Jimmy Buffet even appears in the film, grabbing his margarita before fleeing the pterodactyls, and the sign for Jimmy Buffet's Margaritaville is prominently displayed in multiple scenes (*Jurassic World*). Product placement in the park also becomes product placement in the film, reminding audiences that what they are viewing in a fictional plotline is also a reality in popular culture. Lowery Cruthers, an operator in the park control room, quips that corporations might as well be allowed to name the dinosaurs since they already own all the ball parks (*Jurassic World*). The name "Doritosaurs" is said as a joke, but Cruthers' comments remind viewers that corporations are already heavily invested in the entertainment industry and what seems like a far-fetched joke is frighteningly close to reality.

However, the presentation of the *Indominus rex* as a monster problematizes the economic drive to exploit nature for capital gain The destruction of the technologically advanced, culturally constructed center of the park supports the negative portrayal of corporate exploitation of nature. Previous encounters with the *Indominus rex* took place in the jungles of the island where she was surrounded by trees and an almost natural environment, but the final fight scene in the film takes place in the middle of the constructed theme park town, which is completely destroyed by a plucky raptor, the hero *Tyrannosaurus*, and *Indominus*. Buildings and exhibits are demolished as *Indominus* plunges through a kiosk, a raptor smashes through the window of a gift shop, and *Tyrannosaurus* destroys the front end of a restaurant (*Jurassic World*). The economic ruin of the park is evident through the demolition of capitalistic symbols like gift shops and chain restaurants, and the very creatures the park thought to exploit for profit are the instruments of its

"That's Not a Real Dinosaur": The Indominus Rex

destruction. The *Indominus rex* is created to boost attendance and profits, but she actually brings about the ruin of the park. The monster, in this case, provides an obvious warning to the watching public against only considering profit when implementing technology to surpass natural boundaries.

Conclusion

Although all of the dinosaurs are pieced together from DNA, what makes the *Indominus rex* different is that she is what audiences want to see. The *Indominus rex* is a manipulated creation to provide even bigger thrills and bring even more money into the park. Wu's concern with the fast, nimble dinosaurs of the novel is that they do not meet audience expectations for large, slow animals. The issue of meeting audience expectations is relevant to the entertainment industry where people want to see what they expect, which is not necessarily realism. Pierson mentions that sometimes special effects seem more real than real (172), and this concept of too exacting of detail actually taking away from the audience's experience is relevant to the dinosaurs in the park. They must be the dinosaurs that people expect to see. Wu suggests this when he reminds Hammond that the park is for entertainment, and "entertainment has nothing to do with reality" (Crichton 121). This idea of entertainment as a creation beyond reality is a small section of the novel, but it comes to the forefront of the film *Jurassic World*. The need to entertain visitors leads the park to push the limits of its technology, exploiting what might have been natural into an unnatural, hyper-real creation. Thus Wu's declaration twenty years later in the fourth film that "Nothing in Jurassic World is natural" is accurate (*Jurassic World*). Nothing is natural in the cyborg blend of technology and nature that makes up the park, the result of imposing of cultural ideas upon a once natural space. The insistence in the movie that "these are real animals" (*Jurassic World*) is clearly false, as the entire park proves itself to be a monstrous attempt at blurring binaries for profit.

Audiences, both movie-goers and fictional Jurassic World visitors, want to be thrilled, and the *Indominus rex* provides a warning that there are consequences to ever-increasing technological thrills. Her destruction of the park questions the implementation of technology in order to modify nature, while at the same time the presentation of dinosaurs in IMAX 3D highlights the necessity of developing new technology in order to attract audiences, and ultimately to make money. The *Indominus rex* is a problematic creation of nature, technology, and culture that excites and frightens the audience. She is the contemporary monster commenting on the culture that created her.

Works Cited

Alaimo, Stacy. *Bodily Natures: Science, Environment, and the Material Self.* Bloomington, IN: Indiana UP, 2010.

"All Time Highest Grossing Movies Worldwide." *The Numbers: Where Data and the Movie Business Meet.* Nash Information Services. Web. 30 July 2016.

Baird, Hobart. "Animalizing *Jurassic Park*'s Dinosaurs: Blockbuster Schemata and Cross-Cultural Cognition in the Threat Scene." *Cinema Journal* 37.4 (1998): 82-103.

Briggs, Laura and Jodi I. Kelber-Kaye. "'There Is No Unauthorized Breeding in Jurassic Park': Gender and the Uses of Genetics" *NWSA Journal* 12.3 (2000): 92-113.

Cohen, Jeffrey Jerome, ed. *Monster Theory: Reading Culture.* Minneapolis, MN: University of Minnesota Press, 1996.

Creed, Barbara. *The Monstrous Feminine: Film, Feminism, Psychoanalysis.* New York: Routledge, 1993.

Crichton, Michael. *Jurassic Park.* 1990. New York: Ballantine Books, 2012.

Dyer, Richard. "*Jurassic World* and Procreation Anxiety." *Film Quarterly* 69.2 (2015): 19-24.

Feder, Helena. *Ecocriticism and the Idea of Culture.* Burlington, VT: Ashgate, 2014.

Graham, Elaine. *Representations of the Post/Human: Monsters, Aliens, and Others in Popular Culture.* Manchester UP, 2002.

Haraway, Donna J. "A Manifesto for Cyborgs: Science, Technology, and Socialist Feminism in the 1980s." *The Gendered Cyborg.* Ed. Gill Kirkup, Linda James, Kath Woodward, and Fiona Hovenden. New York: Routledge, 2000. 50-57.

Jurassic Park. Dir. Steven Spielberg. Perf. Sam Neill, Laura Dern, Jeff Goldblum. Universal Studios, 1993.

Jurassic World. Dir. Colin Trevorrow. Perf. Chris Pratt, Bryce Dallas Howard, Vincent D'Onofrio. Universal Studios, 2015.

Pierson, Michele. "CGI Effects in Hollywood Science-Fiction Cinema 1989-95: The Wonder Years." *Screen* 40.2 (1999).

Plumwood, Val. *Feminism and the Mastery of Nature.* New York: Routledge, 1993.

Zizek, Slavoj. *Enjoy Your Symptom!: Jacques Lacan in Hollywood and Out.* New York: Routledge, 2001.

"The Shadow of Saint Nicholas": Dougherty's *Krampus*

ALISSA BURGER AND JENNY COLLINS

> *I was shaking in my damn shoes.*
> *I laughed. I cried. It was an emotional*
> *rollercoaster. It was tremendous. #Krampus*
> (@crazyMILsays, twitter review)

The Christmas season brings to mind a plethora of idyllic and magical associations: dancing sugarplums, dozens of Christmas cookies, piles of presents, Santa Claus, and his flying reindeer. However, there is a darker side to the holiday season, one which can be traced back to 17th-century Bavaria and which recently staked its claim to mainstream Hollywood popularity: the Krampus. *Der Krampus,* or the Krampus, is a monster with its roots in German folklore, a dark version of Saint Nicholas who comes during the Christmas season to punish naughty children rather than to bring presents or treats. As Monte Beauchamp explains in *Krampus: The Devil of Christmas,* "The Krampus terrorized the bad until they promised to be good. Some he spanked. Others he whipped. And some he shackled, stuffed into his large wooden basket, carried away, and hurled into the flames of Hell" (7). Immortalized in stories, images, festivals, and Krampus parades, for hundreds of years this monster has haunted children's nightmares, served as a fantastical reminder of the consequences of bad behavior, and lent a darker cast to the holiday season beyond the twinkling lights and tinsel.

In 2015, the Krampus paid a holiday visit to a more general audience with Michael Dougherty's horror-comedy film *Krampus,* which follows one suburban family's fight for survival against the titular monster and his helpers. With its roots in traditional German lore—here personified in the character of a German grandmother called Omi (played by Krista Stadler)—this film provides a contemporary twist on the familiar figure, exploring the conflicts and anxieties that typify the 21st-century holiday season and the average modern family, from the mad dash of Christmas shopping and school plays to the more domestic pressures of decorating the home, preparing holiday feasts, and straining to achieve domestic harmony, whether within the nuclear or extended family. *Krampus* taps into many of these pressures, with its opening credits featuring a Black Friday-esque stampede of frenzied shoppers before focusing in on the suburban Engel family: father Tom (Adam Scott), mother Sarah (Toni Collette), son Max (Emjay Anthony), daughter Beth (Stefania LaVie Owen), and grandmother Omi. With the arrival of their abrasive and gauche extended family for the holidays, Max finds his faith in the Christmas spirit in general and Santa Claus in particular seriously tested. Amid this volatile mix of inter- and intrapersonal conflict, a mysterious blizzard descends upon their otherwise deserted neighborhood, isolating them first with the weather and then, more violently, with the monsters they encounter when they venture out in search of rescue, and which in turn bring the fight for survival into the Engels' home.

While the figure of the Krampus is not a new one, the monster is never just a monster. As Jeffrey Jerome Cohen argues in *Monster Theory: Reading Culture*, "the monster's body is a cultural body" (4). The monster represents and embodies the fears and anxieties of its surrounding culture, reflecting the surrounding society that breathes life into it, which uses the monster as a site in which to coalesce their fears, where they can be safely faced and fought, if never entirely defeated. As such, Cohen explains, the monster is an embodiment of a certain cultural moment— of a time, a feeling, and a place. The monster's body quite literally incorporates fear, desire, anxiety, and fantasy (ataractic or incendiary), giving them life and an uncanny independence. The monstrous body is pure culture. A construct and a projection, the monster exists only to be read: the *monstrum* is etymologically "that which reveals," "that which warns," a glyph that seeks a hierophant. Like a letter on a page, the monster signifies something other than itself: it is always a displacement, always inhabits the gap between the time of upheaval and the moment into which it is received, to be born again (Cohen 4).

As a result, the Krampus of Bavarian legend communicated a set of cultural mores and values that are distinct from the 21st-century incarnation of this monster, though certain key characteristics continue to resonate between these representations. The fears that kept 17th-century German peasants awake on a cold winter night are vastly different that those which preoccupy the modern man or woman as they try to create a perfect holiday season for their family, though common themes of tradition and togetherness connect these very different

"The Shadow of Saint Nicholas": Dougherty's Krampus

cultural moments and their subjects. By exploring the German Krampus tradition and positioning it in critical discussion with Dougherty's film, we aim to highlight the fears underlying each of these unique social and cultural moments. Dougherty's *Krampus* engages with a dual nostalgia: first, for an idyllic, traditional—and largely imaginary—version of Christmas; second, for the horror-comedy sensibilities of the 1980s, most notably through another dark Christmas classic, Joe Dante's *Gremlins* (1984). These unique cultural moments, their negotiation of the monster, and the intersection of their fears underscore the significance of the Krampus and its enduring legacy, from folklore to popular culture.

Der Krampus

Prior to the terrorizing of a suburban Ohio family, the Krampus emerged in the 17th century in the southern German state of Bavaria and the country of Austria. Conflicting theories exist as to the origin and age of the Krampus stories. Some scholars theorize that Krampus found his way into Germanic folklore by way of the Vikings, as the son of Hel, the Norse goddess of the underworld; however, the Krampus' presence in southern Germany and lack of appearance in any of the northern states would appear to disprove this popular theory. Instead, *der Krampus* emerges like so many fairy-tale monsters from the Black Forest and the mountain regions of southern Germany, where each village appears to have its own version of him. In some towns he is more a man than a monster, with only his cloven-hoofed feet to give him away, while in other towns he bears the more traditionally monstrous appearance of ample fur and goat horns. Differences of appearance aside, however, the Krampus' place as a dark spirit of the Christmas season has always held true. Following Cohen's argument that "the monster's body is a cultural body" (4), a monster is not merely a grotesque but is instead a reflection and result of the anxieties, fears and even desires of the culture in which it originates. The earliest incarnations of Krampus hold strong ties to events and anxieties present in the Germanic states of the 17th century.

The 17th century was a time of tremendous unrest in the majority of the German states, including the mountainous and dark forest regions where the Krampus has its origins. A protestant Union and a Catholic league of competing royalty were formed within months of each other in 1608 and 1609. This sparked off a year of unrest which culminated in the Thirty Years' War from 1618 to 1648, a period in which casualties were catastrophic in Germany. It is unknown what the final death tolls were, but historian John Theibault estimates in his essay, "The Demography of the Thirty Years War Re-revisited" that the losses were perhaps as high as 50% of the population of southern Germany (15). If famine, raids, and war were not enough, witch hunts also became common during the 17th century as those left alive by the conflict sought alternative avenues to make sense of their violent reality. Cohen argues that the monster is at home within a state of "category crisis" and that "the monster notoriously appears at times of crisis as a kind of third term that problematizes the clash of extremes" (Cohen 6). It is perhaps unsurprising then that this unsettled time, with conflicts between Catholics and Protestants, North and South, and even within war-torn families, would lead to the emergence of a monster, tapping into this unrest and uncertainty.

Though now referred to as the Christmas monster, the Krampus of the 17th century, and indeed the Krampus as revived in 21st-century Germany, does not make his visits on Christmas Eve. Early modern Germans reserved Christmas Eve and Christmas Day for the celebration of the Christ child—so St. Nicholas and the Krampus have celebration days separate from Christmas, and in traditional tales arrive together as perhaps the strangest buddy duo in folklore history. *Krampusnacht* or "Krampus Night" falls on December 5th, the night before St. Nicholas' Day on the 6th, when children wake excited to see what the good spirit has left them (see Eddy for details). Krampus acts as a gate keeper for the gifts and good things that Santa brings, a contrasting spirit of darkness to Santa's light, the bad cop to Santa's good. The Krampus is most often represented as a monster who emerges from the mountains in a swirl of snow and traditionally carries with him a bell, a collection of switches, and a basket with which to carry away naughty children ("Horror For The Holidays"). The monster's accessory choices tie into the larger cultural body of Bavaria where copper bells were often used as a way for the wearer to ward off evil spirits, while switches were a common disciplinary tool for children as well as a symbol of order (Raedisch 87).

Considering the cultural happenings of the 17th century, the Krampus' attire identifies him as both a monster and a force of cultural policing. It is the monster, not the jolly old elf, who weighs the good and bad deeds of children. Krampus and Santa Claus, as linked in time by the closeness of their respective holidays and contrasted in appearance, embody Cohen's theory of the monster as a being which "polices the

"The Shadow of Saint Nicholas": Dougherty's Krampus

borders of the possible" (12). While Santa represents celebration, fun, and frivolity, the Krampus is "the monster of prohibition" who "exists to demarcate the bonds that hold together that system of relations we call culture, to call horrid attention to the borders that cannot—must not—be crossed" (Cohen 13). By first depriving bad children of reward and then doubling down the punishment by taking them away to his mountain lair (or bizarrely in some accounts, Spain) to be eaten or condemned to fire and torment, the Krampus is doing his monstrous part to ensure the survival of the culture it occupies. Behavior must be policed and in times as harsh as those found in 17th-century rural Germany, punishment of behaviors outside the limits of society needed to be stopped at an early age, to maintain order and reinforce a sense of proper national identity.

German Christmas tradition is rife with monsters policing the cultural order, of which the Krampus is but one. If children were to survive the first culling on December 5th, another monster was waiting for them on twelfth night. Perchta, a Christmas spirit of strictly pagan origin, is a proto goddess of spinning, weaving and other traditional female arts (Grimm 279). She too is a monster of duality coming in two forms: the first a kindly young woman with blonde hair who leaves silver in the shoes of good children and the second a terrible monster, similar in appearance to the Krampus, who slits the bellies of bad children and stuffs them with straw or wool (Grimm 279). Infractions that will get you in trouble with Perchta are largely the same as those punished by the Krampus, including misbehavior, rebelliousness, and lack of attention to chores or prayers, and today the two monsters are celebrated together during modern-day *Krampusnacht* festivals in Germany (Muller 451). While Perchta has not gained the mainstream recognition the Krampus has in recent years, in Dougherty's *Krampus*, Perchta may well be one of the elves who invade the family home.

"Krampus runs," parades in which townspeople carved masks of Krampus and marched through the streets with torches and the monster's other accouterments, flourished from the 17th century until World War II, a long period of German history marked by unrest and war. The rise of Fascism in Germany and Austria meant a temporary halt for the Krampus tradition in the 20th century, when it was deemed to be "a product of socialist democrats," as well as satanic and paganist by the government and leading Christian groups (Gallon). It was not the end of Krampus though. As Cohen explains, "the monster always escapes" (4) because there is always another cataclysm, another moment of cultural unrest. Culture is fluid and ever changing and so too is the monster, adapting and waiting on the periphery for a moment of resurgence (Cohen 20).

The Krampus was not dormant for long and this figure has seen a huge resurgence in popularity, both in Germany and beyond in the last 20 years. Krampus runs are now a marked event at German *Christkindlmarkt* (Christmas markets) and are even beginning to pop up in American celebrations as well (Eddy). Ironically, many participants in the revived Krampus festivities participate as a way to push back against the commercialization of Christmas and what many Germans see as an invasion of Americanized Christmas celebrations. One participant commented that, "This is a tradition that our great-grandparents were already doing that must be handed down to the next generation. But properly handed down, as it was 40, 50, 60 years ago, not with a lot of commercialization, like from Hollywood films" (qtd. in Eddy). Once again the monster rises to police the borders of the culture, this time against globalization rather than the encroachment of neighboring German states. As the long and colorful history of the Krampus demonstrates, the monster takes many forms, adapting to address the unrest and anxiety which surrounds it, shifting to suit the needs of its audience, regardless of medium, nation, or century.

A Krampus for the 21st Century

The contemporary Christmas season presents very different challenges than those faced by 17th-century Bavarians, including the pressure to achieve a "perfect" holiday for the family, whether nuclear or extended, with myriad commitments both within and outside of the family home. Dougherty's *Krampus* taps into this range of anxieties, making this Krampus—and his rabble of helpers—a distinctly 21st-century monster, a reflection of the contemporary "cultural body" (Cohen 4). This constant and active negotiation is also a hallmark of holiday celebrations and larger cultural traditions; as Bruce David Forbes explains in *Christmas: A Candid History*, these varied meanings are reflected in "the way in which folk and popular traditions morph and borrow from one another as they move through cultures and through time" (93). With *Krampus*, the larger holiday traditions and the malleability of the monster intersect in fascinating and illuminating ways.

144

"The Shadow of Saint Nicholas": Dougherty's Krampus

For many Americans, Christmas is a very important occasion. Whether celebrated as a religious holiday in celebration of the birth of Jesus or more secularly, centered on family meals and gift exchanges, the holiday season often marks a time of family togetherness. As Stephen Nissenbaum explains in *The Battle for Christmas: A Cultural History of America's Most Cherished Holiday,* Christmas traditions "have long served to transfigure our ordinary behavior in an almost magical fashion, in ways that reveal something of what we would like to be, what we once were, or what we are becoming despite ourselves" (xii). Like the monster itself, the celebration of Christmas is a cultural cipher, signifying the values and ideals of those celebrating, whether on the macro level of the larger community or within the microcosm of the family.

The opening scenes of *Krampus* serve as a "to-do" list for modern holiday revelers: rabid consumerism and cut-throat shopping, Christmas pageants, holiday baking, pictures with Santa, the wrapping of gifts, and the traditional family viewing of *A Charlie Brown Christmas.* However, even in these opening moments, as Sarah tries to create an ideal holiday for her family, it remains unattainable and even marred, as Max gets into a fistfight in the middle of the Christmas pageant and, upon inspection of their family photo with Santa, Sarah sees the jolly old elf ogling their teenage daughter. Even the achieved ideals, such as Omi's dozens of immaculate, lovingly crafted homemade Christmas cookies, are undercut, as Tom reminds her that they have plenty of store-bought cookies, suggesting that her dedication to the family and her labor of love are unnecessary and thus devalued. Most significantly, young Max's Christmas spirit is challenged: he is the youngest child and still believes in Santa Claus, though this belief is ridiculed by his classmates — the cause of the pageant fisticuffs — and his cousins, who torment him by stealing and reading aloud his letter to Santa. It is Max's destruction of this letter and the loss of belief that it represents that open the door to Krampus, his minions, and the resulting horrors.

The family dynamics only get more contentious when the extended family arrives, including Sarah's sister Linda (played by Allison Tolman), brother-in-law Howard (David Koechner), and their children (Maverick Flack, Queenie Samuel, Lolo Owen, Sage Hunefeld), as well as crass, drunken Aunt Dorothy (Conchata Ferrell). Sarah has an ideal of what the "perfect" Christmas should look like and her family subverts those expectations at every turn: Max's letter to Santa becomes a source of ridicule and conflict, the elaborate meal Sarah prepares

145

devolves into chaos, and all of the hard work she has put into the home and the meal are criticized and rejected. This reflects a form of angst many families wrestle with during the holiday season, with a fantasy born of popular culture and nostalgia. However, as Forbes argues, "We human beings have a tendency to create golden ages of the past, when all was supposedly wonderful before complicating factors intruded and ruined everything. In most cases, the golden age is an idealized dream" (141). This is exactly the case with Christmas: while many people have an idealized, often less complicated or contentious image of the holiday to which they aspire, Forbes and Nissenbaum's research both prove that this fantasy version of "Christmas as it used to be" is more accurately "Christmas as it never was." The Christmas Sarah yearns to create for her family is a combination of her own childhood memories, as represented by the heirlooms adorning the tree, and suburban refinement, in the designer-grade glitz of the home, its decorations, and the gourmet meal she creates. Max echoes this same sentiment, crying that "I just wanted Christmas to be like it used to be," yearning for a familiar closeness that may never have existed outside of his own imagination and nostalgia-tinted memories. However, this Christmas dream is unattainable, a beautiful set piece that cannot hold once the reality of family and everyday life are set loose upon it, and it all falls apart even before Krampus and his helpers show up.

The class differences between the two families are an especially pronounced point of conflict, with the upper-middle class Engels cast in stark contrast with the working class Burkhausers. Sarah's striving for yuletide perfection is met with a mix of mystified horror and derision, as Aunt Dorothy takes a look at the baubles bedecking the dining room, reflecting that "it looks like Martha Stewart threw up in here." In contrast to Sarah's Cornish hens and crème brûlée, Linda shows up with a homey casserole dish; where the Engels' gifts are artfully presented, the Burkhausers show up bearing boxes wrapped in newspaper. Even the clothes worn by the two families create significant distinction between them. The Engels are dressed in a drab grey pallet, with subdued sweaters that are perfectly in keeping with the stagnant decor of the rest of the home. In contrast, the working class Burkhausers arrive dressed in vivid red hues, reflective of the festive season, including plaid and garish Christmas sweaters, while their children wear weathered sweatshirts and high school athletic letterman jackets. In addition to the monster's body reflecting its surrounding culture, Cohen also argues that the monster is a symbolic negotiator of difference. As Cohen explains,

"The Shadow of Saint Nicholas": Dougherty's Krampus

"Any kind of alterity can be inscribed across (constructed through) the monstrous body, but for the most part monstrous difference tends to be cultural, political, racial, economic, sexual" (7). The two families serve as a shorthand for stereotypes of class in America, with the Burkhausers' gun-toting, Hummer-driving, conservative mentality grating against the polished, liberal, suburban civility of the Engels. As a result of these differences, while Krampus and his helpers pose a supernatural, monstrous threat, that danger is echoed by interpersonal human conflict as well, with the families seeing one another through a more banal lens of Otherness, until that gulf is bridged in their collective fight for survival. As they fight to save their children, their families, and themselves, Tom and Howard forge a particularly significant connection, taking up arms side by side, with Tom even taking on the militaristic, survivalist mantra he dismissed earlier in the film, repeating Howard's words that "a shepherd's gotta protect his flock." Finally, this coming together in some ways takes them back to earlier Christmases, through Sarah and Linda's largely unspoken childhood holiday memories, as they stand before the Christmas tree, looking at their mother's Christmas angel and the ornaments of their own childhood.

Another unique element of *Krampus* is its genre distinction as a hybrid comedy-horror film, as Dougherty "dabbles in Christmas film tropes, as well as horror, comedy and dark fantasy" (Truitt). Set against a backdrop of pop culture Christmas allusions from *A Christmas Carol* to Bing Crosby, Dougherty's *Krampus* shifts between horror and comedy, a genre amalgamation in which "a playful tone predominates, but it is undercut by horrific or startling events or effects" (Gordon). While horror and comedy might, at first glance, appear diametrically opposed, "At their most basic level, both comedy and horror depend on the shock of the unexpected: the subversion of the audience's expectations" (Miller and Van Riper xiv). *Krampus* follows many of the conventions of the traditional horror film, with monsters charging out of the darkness, blood and gore, and death; the barriers of the home prove no match for the horrors that invade it, from a ravenous jack-in-the-box and a rabid teddy bear to a cackling horde of elves and, of course, Krampus himself. The humans prove no match against these terrors and, in the tradition of horror ranging from monster movies to slasher films, they are picked off one by one, attacked, caught, and consumed. These screams of horror are mingled, however, with laughter. The monsters themselves are whimsical and even cartoonish, such as rampaging gingerbread men, their hilarity both heightened and subverted as they

147

lure one of the children to his doom and attack Howard with a nail gun. In effective comedy-horror in general and *Krampus* in particular, both the comedy and the horror take the viewer off guard, upsetting the expectations of reality as they "take their characters' initially stable reality and steadily, relentlessly unravel it around them until—in the moments before the story is resolved—they are left with no safe space in which to rest and catch their breath" (Miller and Van Riper xv). In *Krampus*, the monsters themselves seem too ridiculous to be real and, due to this unbelievability, with the foundations of reality and faith torn out from under them, the family find themselves torn between laughter and screams. There are plenty of moments of near-hysterical hilarity as "The riotous invasion of the family home by Krampus and his allies generates some laugh-out-loud, blackly comic moments, with a genuinely disturbing grotesque undertow" (Diestro-Dópido 80). Despite this comedic undertone, *Krampus* is a horror film at heart, as evidenced by its haunting conclusion, which makes it clear that despite the idyllic Christmas morning façade, no one has—or will—escape this nightmare.

Monsters of Christmas Past: *Krampus* and Nostalgia

Dougherty's *Krampus* engages with dual nostalgia: a desire for the perceived simplicity of Christmases gone by, as evoked by the larger Krampus tradition, and a more kitschy nostalgia for the 1980s comedy-horror genre, with specific and overt allusions to Joe Dante's *Gremlins*.

While the idyllic, carefree holidays of the past have been revealed by many scholars to be more myth than memory, the larger Krampus tradition still strikes a chord with many revelers, who lament the loss of this figure from the mainstream celebrations. As Melissa Eddy explains in her *New York Times article* on the contemporary resurgence of the *Krampuslauf* (a celebration in which Krampus is the central, celebrated figure), the Krampus "tradition dwindled across much of Bavaria during the 1960s and '70s, as postmodern society moved away from its rural past. . . . But with cultural homogenization spreading across an increasingly unified Europe, a new generation is bringing back the customs that defined their childhoods, and those of their parents and grandparents." From this perspective, the renewed interest in Krampus,

"The Shadow of Saint Nicholas": Dougherty's Krampus

particularly in the Bavarian region, can be seen as a push back against the commodified, polished, and perfect Christmas that *Krampus*'s Sarah Engel and so many others strive to create for their families. For the many who lament the commercialization of the holiday season, Krampus may be an ideal solution: with the possibility of a visit from Krampus in the air, young children take a few moments to reflect on their misdeeds of the preceding year, rather than acquisitively brushing up their wish list for Santa Claus. Tom Bierbaumer, one of the proponents and organizers of the contemporary *Krampuslauf*, recalled his own childhood trepidation during the holiday season, when "he would think back over his misdeeds of past months — the days he had refused to clear the supper table, left his homework unfinished or pulled a girl's hair" (Eddy); as he reflected, "When you are a child, you know what you have done wrong the whole year. . . . When the Krampus comes to your house, and you are a child, you are really worried about getting a hit from his switch" (qtd. in Eddy). This contemporary revival of the Krampus tradition has the potential for encouraging self-reflection and perhaps even penance as the year comes to an end, creating the space and mythological context for a more critical, inward looking moment of meditation amid the carols, dancing lights, and piles of wrapping paper that have come to characterize the holiday.

However, the co-opting of the Krampus tradition and its incorporation into contemporary celebrations is, like other discourses of nostalgia surrounding Christmas, problematic. For example, as the Krampus has become mainstream, some concerned traditionalists worry about "Krampus the Christmas demon becom[ing] too commercial" (Jovanovski). Just as Santa Claus made his way into the mainstream growing from his roots as the Catholic Saint Nicholas to a protector of farmers and shepherds (Forbes 74), before taking on his now immediately recognizable incarnation in Clement Clarke Moore's "The Night Before Christmas" in 1823 (Forbes 85), Krampus continues to change with the times, for better or worse. As a result, the contemporary Krampus, according to Eva Kreissl, curator at the Folk Life Museum in Austria, "is falling the way of most holiday traditions . . . as a commodity to be capitalized on" rather than a figure to be feared; instead of fearing his switch and basket, "Krampus chocolates and figurines are very common now and show that this character too is becoming increasingly marketable. Many people also buy devil-type horns that accompany the Santa hats commonly worn around St. Nicholas Day" (qtd. in Jovanovski). Just as Santa and the Krampus showcase the lighter and darker sides of the Christmas season, the nostalgia for the Krampus tradition and its mobilization within the contemporary culture follows two distinct trajectories: the old-fashioned, anti-commercial Krampus versus the monster's commodity value, as just another element of the holidays that can be polished, packaged, and used for profit. Dougherty's *Krampus* arguably engages with both of these impulses, tapping into the traditional significance of the Krampus through Omi's memories of her own childhood, while the filmmakers themselves work to make this monster appealing and relevant to a contemporary audience through the larger conventions of the mainstream Hollywood film tradition.

The second appeal to nostalgia engaged by *Krampus* is in eliciting the viewers' fond memories of comedy-horror films of the 1980s, with Dante's *Gremlins* a particularly salient touchstone mentioned by many of the filmmaking team ("The Naughty Ones: Meet the Cast"). As Joseph Maddrey argues of the blurring lines between comedy and horror, in the late 1970s and early 1980s, an increasing number of horror films began "adopting a lighthearted approach to the old horrors" (81), opening the door for films that challenged expectations of horror, comedy, and family film. Within this liminal space, filmmakers were able to tackle established narratives in inventive new ways and, as Bruce G. Hallenbeck explains, "Although *Gremlins* is essentially a mainstream, family-friendly film, there is a dark and subversive undercurrent that keeps the viewer off guard, wondering which direction it will veer next" (131). *Gremlins'* dual engagement of comedy and horror, with the Christmas holiday at its heart, is distinctly echoed in Dougherty's *Krampus*. In both movies, there are deceptively adorable dangers, such as Mogwai turned gremlins in the former and cartoonish gingerbread men luring children to their doom in the latter; in both films, these horrors are presented through a complex combination of laughter and fear, such as the costumed gremlins' holiday bacchanalia and one of Krampus' helpers being a grotesque, murderous jack-in-the-box so over the top that Tom Engel has no recourse but to exclaim "oh, come on!"

Both films also have a dark and disturbing undercurrent in the remembering and recitation of Christmases gone by. One of the most memorable scenes in *Gremlins* is when Kate (played by Phoebe Cates) tells the story of her father's death, breaking his neck trying to shimmy down the chimney in a Santa suit the Christmas she was nine. Shrouded in dark shadows, with the camera fixed on her wide-eyed, horrified face, she recounts this nightmarish holiday as she and Billy (Zach Galligan) share a quiet moment while they wait for the next disaster to

"The Shadow of Saint Nicholas": Dougherty's Krampus

strike. Part of what makes this scene so effective and memorable is that the way the speech is set up and delivered makes it impossible to pin down which genre tradition the viewer should draw upon to categorize and comprehend it: the scene is by turns horrifying, unsettling, and hilariously over the top. *Krampus* has its own "ghosts of Christmas past" moment, when Omi shares the story of her own childhood encounter with the Krampus, who took her family, highlighting the ways in which "every monster is . . . a double narrative, two living stories: one that describes how the monster came to be and another, its testimony, detailing what cultural use the monster serves" (Cohen 13). In *Krampus*, Omi's story bridges the liminal space of the past and the present, with the film transforming from live-action to stop motion style animation as she tells the gathered family of her childhood experience waiting in what appears to be a post-war bread line, coming home empty handed, and suffering the wrath of her parents. The stop motion aesthetic blurs the lines between live action and animation, creating a visual impact that is both whimsical and surreal. As Weta Workshop's animation supervisor for *Krampus* Dave Clayton explains, "Dougherty wanted the feeling that this piece of animation had been crafted by an incredibly old yet talented Austrian stop motion animator, and the film reel had been sitting in his basement for generations, just waiting to be unearthed" (qtd. in Pattillo). Just as Kate's grim story highlights the less idyllic side of the Christmas season in *Gremlins*, Omi's story takes her family back to a darker time, her childhood fears and frustrations echoed in Max's own decades later.

Nostalgia for *Gremlins* and comedy-horror films like it from the 1980s extends beyond thematic similarities within Krampus, influencing production decisions as well. While the visual style of Omi's flashback is a call back to the holiday stop motion animation of Rankin/Bass Studios (who created the *Rudolph the Red-Nosed Reindeer*, *The Little Drummer Boy*, and *Santa Claus is Comin' to Town* using stop motion techniques during the 1960s and 70s), the special effects in the rest of *Krampus* largely owe influence to the practical effects of the 1980s. The computer-generated effects that would come to dominate modern cinema were only in their infancy during this time period and so practical effects such as painted backdrops, point of view staging, and puppetry were the go-to for bringing monsters to the big screen. *Krampus* connects with the campy horror comedy of the 1980s through its extensive use of puppeteering rather than CGI and other special effects to bring the Krampus and his minions to life.

151

Puppets were used extensively in some of the most iconic films of the 1980s, including *Alien* (1979), *Gremlins* (1982), *E.T.: The Extra-Terrestrial* (1982), *Labyrinth* (1986), *Child's Play* (1988), and *Meet the Feebles* (1989). The use of puppetry spanned across genres but is arguably most memorable in films where it was used to alternatively frighten and delight audiences. There is something thrilling about the realism presented by puppets and the way that actors are able to interact with them. Audiences gasp and cringe when the Alien bursts from William Hurt's chest; they weep when E.T., a creation of foam and simple animatronics, tells Eliot where he can always be found; and fans alternatively coo at the adorable Gizmo of *Gremlins* and cringe from his scaly, hellish counterparts. For individuals who grew up watching these films during their formative years, the use of puppetry in *Krampus* offers a wave of nostalgic familiarity. For younger audiences, many of whom have experienced *Gremlins* or *Labyrinth* as cult classics (and now mainstream classics), the use of practical effects is a charming throwback to films they have enjoyed since childhood.

2015 saw a large influx of directors opting to use practical effects rather than CGI and other methods to add realism to their films. *Mad Max: Fury Road*, one of the top earning films of 2015, was notable for using very little in the way of special effects ("Mad Max"). Instead, the movie relied on practical effects, tightly choreographed stunt work, and the natural landscape of the Namibian desert to tell its story. *Krampus* contains fewer explosions than *Fury Road* but operates under the same idea that a return to practical effects and puppetry represents "a return to form, as a chance to go back to the way things are supposed to be" (Opam). This explanation from film critic Kwame Opam is near-identical to Max's lament throughout *Krampus* that he just wants Christmas to be "like it used to be."

The monsters that besiege the family in the lead up to the arrival of the Krampus himself are (with the exception of the CGI Ginger Bread men) all practical puppets created by WETA workshops, whose head Peter Jackson directed the 1989 puppet comedy-horror film *Meet the Feebles*. Each of *Krampus'* creatures is meticulously designed to be cute but horrifying, twisted versions of childhood toys and Christmas mainstays that come off as a demonic version of the residents of Rudolph's Island of Misfit Toys. A Jack-in-the-Box opens its mouth to reveal row upon row of teeth in a glistening maw before transforming into a writhing creature more reminiscent of Jabba the Hutt than a mainstay of a childhood toy chest. A Teddy Bear and knife-wielding

"The Shadow of Saint Nicholas": Dougherty's Krampus

Rock 'Em Sock 'Em Robot attack the family in the attic, the place of so many childhood nightmares, along with "the Cherub," a grotesque version of the Christmas angel that tops the Engels' Christmas tree. The puppets are viscerally real and delightful even as they commit horrible acts. Like the titular monsters in *Gremlins* they draw gasps, shudders, and laughter from the audience in rapid succession. Director Michael Dougherty (as well as many adult members of his *Krampus* cast) grew up during the late 1970s and '80s, has expressed numerous times his love of films like *Alien, The Exorcist,* and *Gremlins,* and has said that 1980s horror films are his primary influence (qtd. in "10 Questions"). When it came time to make *Krampus,* Dougherty said that practical effects and monsters were the only option, explaining "I was inspired by all the films I loved and it was great because all of the actors were raised on the same movies that I was and they were itching to help bring them back" (qtd. in "The Naughty Ones: Meet the Cast"). In terms of holiday horror, resonant themes of home and family, and the special effects aesthetic that bring their monsters to life, *Krampus* is a 21st-century echo of *Gremlins* and other comedy-horror films of the 1980s, appealing to the audience's sense of nostalgia and their own Christmas memories of childhood and adolescence.

Finally, just as Cohen argues that there is more to the monster than there seems, both *Gremlins* and *Krampus* engage with the monstrous on multiple levels, from critical film analysis to popular fun. As legendary critic Roger Ebert reflected on *Gremlins,* "At the level of Serious Film Criticism, it's a meditation on the myths in our movies: Christmas, families, monsters, retail stores, movies, bogeymen. At the level of Pop Movie-going, it's a sophisticated, witty B movie, in which the monsters are devouring not only the defenseless town, but decades of defenseless clichés." A similar argument could be made of *Krampus.* On the one hand, it follows the B-movie formula, with unbelievable scenarios, dramatic destruction, and creatures that are, by turns, both horrifying and laughable. But from a more critical perspective, *Krampus* engages with the foundational myths and ideals of American culture: the centrality of the family and the magic of Christmas under attack by a horde of monsters that are simultaneously old and new again.

A key point of departure in these two films, however, is in their conclusions. The monster can never really be defeated or eliminated; as Cohen explains, "they can be pushed to the farthest margins of geography and discourse, hidden away at the edges of the world and in the forbidden recesses of our mind, but they always return" (20).

In *Gremlins*, the monsters are destroyed but the threat of monstrosity remains: another drop of water or late night feeding could start the horror all over again. As a result, Gizmo is taken away, removed from the hands of those who have inadvertently destroyed, and a semblance of safety and normalcy returns to Kingston Falls, though it is overshadowed by loss, sorrow, and the weight of newfound knowledge and failed responsibility. In *Krampus*, Max unintentionally calls the monster and his minions down upon his family with his loss of Christmas spirit and in regaining it, he challenges the Krampus, desperate to set things right. However, Dougherty sidesteps the—albeit shaky—return to the status quo offered by *Gremlins*. While Max awakes to a sunny and soft-focused Christmas morning to join his family around the tree, it is not the monsters themselves but this regained normalcy that is the dream, a thin veneer that cannot hold against the nightmare which surrounds them, trapped within the grasp of the Krampus.

Be Good for Goodness Sake: Punishable Behaviors Then and Now

The Krampus is one of many panoptic figures in folklore, a bogeyman who is always watching and ready to dole out punishment to those who overstep the bounds of what is allowed and expected. Following Cohen's reading of the monster as a cultural body, the monster has a symbiotic relationship with the culture it exists within; that culture dictates where the line between what is allowed and what is forbidden (and therefore worthy of punishment) stands. What stands as punishable behavior for a child has naturally evolved in the time between the 17th century and the modern-day Krampus of Dougherty's film. However, while the offenses may have changed, their punishment and purpose carry a common goal as at their core they are still working toward facilitating family harmony and reinforcing the status quo.

In 17th-century Bavaria, where the Thirty Years' War caused mass death, famine, and a breakdown of the traditional and village family structure, the Krampus was a way of ensuring that some order would be maintained in the youngest citizens. Young children, those who still left their shoes out for Santa Claus, were the primary targets of the Krampus. Childhood in the 17th century was short, if indeed children survived infancy to experience it at all, and this left a small window

"The Shadow of Saint Nicholas": Dougherty's Krampus

during which children could be educated on what the society found acceptable and unacceptable in terms of behavior. Children were expected to be modest and quiet, to say their prayers and do their chores without complaint. In her book *Forgotten Children: Parent-Child Relations from 1500 to 1900* author Linda Pollock writes, "From 7 onwards, children were expected to behave as adults, ceasing to be only a 'consumer'; and becoming a 'contributor'" (Pollock 7). There was a strong expectation that even if you were young you needed to contribute to the family, and eventually to the greater community and society, as much as age and ability allowed. It was believed that children carried inherent original sin and the brutal conditions of the 17th century made it all the more imperative for society to make sure that through hard work (and often beatings) the sin in a child was never allowed to manifest in a way that would harm the community (Pollock 15). The greater concern over the moral and spiritual well-being of children in the 17th century works in alignment with the policing offered by the Krampus. The Krampus, like other monsters, is there to warn children to stay on the socially-dictated straight and narrow, reflecting Cohen's argument that "The monster prevents mobility (intellectual, geographical or sexual), eliminating the social spaces through which private bodies may move. To step outside this official geography is to risk attack by some monstrous border patrol" (Cohen 12). The Krampus polices all of the above boundaries; children must not venture away from the home (physically or metaphorically), as their day-to-day lives are bound by the expectations and needs of the family. Failure to perform chores, not showing proper deference to God, or disobeying their parents could lead to the financial, social, or spiritual ruin of the family unit. During the 17th century, outside forces caused increased strain on German families, providing additional urgency to the proper training of the next generation. The monster, by stepping in as an additional protector of the cultural norm, is one more guardian against societal collapse.

Despite what partisan talking heads and doomsday callers on the street preach, things are not nearly as dire in the 21st-century United States as they were in 17th-century Germany. Families are less concerned that marauding bands of soldiers will burn their crops and kill their livestock or that they will lose children to diseases of physical or spiritual origin. During the Christmas season more care is given to the perfect wrapping of packages and to the selection of their contents than to the question of who will be chopping the firewood to ensure that the family will not freeze. Times have changed and the Krampus has changed along with them. The monster of Michael Dougherty's film reflects a different kind of "cultural body" (Cohen 4), adjusting his parameters for punishment to be in alignment with 21st-century values.

The modern monster is concerned about the behavior of the family as a whole, not just that of the youngest members. Family strife and a loss of the Christmas spirit have replaced the more traditional punishable offenses as primary infractions against the societal order that require the Krampus' attention. The Engels' marriage is heavily implied to be on the rocks, Howard wishes he had sons in place of his capable but tomboy daughters, sisters Sarah and Linda have a strained relationship (both between the two of them and with their estranged Aunt Dorothy), and daughter Beth would rather spend the holidays smoking pot and having sex with her boyfriend than spending quality time with her argumentative family. The worst crime committed by the family however is a loss of Christmas spirit, the terrible affliction that makes the rounds in all manner of media around the Christmas season from advertisements to the ever popular assortment of holiday TV specials. Omi, who should be the respected elder as the oldest member of the family, has her labor belittled when her son's only comment on her piles of homemade cookies is that they have plenty of store-bought ones. Beth thinks of Christmas as just another day rather than viewing it as a special time to be with the ones you love. Then there is son Max, who effectively seals the family's fate when he tears up his letter to Santa and hurls the shreds of paper into the night. It is almost immediately after this event that the town is shrouded in darkness and snow, symbolizing that the Krampus is coming to town.

Taken as individual incidents, the behaviors and petty holiday squabbles that lead to the doom of both of these families seem relatively benign. Everyone has a relative who they dread seeing during holidays (in American pop culture it is a well-worn trope), teenagers often would rather spend time with their friends than their family, and all children eventually have to contend with the loss of childhood beliefs and innocence. *Krampus* takes these everyday happenings and punishes them as a threat to the existent social order that holds together American society. It is not enough to merely punish one member of the family, as it was in the 17th century; now all family members contribute to the strain on the bonds of the homogenous nuclear family and so all members must bear the punishment. As Omi says, "This is all our fault. He's come for us all." Monsters patrol the borders of society and often, "these borders are in place . . . to establish strictly homosocial bonds, the

"The Shadow of Saint Nicholas": Dougherty's Krampus

ties between men that keep the patriarchal society functional" (Cohen 13). Each member of the family has tested the bounds of the acceptable with their behavior and the Krampus comes in Dougherty's film in order to make sure that the borders of society remain strong. In the film this is accomplished through purging and then quarantining the family, trapping them forever in one of many snow globes in the Krampus' lair.

The film acts as a cautionary tale against any threat to the patriarchal, nuclear family structure, one that, regardless of socioeconomic background, believes in the ideal American Christmas. The ending scene of the film is Christmas enforced by the Krampus, the dark fulfillment of Max's wish for things to be "like they used to." The family sit together in their pajamas, laughing and opening gifts, while Omi passes out homemade hot cocoa; Aunt Dorothy's 9 am drinking receives no comments or exasperated looks and Sarah is amused rather than horrified by her in-laws' holiday gift of taxidermy. An ominous cover of "Have Yourself a Merry Little Christmas" plays as the family sit together, the lyrics of the song to be taken less as a wishful suggestion and more as a threat of "or else." The Krampus has punished the family and, in doing so, has set an example for others in society. You better watch out, indeed.

Works Cited

"10 Questions: Mike Dougherty & Dan Harris." IGN. IGN, 16 Apr. 2003. Web. 10 July 2016.

Beauchamp, Monte. *Krampus: The Devil of Christmas*. San Francisco: Last Gasp, 2010.

Cohen, Jeffrey Jerome. "Monster Culture (Seven Theses)." *Monster Theory: Reading Culture*. Minneapolis: University of Minnesota Press, 1996. 3-25.

Diestro-Dópido, Mar. "Krampus." *Sight & Sound* 26.2 (2016): 80.

Ebert, Roger. "Gremlins." *RogerEbert.com*. 8 June 1984. Web. 18 July 2016.

Eddy, Melissa. "He Sees You When You're Sleeping, and Gives You Nightmares." *New York Times* 21 Dec. 2014.

Forbes, Bruce David. *Christmas: A Candid History*. Berkeley: University of California Press, 2007.

Gallon, Stephanie. "Christmas Demons II — Krampus and Perchta." *International Gothic Association*. University of Sterling. 18 December 2014. Web. 12 July 2016.

Gordon, Rebecca. "Horror-Comedy." *Oxford Bilbliographies*. Oxford University Press, 2016. Web. 14 July 2016.

Grimm, Jacob. *Teutonic Mythology* Vol. 1. Trans. James Steven Stallybrass. Cambridge: Cambridge University Press, 2012.

Krampus. Dir. Michael Dougherty. Perf. Adam Scott, Toni Collette, David Koechner, Allison Tolman, Conchata Ferrell, Emjay Anthony Legendary/Universal, 2015. DVD.

Hallenbeck, Bruce G. *Comedy-Horror Films: A Chronological History, 1914-2008.* Jefferson, NC: McFarland, 2009.

"Horror For The Holidays: Meet The Anti-Santa." *Weekend Edition Saturday.* NPR, WHYY, Philadelphia. 10 Dec. 2011. Radio.

Jovanovski, Valentina. "Is Krampus the Christmas Demon Becoming Too Commercial?" *Christian Science Monitor* 5 Dec. 2013. Web. 16 July 2016.

Maddrey, Joseph. *Nightmares in Red, White and Blue: The Evolution of the American Horror Film.* Jefferson, NC: McFarland, 2004.

"Mad Max: Fury Road (2015)." *The Numbers: Where Data and Movie Business Meet.* Nash Information Services, LLC, 1 Jan. 2016. Web. 28 Jun. 2016.

Miller, Cynthia J. and A. Bowdoin Van Riper. "Introduction." *The Laughing Dead: The Horror-Comedy Film from* Bride of Frankenstein *to* Zombieland. Ed. Cynthia J. Miller and A. Bowdoin Van Riper. Lanham, MD: Rowman & Littlefield, 2016. xii-xxiii.

Müller, Ulrich. *Dämonen, Monster, Fabelwesen (Mittelalter-Mythen).* München: UVK Verlagsgesellschaft, 2015.

"The Naughty Ones: Meet the Cast." *Krampus.* Dir. Michael Dougherty. Perf. Adam Scott, Toni Collette, David Koechner, Allison Tolman, Conchata Ferrell, Emjay Anthony, Stefania LaVie Owen, Krista Stadler. Legendary/Universal, 2015.

Nissenbaum, Stephen. *The Battle for Christmas: A Cultural History of America's Most Cherished Holiday.* New York: Vintage, 1996.

Opam, Kwame. "2015 is the Year of Hollywood's Practical Effects Comeback." *The Verge.* VOX Media, 4 Aug. 2015. Web. 14 July 2016.

Pattillo, Alice. "The Secrets of Seasonal Horror Krampus Revealed." *Creative Bloq.* Future Publishing Limited. 22 Dec. 2016. Web. 18 July 2016.

Pollock, A. Linda. *Forgotten Children: Parent-Child Relations from 1500 to 1900.* Cambridge: Cambridge University Press, 1983.

Raedisch, Linda. *The Old Magic of Christmas: Yuletide Traditions for the Darkest Days of the Year.* Woodbury, MN: Llewellyn Publications, 2003.

Theibault, John. "The Demography of the 30 Years War Re-revisited: Günther Franz and his Critics." *German History* 15.1 (1997): 1-21.

Truitt, Brian. "Krampus Twists Christmas Magic." *USA Today* 7 September 2015. Web. 14 July 2016.

Unmasking the Bite: Pleasure, Sexuality, and Vulnerability in the Vampire Series

TATIANA PROROKOVA

Introduction: Gender and Monstrosity in the Vampire Series

From the patriarchal image of Dracula to the most recent representations of young female blood-sucking monsters, the vampire films and series raise the problem of gender. Barbara Creed specifies that, with the emergence of the female vampire as a phenomenon in the 1970s, "the vampire film began to explore openly the explicit relationship between sex, violence and death" (59). The interest in these issues has not faded in the twenty-first century, when the vampire genre continues to flourish. Today, fans enjoy vampire stories that are presented not only at the length of a film; instead, they are more and more often drawn by an absolutely new phenomenon—serial stories about vampires that have been holding the attention of their audiences for years. Among such are the story of Elena Gilbert (Nina Dobrev) and her complicated romantic relationship with two vampires, the Salvatore brothers—*The Vampire Diaries* (2009—)—and its spin-off, the story of the original vampires, i.e., the Mikaelson family, and the vampires of New Orleans—*The Originals* (2013—). Among other issues related to popular culture and youth culture, both series overtly deal with the problem of gender. Particularly, this chapter argues that through the multiple portrayals of the vampire bite, along with the issue of violence, the series tackle the ones of pleasure, sexuality, and vulnerability.

The process of biting (and eventual blood sucking) is one of the key constituents of every vampire film. Creed summarizes the classical "symbolic elements" of a vampire tale:

159

> The vampire is one of the undead, a figure who rises from the grave on the full moon in search of young virgins, almost always female. The vampire's resting place is usually a coffin secreted in a dark, cobweb-filled cellar or crypt, which is reached by a long flight of stairs. The vampire sinks his/her two sharp fangs into the victim's neck in order to suck blood. Visual emphasis is usually placed on the two marks, like a snake bite, left by the vampire's fangs. After the attack the victim is transformed into a member of the undead. (62)

While, for the most part, Creed's description is archaic in the twenty-first century, one key element—the bite—is indeed still actual, which only reveals the significance of the act in the formation of the vampire phenomenon. It is through the bite that the twenty-first century vampires feed themselves and transform human beings into vampires. Yet the chapter contends that along with these literal interpretations of the bite, one can also construe it as a symbolic sexual act that happens between the vampire and his/her victim. As a close examination of selected biting scenes from *The Vampire Diaries* and *The Originals* will demonstrate, both series frequently put stress on biting, not as a necessary and unavoidable action that the vampire has to take in order to get food and thus survive, but instead display biting as a process that brings pleasure. The strong focus on the victim's body, however, helps one advance the argument and claim that it is *sexual* pleasure that the vampire bite is usually associated with in the two series. Additionally, the unequal power relationship that develops between the monster and its victim allows one to conclude that along with the problem of sexual penetration, the act of biting is also aimed at unveiling the issue of vulnerability.

Thus, as *The Vampire Diaries* and *The Originals* illustrate, the bite puts on multiple masks, covering its perverse nature. However, apart from figurative masking, the two series present literal scenes of a masquerade that only intensify the problem of perversity and sexual obsession of the twenty-first century vampire. This argument was inspired by Stanley Kubrick's last film *Eyes Wide Shut* (1999), which openly deals with the problems of fidelity and perverse sexuality, particularly through the portrayal of the masked ball. The chapter therefore draws parallels between the two series and Kubrick's film to understand the metaphor of a masquerade as an act of sexual transgression that only corroborates the earlier arguments about the vampire bite as a symbolic sexual act and the vampire nature as a manifestation of a sexually perverse existence.

160

The Metaphor of Biting: *The Vampire Diaries* (2009–) and *The Originals* (2013–)

When construing the vampire bite, one usually thinks of it as a means of feeding, i.e., sucking blood, or as a way of turning the victim into the vampire, thus, as Shannon Winnubst puts it, "giving birth without sex" (7-8). The latter interpretation deserves special attention because it illustrates the important characteristic of every vampire, i.e., their inability to propagate naturally. This, in turn, can be easily explained with the fact that vampires are dead creatures; specifically, they are dead human beings who now possess supernatural powers: "It is the monster that used to be human; it is the undead that used to be alive; it is the monster that *looks like us*" (Hollinger qtd. in Winnubst 7, emphasis in original). It is indeed crucial that although vampires resemble human beings very much, they are not human beings, mostly from a biological perspective. The inability to conceive and give birth allows one to see vampires as not exactly infertile creatures because their reproductive system is not simply afunctional–it is, in principle, dead. This fact allows one to suspect that vampires cannot be characterized by their sex because biologically they become deprived of it as soon as they become monsters. However, as multiple cinematic and serial examples demonstrate, vampires do become romantically and sexually involved with humans, other vampires, and even werewolves. Focusing particularly on the female vampire, Creed claims that she becomes "abject" in many ways, one of which concerns her sexual behavior, namely that "she does not respect the dictates of the law which set down the rules of proper sexual conduct" (61). Improper and aggressive sexual behavior therefore is one of the key characteristics of the vampire, whose desires (including sexual ones) are clearly more intense compared to those of human beings.

The intensified sexual desire of the vampire, leads one to get involved in a romantic and/or sexual relationship. Thus sex becomes one of the key elements in every vampire film and series. *The Vampire Diaries* and *The Originals* even accentuate the difference between vampire sex and human sex, overtly demonstrating that the former is faster, it is more aggressive, and apparently it brings more pleasure. One of the scenes in *The Vampire Diaries* that illustrates this idea takes place in the fourteenth episode of the third season–"Dangerous Liaisons"–when Rebekah Mikaelson (Claire Holt)–one of the original vampires–has sex with the vampire Damon (Ian Somerhalder). Shortly before the scene, Damon says that Rebekah cannot have sex with a human because she "would've broken him in a second;" Rebekah responds: "You're suggesting I can't be gentle?" whereas Damon answers: "No, I'm just saying you should find someone a little more endurable" (*The Vampire Diaries*). The scenes of aggressive and violent sex—that obviously satisfy both Damon and Rebekah—follow the conversation.

Vampire sex can also be seen as an act of transgression. Sexual pleasure is frequently considered a sin. Thomas Aquinas claimed: "The pleasure of sexual intercourse 'seriously corrupts the judgment of moral wisdom.' To multiply such pleasure, therefore, is contrary to good morals" (qtd. in Milhaven 158). Obviously Aquinas wrote about human sex; yet one can argue that the way vampire sex is portrayed in the two series only intensifies its sinful nature. Pivotally, when Elena Gilbert is a human, she dates Stefan (Paul Wesley)—the "good" vampire who refuses to drink human blood, which arguably stands for his fidelity to Elena. After she turns into a vampire, however, she starts to date Damon—a rather selfish vampire who is frequently shown drinking alcohol and feeding from multiple victims. Considering biting equal to having sex, one can claim that in the relationship with Damon, Elena tolerates Damon's "biting affairs" with the others. On the other hand, one can speculate that the vampires' ability to have sex symbolically brings them closer to human beings. Discussing the main vampire character of the *Twilight* saga, Edward Cullen (Robert Pattinson), Tracy L. Bealer writes: "Sexual expression becomes a way for Edward to reclaim the tenderness, empathy, and compassion that he felt was lost along with his human soul" (144). Hence, having sex is not exactly negative for the vampire since it arguably demonstrates that the vampire can express certain feelings and thus possess humanity. That only adds to the general image of the twenty-first century vampire, who, to borrow from Maria Lindgren Leavenworth, frequently provokes "positive identification" (323).

Yet I argue that apart from traditional images of sexual intercourse, the two series overtly focus on its metaphorical depiction that is achieved through the bite. The fact that the vampire bite is depicted multiply in the series only intensifies the idea of sexual transgression and misbehavior of the undead. Creed makes an important observation concerning the nature of the vampire bite: "Sucking blood from a victim's neck places the vampire and victim in an intimate relationship. Unlike other horror-film monsters, the vampire enfolds the victim in an apparent or real erotic embrace. This is as true for the female vampire as

Unmasking the Bite

the male" (59). Moreover, while the bleeding bite can be metaphorically interpreted as "the first menstruation," the most frequently bitten place—the neck—"represents the neck of the uterus" (63). Thus the obvious phallic shape of the fangs allows one to associate them with male genitals, whereas the bite—that is, the actual penetration of human flesh—is figurative sexual intercourse.

Commenting on the nature of the vampire bite by example of both the series and the novel *The Vampire Diaries*, Leavenworth claims: "The vampire's invasion of another's bodily space through the bite has traditionally been figured as particularly evil since it carries with it the threat of transforming the human victim into a monster. When the vampire text falls into the romance genre, this transformation is not always constructed as negative, however, since it also ensures everlasting togetherness" (324). Both *The Vampire Diaries* and *The Originals* seem to suggest that biting can potentially lead to eternal love of two characters. However, the series do not really develop this idea, for neither of them presents such a story; what the audience witnesses instead are multiple breakups that arguably stand for the polygamous nature of both female and male vampires that is manifested not only through their actual sexual liaisons but also through countless bites. Such behavior, in turn, only underscores their sexually perverse nature.

The Vampire Diaries

The Vampire Diaries, which by 2016 comprises a full seven seasons, obviously has its plot twisted in all possible ways. However, the main plot line is devoted to the story of Elena Gilbert and her (complicated) romantic relationship with the vampire brothers Stefan and Damon Salvatore. Elena also has two friends who accompany her in the course of every season and from time to time become central figures—the witch Bonnie Bennett (Katerina Graham) and the blond girl Caroline Forbes (Candice King) who is already in the second season turns into a vampire. Unsurprisingly, biting scenes largely intervene in the stories of the multiple characters. It is impossible to provide even a brief analysis of every scene, which is why the chapter focuses only on selected ones. Yet the various portrayals of the bite arguably carry the same meaning, i.e., they symbolically depict sexual intercourse.

For example, in the first season, Caroline literally serves Damon as food and as a sexual slave at the same time. An important scene takes place when, lying in bed, Damon gets on top of Caroline and, while the audience expects the two to have sex, Damon shows his fangs and bites the screaming girl in her neck. The third episode—"Friday Night Bites"—starts with the two lying in bed. The camera lingers on Caroline, revealing the heroine in her sleep: her arms are on her stomach, the revealing bed gown accentuates her breasts, and her neck is mutilated by multiple bites. She wakes up and stares at her reflection in the mirror, then looks around and sees Damon, sleeping deeply next to her. Scared to death, she tries to leave the bed. Yet she wakes up Damon, and he throws her back on the bed. Scared and desperate, Caroline repeatedly screams "no," when Damon, having smelled her blood on a pillow, returns to his vampire nature and throws himself onto Caroline. The scene overtly plays with the issue of sexuality, mixing the pleasure from feeding with the pleasure of having sex. First, it is crucial that the scene takes place in the bedroom and both characters are practically naked. Second, a strong focus on Caroline's sexuality and eventually on her vulnerability, as she cannot escape from her "prison," hints at her status first as Damon's sex slave and only secondarily as his source of food. Third, the moment when Damon smells her blood on the pillow and the audience observes his visual transformation into a vampire blatantly hints at his being aroused by Caroline's smell. Indeed, female scent is one of the triggering factors for a man as it intensifies his desire to have sex with a woman. This issue is further played with in the fourth episode—"Family Ties"—when Stefan and Elena lie in bed, and as they kiss, Stefan's face changes into that of a vampire. The scene vividly illustrates the tight connection between the vampire's transformation into a real active monster and a sexual act. Thus, one of the moments when the true nature of the vampire awakes is when he/she becomes sexually aroused. One can speculate that biting becomes the final stage—the act that follows arousal—i.e., the moment of penetrating and having sex. Indeed, as soon as Stefan stops kissing Elena, his face gets back to normal and the bite is avoided.

Caroline is obviously a victim; yet, as the scene demonstrates, not because she is kidnapped, but because she is multiply bitten. However, the fact that she is bitten in bed, where her body is hardly covered, obscures the feeding for raping. The bite becomes the man's symbolic penetration of the woman. It is pivotal that when Caroline objects and begs Damon to stop feeding from her, she is in bed, which fully constructs her image as a rape victim. The sexual relationship between Damon and Caroline is developed in the fourth episode, when in one of

Unmasking the Bite

the scenes the audience witnesses Damon pulling Caroline into bed. He lies on top of her and tenderly kisses her, without biting. Toward the end of the episode, the viewer observes Damon hugging Caroline from behind, kissing her, and saying: "You make me crazy, you know that?" (*The Vampire Diaries*). He then brutally bites into her neck and starts sucking blood. Importantly, he slowly puts her on the ground, thus making the scene reminiscent of the ones in which he was biting her in bed. This moment proves again that Caroline is not only Damon's food but also a woman with whom he can have sex repeatedly.

Later, in the thirteenth episode of the second season—"Daddy Issues"—one witnesses Damon and his female victim lying in a bath full of foam, having a glass of wine. They start to kiss passionately, when Damon reveals his fangs and thrust them into the woman's neck. Her facial expression reveals that she is both scared of and dislikes what he is doing, most probably because of the pain that she feels. Yet, as more blood runs down her back, her face relaxes and she obviously starts to enjoy the bite. One can speculate that the scene is a metaphoric depiction of the first sexual intercourse that the woman has. While a virgin is scared of the first painful penetration (which is frequently accompanied with bleeding), as soon as this is done, a woman can finally get pleasure from sex. In this scene, the bite is therefore an overt representation of a sexual act. Nevertheless, it is important to note that both Caroline and this woman are "under compulsion," i.e., they cannot control their actions and have to obey the vampire, which openly displays their vulnerability.

Later in the season, in the nineteenth episode—"Klaus"—the audience witnesses the same woman wearing only her underwear and sharing with Damon that she has developed feelings for him: "You need to know that somebody cares about you. I care about you, Damon" (*The Vampire Diaries*). This confession, however, brings Damon in rage, and he, first, savagely bites the woman in her neck and then throws her on the floor. The fact that she is practically naked, weeping on the floor, and that she is not physically capable of fighting back create an image of her as a rape victim (the rape, in this case, is the brutal bite). Even more explicitly, the issue of rape is raised in the twenty-second episode—"As I Lay Dying"—when Klaus Mikaelson (Joseph Morgan)—one of the original, hence, most powerful vampires—invites Stefan for a "hunt" (*The Vampire Diaries*). Klaus bites a girl in her neck and lets her run, which only teases Stefan to catch and bite her, too. The scene is very similar to those depicted in "rape-revenge" (Schubart

83) films, among which are, for example, Wes Craven's *The Last House on the Left* (1972) and Meir Zarchi's *Day of the Woman* (1978), as well as their recent remakes that include scenes in which the female victim is raped by several men in a row. In the vampire series, biting therefore symbolically turns into the rape of the girl by two vampires.

A more complex scene of symbolic rape takes place in the seventeenth episode of the sixth season — "A Bird in a Gilded Cage" — when Stefan offers Caroline to "share" a girl. He greedily sucks blood out of the victim's neck and then invites Caroline to do the same. After she bites the girl, however, she turns to Stefan and as greedily kisses him on the mouth. The scene of aggressive vampire sex follows. The inclusion of the female vampire in this heterosexual relationship between the male vampire and his female victim makes the sequence problematic. On the one hand, considering the bite a symbolic act of having sex, one can speculate that the scene suggests the lesbian nature of the female vampire. Yet the following sex scene with the male vampire obviously refutes this argument. Or does the scene illustrate the nature of the vampire as a non-gendered creature, therefore suggesting that sex is only a mechanical act and the vampire can have it both with men and women? With regard to *The Vampire Diaries*, this argument also seems rather far-fetched, since the series builds its multiple plot lines on heterosexual romantic relationships between the characters.

The series is also rich in scenes in which female vampires bite their female victims. Employing the theory of the bite as a sexual act to these scenes, it seems plausible to claim that they suggest the vampires' homosexuality. With the fangs, a female vampire arguably turns into, what scholars refer to as a "phallic woman" (Creed 156), who, with the help of these very fangs, penetrates her victim. Thus, when the female vampire bites the female victim, she is arguably portrayed as lesbian. However, it is hard to foster this argument by example of *The Vampire Diaries*, where every female vampire has a boyfriend (or wants to have one). The only lesbian couple introduced in the series — Mary Louise (Teressa Liane) and Nora (Scarlett Byrne) — are heretics, i.e., half witches and half vampires. Their nature therefore does not allow one to consider them an example of the homosexual relationship between vampires, since they are not pure vampires. Finally, the fact that the heroines are introduced relatively late in the series and that they die already in the seventh season underscore *The Vampire Diaries'* intention to focus on the heterosexual relations only.

Unmasking the Bite

The scenes in which the female vampire bites the male victim, on the other hand, illustrate her masculinity and her ability to be more powerful than the man. Therefore, although particular scenes invite the analysis of the characters' (possible) homosexuality, the series still largely comments on the heterosexual relations among vampires or vampires and humans (rarely, werewolves), where the bite becomes an overtly sexualized act that only reinforces the intensified and exaggerated sexual desires of vampires.

The Originals

In 2013, one of the stories from *The Vampire Diaries* was developed into the independent series *The Originals*, which, by 2016, consists of three full seasons. *The Originals* focuses on the family of the first vampires, the Mikaelsons, geographically placing the action in New Orleans, and connecting the lives of the local vampires, werewolves, and witches.

Just like *The Vampire Diaries*, *The Originals* arguably depicts the bite as a symbolic sexual act. There are multiple biting scenes in the series that display the male vampire hunting for the female victim. For example, the fifth episode of the second season—"Red Door"— includes a flashback that displays Elijah Mikaelson (Daniel Gillies) attacking his beloved Tatia (Nina Dobrev). Tatia has just found out that Elijah has turned into a "monster" (*The Originals*), and although Elijah tries to prove the opposite, as soon as he smells blood on Tatia's injured palm, his face turns into that of a vampire. He orders the girl to run as he realizes that he will not be able to control himself. Yet he eventually catches her. The camera focuses on Tatia's neck, and then the vampire brutally bites the girl. As he sucks her blood, Tatia's face is distorted with terror, pain, and helplessness. The scene is intensified by Elijah's earlier memory that precedes the just-described moment, when scared Tatia runs toward the door through a long corridor, trying to escape from Elijah. Yet the door is locked and Elijah easily gets his take. The scene is visually striking because while Tatia is wearing a white dress that overtly hints at her innocence, Elijah's trunk is uncovered from clothes, but his mouth, neck, and chest are heavily covered with blood, which vigorously creates the image of a monster. The attack therefore can be symbolically interpreted as rape: Tatia is depicted as a virgin because of her snow-white dress that eventually is spoiled with her own blood and that from Elijah's body, which metaphorically stands for a sexual damage of the pure girl.

Another important scene that perhaps most explicitly demonstrates the symbolic connection between sex and biting takes place in the second episode of the third season — "You Hung the Moon" — when the vampire Lucien Castle (Andrew Lees) is shown sucking blood from a girl. The scene opens with his hand greedily touching the victim's naked legs. The camera reveals his hand moving up toward the girl's dress and then focuses on her breasts, whose shape is revealed in a sexy way. The audience hears the vampire sucking blood from the girl's neck and then moving away in satisfaction, licking his fangs. He continues holding his hand on the girl's knee, when he hears a door bell ringing. The biting scene ends. The girl is obviously perplexed and does not understand what is going on because she is under compulsion. This reveals her vulnerability and powerlessness as Lucien uses her in the ways he finds appropriate, whereas she cannot object.

Unlike *The Vampire Diaries*, *The Originals* seems to be more tolerant toward vampire homosexuality. First, it includes the story of the gay vampire Josh Rosza (Steven Krueger). Second, the series shows a considerable number of scenes in which a man bites another man. Yet, both aspects are quite complex. For example, while Josh is explicitly gay, he is in a relationship with a werewolf, i.e., a man who belongs to another "breed." Therefore, while the same sex of the characters indeed makes their relationship homosexual, the fact that they are different "species" apparently complicates this. This couple seems to suggest how perverse homosexual relationship is because it is a certain deviation from a norm. To specify, if Josh had been in love with another vampire, or his werewolf partner had fallen for another werewolf, the series would have celebrated homosexuality. In the current state, however, *The Originals* seems to censure it. As for the large number of biting scenes between men, they can be suggestive of the characters' homosexuality. Yet it is significant that very often it is Klaus Mikaelson who bites male vampires or werewolves. But Klaus is a hybrid (half vampire and half werewolf), and the series articulates it too often that his nature is a deviation, thus making Klaus the most powerful character yet an outsider. Klaus' nature therefore also complicates one's interpretation of the series' attitude toward homosexuality because it seems to both celebrate and censure it. Hence, while *The Originals* raises

Unmasking the Bite

the problem of homosexuality more explicitly compared to *The Vampire Diaries*, it does not make its stand with regard to the issue clear to the audience.

Finally, the important plot line that supports the idea of dangerous, perverse, and harmful nature of the vampire includes the tender relationship between Klaus and Camille O'Connell (Leah Pipes). Whereas the viewer understands that the two characters are in love, this story never really develops any further, for Klaus understands that this relationship can be life-threatening for the woman who can easily become a victim of Klaus' multiple enemies. In addition, the vampire tries to protect the woman from the violence of the supernatural world — both by not getting involved with her and by literally saving her many times. While Camille seems rather courageous, Klaus understands the danger that (mainly) vampires pose to her and therefore constantly rescues her from possible bites. He thus symbolically protects her purity as a human being and, most importantly, as a female. The similar relationship can be witnessed between the vampire Marcel Gerard (Charles Michael Davis) and the witch-girl Davina Claire (Danielle Campbell), whose purity is intensified even more due to her youth. This motif is also noticeable in the early seasons of *The Vampire Diaries* when Elena, still being a human, is constantly protected by the Salvatore brothers from being bitten, murdered, or turned into a vampire. All these subplots only reinforce the image of the vampire bite as not only a life-threatening act, but also, and arguably even more importantly, as a threat to female purity and virginity.

Perversity of Masquerade: Disguising Pleasure

The vampire bite, as it is represented in *The Vampire Diaries* and *The Originals*, is a metaphor for a sexual act. The real nature of the bite is therefore skillfully masked behind its visible brutality that superficially stands for the vampire's feeding. Behind savageness, the bite hides sexual pleasure; and it is exactly through the combination of sex and violence that the bite can be perceived as "perverse." Perversity therefore can be metaphorically disguised. It is, however, possible to argue that the literal masking or masquerading depicted in both series disguises perversity, too.

The most apparent scene that includes masking and sexual perversity is vividly demonstrated in Stanley Kubrick's *Eyes Wide*

169

Shut — the film that can succinctly be described as "an existential film about human nature, sexuality, marital fidelity, and the nature and significance of choice" (Hoffman 59). Although the film demonstrates how William Harford (Tom Cruise) and his wife Alice Harford (Nicole Kidman) "remove their literal and metaphorical masks" (59), the film's arguably most equivocal scene takes place at a masked ball where the participants, including Bill, wear real masks.

The main attribute of any masquerade is a mask and a costume. Thus at a masquerade one pretends to be someone else, hiding his/her own identity. Defining a "carnival," Mikhail Bakhtin claimed that it is a "second life" (qtd. in Jordan and Haladyn 189). To put it differently, "the carnivalesque is a turning inside out of everyday life, in which prevailing norms and social prohibitions are temporarily suspended and a second life of new possibilities is born" (Jordan and Haladyn 189). Yet carnival does not necessarily presuppose one's wearing a mask; therefore, employing Bakhtin's theory to the characterization of the nature of a masquerade, one can speculate that a masquerade is a more complex play that involves not exactly pretense but rather one's full adoption of another identity for a specific period of time. Discussing English masquerades in the eighteenth century, Terry Castle claims that a masquerade is usually linked to the problem of "the varieties of libidinous freedom" (160). The scholar adds that at that time, a masquerade was perhaps the only opportunity for women to be equal to men in terms of freedom of behavior: "Women, notably, were as free as men to initiate verbal or physical contacts with strangers" (161-62). It is also important that, for example, at carnivals, female performers "expose their bodies in order to reclaim them, to assert their own pleasure and sexuality, thus denying the fetishistic pursuit [by men] . . ." (Forte qtd. in Bettelheim 69). Thus a masquerade (as well as a carnival) facilitates a particular type of freedom that participants can experience only at this event but not in real life. Grotesqueness and exaggeration become the key characteristics of a masquerade.

To illustrate the idea of sexual freedom that a masquerade guarantees, I turn to the analysis of one of the most controversial scenes in *Eyes Wide Shut* — the masked ball. Confused with and jealous of Alice's thoughts of having sex with another man, Bill decides to attend a masked ball that his friend Nick Nightingale (Todd Field) tells him about. The ball is a closed event, and in order to partake one needs to know the password and have a mask with him/her. As Bill gets inside the mansion where the masquerade takes place, he is met

Unmasking the Bite

by people in masks, who ask him for the password. Approved, Bill puts on his mask as well as a hood, thus completely disguising his own self. Having entered the main hall, Bill joins those who witness a mysterious ritual. The ritual involves women who are being prepared for an important event. It is crucial that both the audience and the participants of the ritual wear masks. When at some point of the ritual women have to uncover themselves and remain practically naked, their masks are still on. The ritual concludes as the women kiss each other in a symbolic touch of their masks and then leave the circle to choose one person from the crowd. Bill is chosen, too, and leaving the main hall, he eventually walks through the rooms in the mansion to witness the people having sex: "[H]e [Bill] wanders through room after room of groups and couples mechanically copulating in an array of sexual permutations, a spectacle of just as much jiggling, pumping flesh that it simply leaves the viewer cold" (Ransom 34). The scenes are surreal not only because they overwhelm with the number of participants who have sexual intercourse with and in front of each other, creating a spectacle out of it, but also because despite their nakedness, all the participants continue wearing masks. Bill is eventually identified as the one who does not belong to this secret society and asked to take his mask off, thus allowing the people around him to see his true self. He takes off his mask but refuses to obey the next order, namely to undress. Eventually, the woman who has chosen him (and then warned him several times that he should have left the place) offers to sacrifice herself for him. Bill is let go.

The scene aptly combines sex with (possible) violence, particularly at the moment when Bill is unmasked, as "eroticism has been replaced with fear" (Ransom 34). Importantly, while the scene overtly portrays sex and, for that matter, pornography, it arguably "is not meant to be erotic; it is not meant to offer pleasure" (37). Christiane Kubrick—the wife of Stanley Kubrick—accurately pinpoints that the scene "has nothing to do with sex and everything to do with fear" (qtd. in Ransom 37). Other commentators underline that "frank frontal nudity . . . is used to disturbing effect" (Maslin qtd. in Ransom 37), whereas the masks are simply as "creepy as hell" (Kreider qtd. in Ransom 37). The combination of sex with violence is arguably achieved and is only possible in *Eyes Wide Shut* because of the mask. The mask continues to play the role of a dangerous object, when toward the end of the film Bill finds his mask on a pillow in his and Alice's bedroom. Amy J. Ransom contends: "The presence of the mask not only suggests a continuing

171

menace to the protagonist's safety, but by that very menace, it also signifies the reality of the evil and the power of the secret society that underlines a beneficial surface image of his society's leaders that he previously took for granted" (42). The masquerade in Kubrick's film is therefore not only a pervert fantasy, but it is also the place where sex and violence can be put up and manifested.

Just like *Eyes Wide Shut*, both *The Vampire Diaries* and *The Originals* include masquerade scenes that, I argue, unveil similar issues, i.e., violence and sex that the masquerade freedom facilitates. Moreover, in the case of the two series, the inclusion of the masquerade scenes is aimed at intensifying the exaggerated perversity of the vampire's desires. Whereas the masquerade scenes in *The Vampire Diaries* and *The Originals* differ considerably in terms of aesthetical representation from the one the viewer witnesses in *Eyes Wide Shut*, mostly because none of the series' masquerade scenes include nudity, they still aptly underline the vampire's thirst for sex and violence that is usually manifested through the bite. The two series therefore arguably adopt Kubrick's idea of representing desire in a masquerade setting, when one's identity is disguised.

Whereas *The Vampire Diaries* shows quite a number of ball scenes, especially during the first seasons, when the main characters are still high school students, none of these scenes include the characters wearing masks. Yet there is a "masquerade ball" (*The Vampire Diaries*) in the seventh episode of the second season, titled "Masquerade." In this episode, Stefan, Damon, Bonnie, and Elena's younger brother Jeremy (Steven R. McQueen) try to kill Elena's doppelganger — the vampire Katherine Pierce (Nina Dobrev). The action takes place at a masquerade, where Katherine is easily taken for Elena by everyone around (excluding her four potential killers). The audience witnesses the moments when Stefan and Damon discuss how they will kill Katherine, then Jeremy and Bonnie going upstairs in the house where the party takes place, carrying weapons and Bonnie's spell books. In both cases, the characters wear masks.

Shortly before, the viewer observes Katherine getting ready for the masquerade. It is crucial that it is with the help of the mask, as Katherine thinks, that no one will be able to distinguish her from Elena (although the girls do look identical in any way). Katherine, however, goes to the ball together with her friend, a witch. Whereas Katherine is happy that the woman will join her, the witch explains: "You know I love you." She then puts on a mask on her face and asks Katherine where they will be able to wear masks, whereas Katherine tells her

Unmasking the Bite

about the masquerade, and then adds: "You wanna be my date?" (*The Vampire Diaries*). While the scene does not proclaim the heroines' homosexuality, instead underlining the close friendship between the two, it overtly foregrounds the perversity of such a relationship. This perversity, however, is not based on sex but rather on violence; explicit references to the possible sexual relations between the two only intensify their evil nature.

Katherine appears in the masquerade in a short and tight black dress, she wears a bright red lipstick and a laced black mask. Despite the fact that she is disguised, she can be easily recognized. Nevertheless, her outfit underlines the vampire's seductive nature, thus she becomes dangerous not only because she is a supernatural creature but also because her exaggerated sexuality makes her threatening both to men and women. She invites Stefan for a dance and when he refuses, she responds: "Fine. Then tell me who I should kill." Searching for a potential victim she says, "She looks delicious," and then immediately bites off a piece of a strawberry (*The Vampire Diaries*). Thus after being rejected, Katherine tries to force Stefan to do what she wants, demonstrating that she is both violent and sexy. This motif continues later when, dancing with Stefan, Katherine is both cold and seductive. She reminds Stefan how she injured Elena's aunt. She then kills a girl right in front of Stefan, explaining that she will continue killing if he does not give her a moonstone. Later in the episode, Katherine also demonstrates Jeremy that she can be both violent and sexy: while adjusting his tie, she asks whether his uncle managed "to sew his fingers back on" (obviously after Katherine had injured the man) (*The Vampire Diaries*).

It is only when the characters are ready to kill Katherine that they become unmasked. Nevertheless, they soon realize that they cannot kill the vampire because the doppelganger is connected to Elena by a spell. Katherine feels free again and continues to play with her violence and sexuality. She says to Stefan: "You'll hurt me? . . . Everything that I feel Elena feels. So go ahead." Then turns to Damon: "Or better yet, kiss me Damon. She'll feel that too" (*The Vampire Diaries*). Katherine does not simply invite violence and sex. Including both brothers in her plan, she is ready to start an orgy. Later in the episode, enraged Damon tries to stab Katherine, but Stefan prevents him from doing that. Yet Katherine only encourages Damon to hurt her, realizing that Elena will suffer, too. Moreover, she comments on Damon's actions and appearance: "God, you are hot" (*The Vampire Diaries*), thus again combining sex and violence.

173

The masquerade therefore turns into the place of violence and sexual perversion mainly for the reason that the disguise helps the vampires have more freedom. While the vampires' desires, which are violence and sexual perversion, are generally intensified by their supernatural selves, the mask helps them manifest these desires in a greater extent. It is interesting that the masquerade produces such an effect not only on the vampires but also on humans. For example, while in normal life Jeremy is scared to tell Bonnie that he has fallen for her, at the ball one witnesses them talking about Bonnie's magic abilities, when Jeremy says that he would be happy to learn some "sex spell" and soon invites the girl for a dance (*The Vampire Diaries*). Importantly, their masks are on. *The Vampire Diaries* therefore claims that the mask gives one more freedom, particularly with regard to sexual and physical freedoms. The episode finishes with Elena being kidnapped by a person in a mask, thus claiming that the circle of violence (including a potential sexual threat) continues.

The Originals seems to adopt the idea of a masquerade as the space for sex and violence, presenting two masquerade scenes. The first one takes place in the third episode of the first season—"Tangled Up in Blue." The viewer is immersed into the atmosphere of the surreal world, when the masquerade starts. Everyone is dressed in an exquisite costume; there are dancers and acrobats that bring magic into the room. As Camille enters the hall, one notices that her image contradicts all the others in the room. She is dressed up as an angel (white dress and wings obviously render her innocence). Her costume becomes especially important as the audience realizes soon that Camille is the only human among the guests, who are vampires. Thus her innocence and vulnerability are not only symbolic but also literal. Lana Del Rey's song "Dark Paradise" that accompanies some of the masquerade scenes aptly underlines the innocent nature of Camille, who is disguised as a pure angel but surrounded by demons. Violence therefore becomes disguised behind the masks of the others who pose a potential threat to Camille's life. Additionally, the scene plays with the issue of sex. First, when Camille mistakenly takes Rebekah for Klaus' girlfriend, and later, when Rebekah is jealous of Marcel dancing with Camille. The impossibility for the two couples to be together creates tension as well as the atmosphere of sexual dissatisfaction and competitiveness.

The fourth episode of the third season—"A Walk on the Wild Side"—depicts another masquerade. The main characters here are Hayley (Phoebe Tonkin)—the mother of Klaus' daughter—and Elijah,

Unmasking the Bite

who are invited to a masquerade organized by Tristan de Martel (Oliver Ackland) and his "most dangerous" organization of vampires in the world (*The Originals*). Just like *Eyes Wide Shut*, the episode introduces the masquerade with the image of the mansion where the event will take place. Inside the house, everyone wears a mask; people and vampires dance, one witnesses a vampire sucking blood and a couple kissing in the corner. The masquerade is again represented as the space of transgression — the place of sin, where violence and sex coexist. Yet violence dominates the atmosphere in the scene, since Marcel has to find his stolen ring and fight against another vampire or die himself. The search for the ring (whose absence is the threat to Marcel's existence) and the eventual fight are part of the "initiation" (*The Originals*), and having gone through it, Marcel becomes a member of the group. While violence is explicit in the scene, sexual tension is noticeable, too. For example, Hayley and Elijah come together, as a couple, although the audience is aware that the two are not together (despite the fact that both really want to). When Tristan eventually asks Hayley to dance, Elijah obviously becomes jealous. Additionally, it is interesting that looking for his ring, Marcel chooses to kiss the woman (who, he believes, has stolen it) because he sees it as the easiest way to search her.

Following the tradition of *Eyes Wide Shut*, both *The Vampire Diaries* and *The Originals* include masquerade scenes to reflect the atmosphere of freedom and permissiveness. Yet, while Kubrick's film deals with these issues on the level of human relations, discussing, among others, the problem of fidelity and sexual fantasies, the series use the masquerade to render the vampire nature in a more illustrative, grotesque way, underlining violence and sex as the main desires that govern the monsters, just like the ordinary-to-their-existence bite does.

Conclusion

The only scene that is always included in literally every text about vampires — whether it is literature, film, or TV — is that depicting the bite. The bite is important because it is through biting that the vampire feeds itself. It is also though the bite that the vampire demonstrates its superiority over the human being. Yet, while biting and consequential blood sucking can indeed be interpreted as the process of feeding, series like *The Vampire Diaries* and *The Originals* seem to suggest other interpretations of the bite. Precisely, while both do not refute the idea that the vampire has to suck blood in order to exist, they load the bite with other meanings, too. While the vampire needs blood to "eat," it does not necessarily have to bite for it, and the multiple scenes from the series, when vampires drink from blood bags, prove that. The bite therefore loses its traditional function as the way of getting access to human blood. But it accumulates some other ones. Specifically, as the chapter has argued throughout, the bite is still essential in both series, yet it serves to reveal not only violence that is inherent in the vampire nature but also the vampire's intensified sexual desires. While being disguised as a brutal act, the vampire bite also stands for perverse sexual intercourse between the vampire as an initiator and the human being (in some cases, between vampires or vampires and werewolves). Combining violence with sex, the bite becomes the means of achieving pleasure. The masquerade scenes that are included in both series reveal the perverse nature of the vampire, thus implicitly supporting the idea of biting as both a violent and sexual act. The series provide an important contribution to the construction of the vampire image in general and of the bite in particular, discussing rather conventional understanding of the relationship between human beings and vampires based on unequal power, yet to a great extent addressing the problems of pleasure, sexuality, and vulnerability that emerge in connection to vampires and the bite.

Works Cited

Bealer, Tracy L. "Of Monsters and Men: Toxic Masculinity and the Twenty-First Century Vampire in the *Twilight Saga*." *Bringing Light to* Twilight: *Perspectives on the Pop Culture Phenomenon*. Ed. Giselle Liza Anatol. Basingstoke: Palgrave Macmillan, 2011. 139-52.

Bettelheim, Judith. "Women in Masquerade and Performance." *African Arts* 31.2, Special Issue: "Women's Masquerades in Africa and the Diaspora" (1998): 68-70+93-94.

Castle, Terry. "Eros and Liberty at the English Masquerade, 1710-90." *Eighteenth-Century Studies* 17.2 (1983-84): 156-76.

Creed, Barbara. *The Monstrous Feminine: Film, Feminism, Psychoanalysis*. London: Routledge, 1993.

Eyes Wide Shut. Dir. Stanley Kubrick. Perfs. Tom Cruise, Nicole Kidman, Sydney Pollack, and Marie Richardson. Warner Bros., 1999.

Unmasking the Bite

Hoffman, Karen D. "Where the Rainbow Ends: *Eyes Wide Shut*." *The Philosophy of Stanley Kubrick*. Ed. Jerold J. Abrams. Lexington: The UP of Kentucky, 2007. 59-83.

Jordan, Miriam, and Julian Jason Haladyn. "Carnivalesque and Grotesque Bodies in *Eyes Wide Shut*." *Stanley Kubrick: Essays on His Films and Legacy*. Ed. Gary D. Rhodes. Jefferson: McFarland & Company, Inc., 2008. 182-95.

Leavenworth, Maria Lindgren. "Transmedial Narration and Fan Fiction: The Storyworld of *The Vampire Diaries*." *Storyworlds across Media: Toward a Media-Conscious Narratology*. Eds. Marie-Laure Ryan and Jan-Noël Thon. Lincoln: U of Nebraska P, 2014. 315-31.

Milhaven, John Giles. "Thomas Aquinas on Sexual Pleasure." *The Journal of Religious Ethics* 5.2 (1977): 157-81.

Ransom, Amy J. "Opening Eyes Wide Shut: Genre, Reception, and Kubrick's Last Film." *Journal of Film and Video* 62.4 (2010): 31-46.

Schubart, Rikke. *Super Bitches and Action Babes: The Female Hero in Popular Cinema, 1970-2006*. Jefferson, NC: McFarland & Company, 2007.

The Originals. Dir. Matthew Hastings et al. Perf. Joseph Morgan, Daniel Gillies, Phoebe Tonkin, Charles Michael Davis. Warner Bros. 2013–.

The Vampire Diaries. Dirs. Chris Grismer, et al. Perf. Nina Dobrev, Paul Wesley, Ian Somerhalder, Katerina Graham. Warner Bros. 2009–.

Winnubst, Shannon. "Vampires, Anxieties, and Dreams: Race and Sex in the Contemporary United States." *Hypatia* 18.3 (2003): 1-20.

Zombie Blues:
The Rise of the Sorrowful Living Dead in Contemporary Television[1]

ALBERTO N. GARCÍA

> "I'm ready to feel again. Anything, good or bad.
> I want to be alive, now, more than ever" (Liv, *iZombie*, 1.5)
> "When you died, everything turned to shit.
> Life didn't mean anything anymore" (Kieran, *In the Flesh*, 1.2)
> "You can feel things that people try to hide from you"
> (Virgil, *Les Revenants*, 2.3)

1. Introduction

The three quotations that open this article show anguished characters, worried about their feelings and confused about their identity. They are dialogues that correspond to the types of listless, depressed or existentialist characters, common features in any contemporary television drama. But there is another, very remarkable feature in each of them: the three characters ruminating on their situations in this way are... undead.

The figure of the zombie has infected contemporary popular culture. Something which for many years remained a subgenre found mostly in B movies with relatively few viewers, has in the past decade made its way into the mainstream (Hubner, Leaning & Manning 3-10; Bishop, *How Zombies Conquered* 5-21), even serving as a device on fitness apps that simulate the grunts of undead to stimulate the user to sprint faster. The presence of the zombie currently enjoys an extraordinary vitality in the field of video games (*State of Decay*), Hollywood movies (*World War Z*), literature (*Jane Eyre Z*), graphic novels (*The Walking Dead*) and, as addressed in this article, in contemporary television fiction. Not surprisingly, the TV adaptation of *The Walking Dead* (AMC, 2010 –) has spent six successful seasons garnering global resonance.

[1] This article is based on an earlier one ("Prozac para zombies. La sentimentalización contemporánea del muerto viviente en la televisión.") published in Spanish in the journal *Brumal*.

178

Zombie Blues

While vampire mythology muses about love and sexual desire, and werewolves point to the animalistic nature of man, zombies—brutish, one-dimensional beings who never feel anything for their victims—usually offer a reading that is essentially sociopolitical in nature, or, as summarized by *The New York Times*, "Zombies are from Mars and vampires from Venus" (Stanley). However, following trends in literature and cinema in recent years, it has become possible to detect how zombie television stories have begun to propose a more empathetic, emotional, and complex vision of the undead.

In order to analyze this phenomenon, this article will be divided into three parts. First, we will review the genesis of the figure of the zombie, with special attention paid to its metaphorical power to reflect cultural anxieties of a particular period. Next, we will place the process of sentimentalizing the figure of the zombie that has supported this myth in context, a context that sociology calls "emotional culture." And finally, following the perspective and methodology of cultural studies, we will take a look at three series which, from complementary ideological therapeutic nuances, show the evolution of the undead in contemporary television: the British TV series *In the Flesh* (BBC Three, 2013-14), the French *Les Revenants* (Canal Plus France, 2012 −) and the American *iZombie* (the CW, 2015 −).

Choosing these three TV shows allows us, first of all, to give our analysis a global character. They have been produced in different parts of the world, with different traditions and styles of television; however, they reflect a similar thematic pattern, showing the zombie phenomena to be a cultural and aesthetic trend. In addition, all three are proposals that have enjoyed success with the public: *In the Flesh* had a short first season, even by British standards, and was renewed for a second, while enjoying broad critical acceptance in Great Britain both in general-interest newspapers as well as in specialized publications (Jeffries; Mellor). *Les Revenants* has been one of the stalwarts of the new wave of European television production, with series like *Engrenages* (Canal Plus France, 2005 −), *Borgen* (DR1, 2010-13), *Gomorrah* (Sky Italia, 2014) and a large etcetera. With its *high-concept* as a lure, this French offering has been broadcast in many European countries, was bought by the US Sundance Channel and even led to an American remake.

Critics as notable as James Poniewozik of *The New York Times* and Todd Van der Werf in *The A.V. Club* greeted its arrival effusively. The third series chosen, *iZombie*, demonstrates less artistic ambition, but its concept—in the context of a channel aimed at a post-adolescent audience — has been firmly established and the series renewed for a third season, which in the current crowded ecosystem of American television fiction is synonymous with success, especially on the networks.

2. The zombie as sociopolitical metaphor

The metaphorical role of the zombie is not a new one. On the contrary, it is present from its filmic origins, when Halperin's *White Zombie* (1932) suggested an implicit reading about the fear of a racial insurgency, both in the Southern United States as well as in the colonies. Since then, its symbolic capacity has moved to the rhythm of the society that engendered it as a cultural product. As Ted E. Tollefson has written: "Films can be an ideal means for generating myths that map the rapidly changing landscape of the twentieth century. . . . These film-myths . . . always bear the stamp of a time, place and specific culture" (qtd. in Browning 14). Much has changed, therefore, in the semantic capacity of the zombie from the decade of the thirties in the last century until today.

2.1. From voodoo to *The Night of the Living Dead*

Unlike the Central European origins of most monsters and supernatural beings that have characterized the horror genre, the zombie is a figure born of Caribbean folklore. It was originally linked to Haiti and the use of voodoo, revived by the use of black magic, whose sociopolitical readings were bound up with slavery and colonialism. Literary references are scarce — Lovecraft, Shelley, Matheson — and they were portrayed on the big screen only rarely, as in the case of Tourneur and the aforementioned Halperin. This lack of robust narrative precedents allowed George A. Romero to re-found zombie mythology, establishing the characteristics of the creature from which today's subgenre still draws. First of all, unlike other monsters, the zombie exhibits in its own flesh the wounds and putrefaction of its death. Zombies "threaten stability and security not only through their menace to life, but through their very bodies, a stark image of disintegration and harbinger of a crumbling civilization" (Tenga & Zimmerman 78-9).

Despite an animal impulse that leads them to feed on other humans, despite its abject features and disintegrating body, the zombie retains an ominous similarity to that of other humans (especially when the undead

180

Zombie Blues

are known to or recognized by other characters),[2] but are emptied of any hint of cognitive or emotional awareness. The zombies of *Night of the Living Dead* (Romero, 1968) neither feel nor suffer; they only emit guttural sounds and crave human viscera to devour. Consequently, the terror they provoke comes from the persistent threat of an infectious and cannibalistic death.

But additionally, as Kyle W. Bishop summarizes, these stories are always placed in an apocalyptic landscape that peppers the subgenre with three critical features: the collapse of social infrastructure, the cultivation of survivalist fantasies, and the fear of other humans, a suspicion that reaches levels of paranoia because of the accompanying anarchy and scarcity of resources, and because of the ease with which survivors—even one's own family and friends—can become zombies with the speed of an unexpected bite (*American Zombie Gothic* 21).

These features allow for the repetition of a basic plot device, with logical variations, within the zombie subgenre: a group of survivors seek refuge in a safe environment in order to deal with a threat that comes from both zombies and another group of human beings (Verevis 17). The survival instinct involves a dramatic leap: "the journey from survivor to vigilante is a short one; with the total collapse of all governmental law-enforcement systems, survival of the fittest becomes a very literal and grim reality" (Bishop, "Dead Man *Still* Walking" 22). In fact, if we look at the long narrative distance traveled by the characters in *The Walking Dead*, we find that the same basic vicissitude—constantly seeking shelter to hide from the menace—is repeated cyclically: Hershel's farm, Terminus, Alexandria. The novelty the serial story—forced to renew their conflicts—introduces, is the perpetual journey due to the lack of a safe place the characters can inhabit continuously. This implies a nihilistic vision in which the Apocalypse, unlike the first Romero, has already taken place. And it is irreversible.

2.2. Constructing allegories

As we have noted, one of the most striking features of the zombie narrative is its ability to take on sociopolitical and cultural readings. Joe

---

2 It is the same mirage of humanity which, in the popular series *The Walking Dead*, made it impossible for Morgan Jones to pull the trigger in the pilot episode (1.1), gave emotional force to the melancholy "Test Subject 19" (1.6) or turned the unexpected appearance of Sophia on the Hershel's farm into a kick in the stomach for the viewer (2.7). Even a villain such as the Governor softened in his perversity, during the third season, upon refusing to accept the transformation of his daughter into a zombie.

181

Tompkins noted how both academic and specialized criticism fall into the over-interpretation of the horror film as a way to "enshrine their own interpretive authority and exert their own cultural power" (36). Even bearing in mind Tompkins' critique, the inexhaustible semantic capacity of the zombie is surprising.[3] It is precisely its minimalism — zombies originally were slow, expressionless, cannibalistic, gregarious, primal and instinctive — which allowed them to become creatures open to different meanings, capable of constructing allegories that pointed to the communist terror, repressed desires, civil rights for minorities, militarism and Vietnam, consumerism, pandemic fear or even class struggle.[4]

So, zombies share the symbolic nature traditionally attributed to the Neo-Gothic horror literature, which "helps us address and disguise some of the most important desires, quandaries, and sources of anxiety, from the most internal and mental to the widely social and cultural" (Hogle 4). As will be detailed below, the uniqueness of the zombie, unlike the vampire's, is more confined to collective, sociocultural aspects: zombies move in hordes; they are radically impersonal monsters, lacking in will and possessed of a cannibalistic instinct. Consequently, as Verevis writes, it is not surprising that "zombies and zombification become the perfect vehicle for encapsulating cold war anxieties about the loss of individuality, political subversion and brainwashing" (13). However, it is precisely the flat, one-dimensional nature of the zombie — beyond the empty gore of exploitation-type films in the style of Lucio Fulci — which makes these sociopolitical readings unduly literal. This happens, for example, with the criticism of consumerism and media in *Dawn of the Dead* (Romero, 1978). The four protagonists flee the city and seek refuge in a shopping mall outside Pittsburgh. While watching the throng surrounding the facilities, Francine asks Peter: "Why do they [the zombies] come here?" He answers: "Some kind of instinct. Memory of what they used to do. This was an important place in their lives." Or, later: "What the hell are they?" to which Peter replies with a resounding: "They're us. That's all."

This *they are us* also enables a Hobbesian reading of society, repeated in almost all the stories of zombies: there are often humans

3 For example, two recent books by Lauro, Carrington et. al. attest to the metaphorical survival of the zombie.
4 "The zombies enact a kind of hysterical imagining of a proletarian revolution; they are a distorted fantasy of a postapocalyptic, classless society that articulates twentieth-century anxieties toward crowd and mob behavior" (Boluk & Lenz 141).

Zombie Blues

who are much more savage and wicked that the undead themselves. This is one of the recurring motifs the zombie genre, and is present even today in *The Walking Dead*: "All this time, running from walkers—you forget what people do, have always done," Maggie laments in "Made to Suffer" (3.8). In fact, the substratum of *homo homini lupus est* permeates the entire canon of zombie narratives, to the point of raising these dilemmas to the category of a pre-political status:

> Rick: You really want to debate about saving a guy who will lead his buddies right to our door?
> Dale: That's what a civilized society does.
> Rick: Who says we're civilized anymore?
> Dale: No, the world we knew is gone. But, keeping our humanity? That's a choice. (*The Walking Dead*, "Judge, Jury, Executioner," 2.11)

In this dialogue between society, civilization, violence and humanity, the classic zombie tale, located in an agonized and apocalyptic landscape, exhibits a paradox: for the human race to survive, you have to stop being human for a time; one must behave in a wild, ruthless, and even utilitarian fashion, if necessary.

2.3. Classicism, generic fatigue and subversion

Every genre implies, as Steve Neale writes, "a contained and controlled heterogeneity," which plays a balance between "repetition and difference," between "discursive tension and contradiction." Thus, following Neale, we could define a genre as a "systems of orientations, expectations and conventions that circulate between industry, text and subject" (6). This formulation is also applicable to subgenres, as is the zombie with respect to horror; it simply further restricts the defining characteristics, closing the focus in order to isolate a number of common and exclusive features.

But at the same time, genres can also be approached diachronically. It is customary to demarcate stages of experimentation—classicism, mannerism and deconstructionism—in any genre. As Thomas Schatz explains, this evolution comes from the fact that genres "must continually vary and reinvent the generic formula" (36). Leo Baudry explains this tension between familiarity and difference even more explicitly:

183

> Genre films essentially ask the audience, "Do you still want to believe this?" Popularity is the audience answering "Yes." Change in genres occurs when the audience says, "That's too infantile a form of what we believe. Show us something more complicated." (179)

However, it is unreasonable to view this timeline as being something rigid and shaped like an arrowhead; quite the contrary, it is common for more classical proposals to exist alongside other proposals that renew, disrupt or parody established codes. As Gallagher insists, "a superficial glance at film history suggests cyclicism rather than evolution" (qtd. in Keith Grant 36). So, as we shall see below, it is currently possible for series that stick fairly closely to the essential aesthetic and landscape features of the zombie subgenre (*The Walking Dead, Z Nation*) to coexist with others that boldly violate some of its thematic or iconographic constants (*In the Flesh, iZombie*).

This fluctuation within the zombie genre, evolutionary and cyclical at the same time, can be synthesized in the work of George A. Romero himself. The psychology of the zombie progresses in his films until, in 2008, he returns to a pre-apocalyptic situation with *Diary of the Dead* and monsters who are once more "pure desiring machines — they are creatures composed entirely of excess desire" (Boluk & Lenz 136). Furthermore, the coexistence of classical, mannerist and parodic periods can be seen, for example, when we note that at almost the same time in which Hollywood's remake of *Dawn of the Dead* (Snyder, 2004) was enjoying intense media attention with its enraged runners, two other landmarks were released: the insurgent zombie leader Big Daddy (*Land of the Dead*, Romero, 2005), and the ironic and funny look at the genre taken by *Shaun of the Dead* (Wright, 2004). Something similar would occur years later: *World War Z* (Forster, 2013) starring Brad Pitt, or the blood and guts episodes of the third season of *The Walking Dead*, coexisted with a "romantic zombedy," *Warm Bodies* (Levine, 2013).

Following the bloody European take on the genre from the late seventies and early eighties there came *The Return of the Living Dead* (O'Bannon, 1985), which led to a certain renewal of the genre by mixing humor with horror and, above all, by avoiding some of the usual zombie characteristics: they were now able to talk, run, and even keep moving once their heads had been severed. In the early 2000s, at a crossroads where the success of videogames such as *Resident Evil* or *Silent Hill*, the gruesome imagery of a post-9/11 world, and the viral terrors of

Zombie Blues

mad cow and avian flu can be traced, the zombie made a permanent comeback, especially following the success of the rabid and accelerated monstrosities of *28 Days Later* (Boyle, 2002). One of the novelties of Danny Boyle's film was that the zombies were not completely dead, but infected. This undead condition is precisely what will serve to rehabilitate them in some of the contemporary TV series. The generic "sentient zombie" emerges as part of this reinvention.

3. The humanization of the zombie

The thesis of this article is that the humanization that the zombie has undergone in pop culture—more pronounced in recent years—represents an example of a trend that sociology has been termed as "the affective turn" (Clough & Haley). This attitude is linked to the concept of "emotional culture," which refers, *inter alia*, to the growing presence of therapeutic discourse and sentimentalization in all spheres of social life. "Emotional culture" is understood as a "set of cultural meanings and operational codes by which people manage, deploy and understand their emotions and actions" (García Martínez & González 13). As González adds elsewhere, "contemporary selves are not only highly reflexive selves, but, specifically, *emotionally* reflexive selves who continually turn to their emotions for self-knowledge" (González 5).

In this regard, studying the evolution of the zombie while dwelling on some of the latest televised innovations of the monster helps us to think about some of the more prominent manifestations of human behavior in contemporary life. Because it is only from the perspective of this contemporary "self"—obsessed with knowledge filtered through sentiment—that it is possible to understand the tendency to romanticize and sweeten the grisly. This domestication of the horrific is also displayed as a therapeutic vehicle for overcoming trauma, a means of alleviating or living with grief, and a vehicle for resolving questions about our own identity.

3.1. Dreaming robots, vegetarian vampires, depressed zombies

This trend towards emotionalization in every sphere of public life is what explains the humanization of, and empathy with, many of the traditional villains of the fantasy genre. This idea has always been

185

present in science fiction, where one of the generic constants has been precisely the human capabilities of robots, machines and replicants, from Frank Baum's Tik Tok to the cyber dolls of Dr. Calvin in Asimov's *I, Robot* in literature; from the figure of Maria in *Metropolis* to Roy Batty in *Blade Runner* in cinema; or, focusing on television fiction, from Number Eight Boomer in *Battlestar Galactica* (Sci-Fi, 2004-09), to the synthetic Ash of *Black Mirror* (Channel 4, 2011—), or the group of rebel androids in *AKTA människor/Real Humans* (SVT1, 2012-14) and its American remake *Humans* (AMC, 2015—). In all of these works, the question of what makes us human, and issues involving the emotional limits of robotic creations, their uprising against their creators and other issues of a fertile metaphorical, anthropological and metaphysical reading are fundamental.

A similar movement can be found surrounding the figure of the vampire. The breadth of the academic literature on this metamorphosis (Kane; Abbott, *Celluloid Vampires*; Clements; Silver & Ursini) pinpoints how the original evil vampire has been exorcised, and softened through a process of "Ricification" – an allusion to the *Vampire Chronicles* series of novels by Anne Rice—in which numerous blood-sucking creatures of the night have eliminated human blood from their diet altogether, sometimes substituting animal blood (Louis de Pointe du Lac in *Interview with the Vampire*) or synthetic drinks (*True Blood*, HBO, 2008-14) for the blood of their human prey. The "fangs of the night" are also found mixing in the most dynamic of social environments (the *Twilight* franchise) or even displaying the most enviable skin tone and physical figures, such as the brothers Stefan and Damon Salvatore in *The Vampire Diaries* (The CW, 2009—).

This updating of the bloodsucker into someone harmless and cool has led Tenga and Zimmerman to state that "the zombie has surpassed the vampire as a source of horror and revulsion because the vampire has become so 'civilised' that it needs an alter ego to bear the burden of true monstrosity" (76). Aldana sees in the corpse as a source of abjection one of the reasons for the differences in the reception that the zombie and the vampire have enjoyed; the body of the latter circumvents corruption and decay, so that "their capacity to stay pristine and untouched by time has, in fact, had a crucial impact on their mainstreaming" (Aldana 61). However, as we are trying to demonstrate in this article, the zombie has in recent years also undergone a similar process of civilization and whitewashing.

Zombie Blues

3.2. From Bub to R. via Big Daddy[5]

Like many elements of popular culture, the zombie has been recycled in every format imaginable: from legendary music videos (*Thriller* by Michael Jackson, 1983) to recent television commercials (for the courier company FedEx, DieHard car batteries, and the Honda Civic automobile, for example), and even animation for children, such as the delicious and touching *Paranorman* (Fell & Butler, 2012), or a funny episode of *George of the Jungle* ("FrankenGeorge," 1.11).

However, beyond these playful readings, it is important to note how the progressive humanization of zombies in films that make up the canon of the subgenre can be seen. In order to achieve this, it was necessary for the interstitial, the impure — to use the notion of horror in Carroll (55-6) — to cease to exist and a progressive recovery of the human form occur: that is, that beings capable of thinking, expressing will and showing emotions emerge to take the place of the classic figure of the zombie. Consequently, it is easier for the viewer to identify with and feel empathy towards the monster. Without being exhaustive, we can recall, once again, how George A. Romero was the first to open the way for this humanization in *Day of the Dead* (1985). The character of Bub, a pupil of Dr. Logan, had the ability to recall certain actions from when he was a living being (such as a military salute or shaving), to experience feelings of anger upon learning of the murder of his trainer, and even to display a basic cognitive ability (his capacity to be triggered into a rage and pursue Rhodes until he succeeds in killing him).

From the perspective of parody, the outcome of *Shaun of the Dead* "projects a future in which the horror is domesticated and integrated into quotidian living" (Boluk & Lenz 139). Giving an ironic twist to the slavish nature of the original, pre-Romero figure of the zombie, the closing of Wright's film defuses any hint of a purulent bogeyman by inserting it into relief efforts or domestic help. Not for nothing does he have Ed, Shaun's inseparable friend, close the film in the shed, extending one of the visual motifs from the beginning of the film: the two thirty-somethings wasting time playing videogames. Ed is now literally, and not just metaphorically as at the beginning of the film, a zombie. A similar use — as servants — awaits the zombies that have been domesticated in *Fido* (Currie, 2006), a Canadian zombedy set in the Fifties.

---

5 A more detailed analysis of these film characters who gradually humanize the figure of the zombie can be found in Bishop (*American Zombie Gothic* 158-96; and *How Zombies Conquered* 163-79).

187

In 2005, with *Land of the Dead*, Romero returned to the subgenre that had made him most popular. This time, the plot is situated years after the outbreak, in a walled city that confronted with a fierce class struggle. In this environment, Romero presents zombies, led by former gas station attendant Big Daddy, capable not only of feeling sorry for the death of the other members of their "race" and anxious for revenge on the villain of the film (the treacherous ruler of the city), but also of organizing a quasi-military army to storm the fortress where the privileged of the city dwell.

In this evolution, the zombie continues to acquire an ever-greater ability to feel and act with free will (in the dramatic proposals by Romero), and even become someone who is well-regarded by humans (in the *Fido* and *Shaun* comedies). The next step in the genre's innovation was to make the zombie into the object of romantic love—and this is what *Warm Bodies* accomplishes. Additionally, the story in this film is told from the point of view of the monster, named R. These precedents have paved the way for the arrival of the zombie in the broader, mass medium of television, and, what is of most interest to us here, in portrayals that continue delving into the humanization of a creature that, until recently, was exclusively viewed as terrifying and slimy.

4. TV Zombies: viscera become mainstream

This grotesque and bloody figure has become the common currency of television fiction. Beyond appearances on episodic classics like *Buffy the Vampire Slayer* (The WB/UPN, 1997-2003), *Supernatural* (The BW/The CW, 2005–) or even *The Simpsons* (Fox, 1989–), it was a British miniseries that first captured the *zeitgeist* of gore and recycled it for the general public on the small screen. Created by Charlie Brooker, *Dead Set* (E4, 2008) consists of five episodes which, full of hematologic excesses, slips glaringly into a critique of society and the media from its very first episode, in which a virus zombifies the entire UK, except for the isolated inhabitants of the house on the reality show Big Brother.

But the real punch was delivered, as we have noted previously, by one of the most successful series of the last decade: *The Walking Dead*. The AMC epic successfully updated the classic tropes of the subgenre: a mob of slow, hungry zombies; post-apocalyptic scenarios; explicit violence; the collective imaginary of fear; the Other (human) as a threat; the openness of the text to political readings; and a plot involving the

Zombie Blues

impossibility of escape and the search for fragile refuge. In *The Walking Dead*'s wake, a number of other TV fictions have appeared: *Z Nation* (Syfy, 2014–) is an approximation to the classic formula, albeit with an absurd script and sometimes self-parodying tone; or *Helix* (Syfy, 2014-15), which presents a group of scientists stranded in an Arctic research station, where a virus is infecting their workers. This trend has continued to adopt innovative points of departure that provide new horizons for the genre, as we will see below.

4.1. *In the Flesh*: guilt and identity politics

Following a civil war against the zombies, humans have emerged victorious and society has managed to partially cure the state of the "rabids" —as they are called in this British TV series—and categorize it as a chronic disease. They have been confined to enormous health centers where physicians, biologists, and psychiatrists treat those affected by "Partially Deceased Syndrome;" when they are "cured," they are sent back home to resume their former lives. The series explores, therefore, themes such as returning home to a family that has no instruction manual for the return of the dead; the confrontation with a hostile environment, in a small town that had created a militia to fight the savages; and, above all, the teenaged drama of someone who cannot find his place in the world. It is no coincidence that one of the first scenes shows us the protagonist receiving —as if he were a patient with depression—a kind of therapy in which the physician-scientist tries to convince him of his lack of guilt, and having to go out into the world as soon as possible: "That's exactly why you're ready: you're feeling!" The "emotional culture" which we cited earlier is presented here explicitly as a catalyst: what makes the character socially adept, even acceptably human, is his ability to feel.

Shortly afterwards, when Kieran expresses his fear that his parents will not accept him because he is a "rotter" and has killed people, the doctor forces him to repeat to himself a phrase that dispels the stigma of everything he has done, even of his own nickname, "zombie:" "I am a Partially Deceased Syndrome sufferer. . . . And what I did in my untreated state was not my fault" (1.1). This scene from the pilot makes clear that the "rabids" who were defeated by the humans retain their memories of the barbaric actions committed after rising from their graves, which burdens their social and family reintegration with additional layers of

189

guilt and shame. As Abbott has noticed, proposals like this one on BBC Three are symptomatic of the contradictory relationship that Western society maintains with death:

> If, as Gorer and Kamerman argue, contemporary society is uncomfortable with the reality of death, preferring to keep "death out of our sight" (Kamerman 30) and avoid the hard truths of death and decomposition through denial, the zombie narrative forces both the audience and the characters to face this reality through the zombie's corpse-like appearance, maintaining the evidence of its death. ("Loss is Part" 164-5)

So, in *In the Flesh*, for example, Kieran still has the scars from when he cut his wrists and needs, like all rehabilitated zombies, contact lenses and makeup to simulate an outwardly human appearance. That is, differences are concealed in order to appear normal, which leads to Amy's revolt in the first season, and that of Simon, one of the leaders of the "Undead Liberation Army," in the second. The zombies of *In the Flesh* not only struggle to regain their individuality, but to demonstrate it in the social sphere. In this sense, the series rejects the mass, assimilatory drive that characterizes the traditional zombie narrative: that of a creature seeking to infect others with the radical depersonalization to which it has succumbed. However, although this may sound paradoxical, the plot transforms Kieran's initial aspiration to externalize his own personal identity into the expression of a collective identity.

For this reason, beyond the subsidiary, symbolic function horror fiction can have on the viewer by naturalizing death, *In the Flesh* also demonstrates the current validity of what has been called identity politics. As Carolyn D'Cruz writes, in *identity politics*[6] "markers such as gender, race, sexuality, class, and nation attempt to maintain their grounds as fundamental organising principles from which to position theoretical perspectives and political strategies for changing relations of powers" (2); political strategies that necessarily require visibility in order to achieve the political goals of one group or another.

---

6 "Rather than organizing solely around belief systems, programmatic manifestos, or party affiliation, identity political formations typically aim to secure the political freedom of a specific constituency marginalized within its larger context. Members of that constituency assert or reclaim ways of understanding their distinctiveness that challenge dominant oppressive characterizations, with the goal of greater self-determination" (Heyes).

Zombie Blues

Thus, according to the open work that characterizes the subgenre, Dominic Mitchell, the creator of the series, deploys a premise where allegories can range from the difficulties of the conflict in Northern Ireland or post-traumatic stress, to racism, homophobia, AIDS or euthanasia. It is no coincidence that, in the first season, the three characters most affected by "Partially Deceased Syndrome" are a soldier killed in Afghanistan, a victim of leukemia and an unstable young man who committed suicide. That is, in all three cases, the lives of the now resurrected and cured had violent, agonizing, or unexpected deaths. In any case, the ex-zombies are outsiders; people who fall outside what is considered normal. The series itself strives to present them in an environment that welcomes visitors with hostility, where the prevailing prejudice, hatred and social humiliation in the second season, for example, forces everyone to go through a course in social reintegration, perform community work and wear phosphorescent vests reading "I am a Partially Deceased and I'm giving back [what I've taken away from society]." This oppression, which may be real or perceived, is what allows us to connect *In the Flesh* with the contemporary trend of identity politics: the self is, above all, defined by its collective features, assiduously linked to victimization, and a political agenda guided by feelings rather than by reason.

4.2. *Les Revenants*: mourning and the *unheimlich*

Clearly, including here this mysterious and hypnotic story set in a small town in the French Alps creates taxonomic problems. The revenant is not a zombie; however, as part of the evolution and domestication of the living dead, the French series is a step in the same direction. As explained in the *Encyclopedia of the Zombie: The Walking Dead in Popular Culture and Myth*, the revenant (sometimes referred to as the revenging revenant) is "[t]he form of the ghost which most resembles the zombie. . . . This reanimated creature is typically the corpse of a deceased person who returns from the dead to haunt the living, usually the individual(s) who wronged the person while in life" (Fonseca 110).

The Canal Plus France series, which underwent a failed remake entitled *The Departed* (2015) on the US network A&E, and which shares a similar premise with *Resurrection* (ABC, 2014−), draws upon this creature to establish a reflection on the sorrow of absence and mourning the death of loved ones. *Les Revenants* possesses an enigmatic, fascinating and poetic style that departs from the traditional visual elements of the horror genre. At the same time, its schematized plot connects with the

191

genre's typical tropes; what changes is the deliberately ambiguous way it confronts the prodigy of the dead returning in body and soul.

As Jowett and Abbott explain, this is one of the elements that differentiates the cinematographic narrative from the televised one: instead of focusing on the shock, and the repeated and explicit spread of horror, the expanded story allows for the exploration of issues such as the collective fears and emotional responses of the characters to paranormal, horrific, or supernatural events (31-55). In a metaphysical movement similar to the one later used in *The Leftovers* (HBO, 2014 –), *Les Revenants* uses the inexplicable to explore family ties, the desire for motherhood, post-traumatic stress, the validity of religious faith or the weight of the past. Consequently, with *Les Revenants* the figure of the risen veers from a social and political interpretation to a deeply intimate and psychological reading.

It is no coincidence, therefore, that the mise-en-scène aspires to the precious aesthetic smoothness of melodrama while the traditional shocking elements of the horror genre remain virtually absent. In fact, despite the disturbing nature of aggressive *revenants* such as Milan, graphic violence seldom emerges in the series. Zombie iconography is also sparsely employed: Camille's decomposition at the end of the first season (1.8); the silent and gregarious nature of the group of undead who, in the second season, are on the other side of the flood; the brutal kicks Adèle receives in her stomach (2.1) from the child she conceived with Simon, who now feels like an aberration; and, above all, the guts of Sandrine being devoured by her daughter (2.8), in a direct visual reference to Romero's seminal *The Night of the Living Dead*.

Precisely as a result of its glacial pace, its refined style and its contempt for providing answers to mysteries, *Les Revenants* emphasizes its exploration of the emotions of loss and grief, and it does add some nuances to what Freud termed the uncanny (*unheimlich*): "That species of the frightening that goes back to what was once well known and had long been familiar" (124). The characters who return from the grave maintain their appearance intact; they are "well known" and "familiar," without any external mark that distances the living from the *revenants*. On the one hand, the addition of this kind of emotional upheaval — being able to once more embrace a loved one believed to have been lost forever — allows the writers more latitude in playing with the characters' emotions. But it also implies confronting the unfathomable mystery of their return from the dead, and the inability to discern the "us" from "them" implies a constant source of anxiety.

Zombie Blues

The return of Camille, Simon, Serge, Madame Costa, or the inexplicable presence of little Victor has almost nothing of the monstrous or threatening in it; on the contrary, they are not even aware of their own deaths, nor of the time that has passed, which supposes a painful surprise and sometimes unbearable contradiction for those who are once more able to enjoy their presence, long after having mourned their loss. The undead act as emotional engines: they bring up the past, stirring up guilt and remorse in the process (Pierre's involvement in the murder of a child, the barbaric crimes of Serge); they complicate the course of present events (as happens with Adèle's pregnancy and the death of Thomas); and determine the future, as evidenced by the redemption of Jérôme within his family, Lena and Claire's situation, or the happy beach scene where we bid farewell to Julie and Victor.

Thus, *Les Revenants* confirms Abbott's intuition: contemporary horror TV aims "to evoke not the fear of pain and death to oneself but the fear of death to family and loved ones, thus triggering the trauma of loss, grief and mourning" ("Loss is Part" 158). A trauma that also benefits from the elasticity of the television format: the ability to have 20 hours to tell this story of dead returning allows a palette of much wider emotions for each character, providing emotional echoes, dramatic iterations and a long, narrative progress in the lives of this bunch of the undead and their loved ones. The six-month time jump that triggers the second season means *Les Revenants* doesn't have to deal with the suffering of mourning interrupted by the enigmatic, as in the first season, but with the trauma in a community devastated by the scourge of the inexplicable.

Thus, with the revenants transformed into a kind of zombie existentialists, both the living and resurrected in this small Alpine village share the same eternal concerns: Who am I? Why am I here? Is there life beyond death? So, we hear Virgil instruct Camille about his identity, "How do you know you're immortal?" (2.2); or Milan lamenting his violent personality, "I was mistaken. Death has no meaning" (2.8). For all the characters, the return of the past implies that emotionality, peppered with existential doubt, comes radically to the foreground in a vain attempt to make sense of the inexplicable.

4.3. *iZombie*: empathy and heroism

"It's probably wrong that every time I see a dead body I think, 'what the hell am I doing with my life'?" This thought, articulated in a voiceover by Olivia "Liv" Moore, the main character of *iZombie*, encapsulates many of the innovations that the series created by Ruggiero-Wright and Thomas offers with respect to the subgenre we are studying. The plot premise revolves around a young, dynamic medical student who suffers a zombie attack and, as a result, her everyday life, in both the professional and romantic spheres, changes drastically. She leaves her fiancé, becomes withdrawn and starts working in a morgue in order to have easy access to brains, which keep her "stable." That is, zombies retain a normal appearance and personality, memory and intelligence... provided they do not neglect their diet of human brains. In fact, *iZombie* is not "a show about zombies, but rather a show about people *trying not* to turn into zombies after they have been infected" (Brown). Actually, this produces the series' first break with the canon of zombie narratives: the evil of the myth can be contained. As was the case in the humanized vampires of *True Blood* and *The Vampire Diaries*, Liv has found a formula for controlling her wild, bloody impulses.

This lack of cannibalistic violence — an integral part of series such as *The Walking Dead* — is no coincidence. *iZombie* airs on The CW, a youth-and-teen-oriented public network, responsible for series such as *Smallville* (2001-11), *Gossip Girl* (2007-12), or *Arrow* (2012 —). The network has traditionally been accused of offering up shows with excessively melodramatic touches, aimed at the broadest possible audience in their morality. *iZombie*, therefore, usually opts for black humor, virtually parodying its most potentially bloody situations, while facilitating its audience's identification with the zombie protagonist in choosing an attractive young actress, Rose McIver.

The use of voice-over also presents a self-aware zombie, using this cinematographic device to make the viewer complicit in the intimate doubts and problems of the creature in adapting to its new condition. Nor is this the only narrative resource it shares with *Warm Bodies*. In Levine's film, R. falls in love with Julie after she has eaten her boyfriend's brains. In an analogous way, in *iZombie* the brains stolen from the morgue on which Liv feeds allow her to develop an extreme form of empathy: she has flashbacks from the memories of the dead, sharing their skills and even adopting certain personality traits from the offal she has just consumed. This converts the CW series into a psychological thriller *stricto sensu*: every brain serves to start a new case each week. Liv works with the police, hiding her knowledge of the secrets of this or that victim under the excuse that she possesses psychic powers. This revolutionizes the genre completely: the zombie, a mythical figure of

Zombie Blues

terror in the sixties, was previously pure animal instinct, incapable of feeling; here it has been transmuted into a being that can literally take on the minds and souls of others. It can recall their memories, use their skills and feel their affections. This radical metamorphosis contradicts Tenga and Zimmerman's assertion (76), which was cited above: the zombie is no longer outdoing the vampire as a source of fear and disgust; on the contrary, it is imitating it in its socially-positive, civilizational, and inclusive process.

Because the other grand innovation of *iZombie* is the introduction of yet another 180-degree turn in zombie morality: it's not just that it is no longer the villain of the story—something that other projects have conjured up, as we have already discussed in these pages—but that here it is directly cast as the hero, even possessing some empathetic abilities approaching superheroism. The parallel is such that the series even emulates a standard trope in the comics' universes of Marvel and DC Comics: Liv enjoys the complicity of a confidant, Doctor Ravi Chakrabarti, who knows her secret identity. From those grotesque, violent, and lawless hordes has emerged a beautiful superheroine, capable of solving the most intricate cases, thanks precisely to her status as one of the living dead.

5. Conclusion

As we have tried to show throughout these pages, the zombie, not only in cinema but also on television, is being tamed and humanized, transformed from being the monstrous and nauseating horror device that defined its essential nature for decades. Three elements go hand in hand in this change: first, the innovative logic of a particularly fertile time on television and the need to overcome mere shock, in order to engage viewers in a more emotional, and therefore lasting, way. Second, the persistence of a dynamic proper to artistic genres in which innovation is a vital necessity. And finally, the omnipresence of an emotional culture that allows even the greatest taboos to act as vehicle for therapy, bereavement and grief.

To illustrate the transition of the zombie, our article has detailed how the undead are presented in three, successful contemporary television series. *In the Flesh* neutralizes the emotion of guilt and demands individuality while making a commitment to collective identity to portray "the rabid" as a denunciatory allegory of various social ills. In *Les Revenants*, meanwhile, the boundaries between life and death are diluted to construct a story—sometimes sinister, always melancholy—in which the wounds of loss, grief, and bereavement can never heal. Finally, the juvenile and friendly offering, *iZombie*, subverts the myth of the undead, marrying it with the heroism and generosity of its protagonist. Liv is infected, but far from generating terror and repulsion, she becomes a key figure in fighting crime, injustice and seeking the common good.

After analyzing these examples in depth, in which zombies embrace all the characteristics of contemporary emotional culture, it seems that the witty phrase of Alessandra Stanley with which we opened this article ("Zombies are from Mars, vampires are from Venus") is no longer relevant. We will have to find newer, more horrifying monsters on the red planet of the horror genre, now that even zombies demand hugs and get prescriptions for anti-depressants to turn around the blues.

Works Cited

Abbott, Stacey. *Celluloid Vampires: Life After Death in the Modern World*. Austin: University of Texas Press, 2007.

_____. "Loss is Part of the Deal: Love, Fear and Mourning in TV Horror." *Emotions in Contemporary TV Series*. Ed. Alberto N. García. New York: Palgrave Macmillan, 2016. 155-71.

Aldana Reyes, Xavier. *Horror Film and Affect: Towards a Corporeal Model of Viewership*. London: Routledge, 2016.

Baudry, Leo. *The World in a Frame: What We See in Films*. Chicago: Chicago University Press, 2002.

Bishop, Kyle W. "Dead Man *Still* Walking: Explaining the Zombie Renaissance." *Journal of Popular Film and Television*, vol. 37, no. 1, 2009, pp. 16-25.

_____. *American Zombie Gothic: The Rise and Fall (and Rise) of the Walking Dead in Popular Culture*. Jefferson, NC: McFarland, 2010.

_____. *How Zombies Conquered Popular Culture. The Mutifarious Walking Dead in the 21st Century*. Jefferson, NC: McFarland, 2015.

Boluk, Stephanie, and Wylie Lenz. "Infection, Media, and Capitalism: From Early Modern Plagues to Postmodern Zombies." *Journal for Early Modern Cultural Studies* 10.2 (2010): 126-47.

Brown, Cameron. "*iZombie* Season 1 Review Is This a Zom-com?" *Couch Potato Psychology*. 15 November 2015. Web. 3 July 2016.

Browning, John Edgar. "Survival Horrors, Survival Spaces: Tracing the Modern Zombie (Cine)Myth." *Horror Studies* 2.1 (2011): 41-59.

Zombie Blues

Carrington, Victoria, Jennifer Rowsell, Esther Priyadharshini, and Rebecca Westrup, eds. *Generation Z. Zombies, Popular Culture and Educating Youth.* Singapore: Springer, 2016.

Carroll, Noël. "The Nature of Horror." *The Journal of Aesthetics and Art Criticism* 46.1 (1987): 51-59.

Clements, Susannah. *The Vampire Defanged: How the Embodiment of Evil Became a Romantic Hero.* Grand Rapids, MI: Brazos Press, 2011.

Clough, Patricia Ticineto, and Jean O'Malley Halley. *The Affective Turn: Theorizing the Social.* Durham, NC: Duke University Press, 2007.

D'Cruz, Carolyn. *Identity Politics in Deconstruction: Calculating with the Incalculable.* Aldershot, UK: Ashgate, 2008.

Fonseca, Anthony J. "Ghosts." *Encyclopedia of the Zombie: The Walking Dead in the Popular Culture and Myth.* Eds. June Michele Pulliam and Anthony J. Fonseca. Santa Barbara: Greenwood, 2014. 109-110.

Freud, Sigmund. *The Uncanny.* Trans. David McLintock. New York: Penguin Books, 2003.

García, Alberto N. "Prozac para zombies. La sentimentalización contemporánea del muerto viviente en la televisión." *Brumal. Revista de investigación sobre lo Fantástico* [Online]. 4. 1 (2016): 13-34.

García Martínez, Alejandro, and Ana Marta González. "Emotional Culture and TV Narratives." *Emotions in Contemporary TV Series.* Ed. Alberto N. García. New York: Palgrave Macmillan, 2016. 13-25.

González, Ana Marta. "Introduction: Emotional Culture and the Role of Emotions in Cultural Analysis." *The Emotions and Cultural Analysis.* Ed. Ana Marta González. Burlington, VT: Ashgate, 2012. 1-15.

Heyes, Cressida. "Identity Politics." *The Stanford Encyclopedia of Philosophy (Winter 2014 Edition).* Ed. Edward N. Zalta. 2014. Web. 20 June 2016.

Hogle, Jerrold E. "Introduction: The Gothic in Western Culture." *The Cambridge Companion to Gothic Fiction.* Ed. Jerrold E. Hogle. Cambridge: Cambridge University Press, 2002. 1-20.

Hubner, Laura, Marcus Leaning, and Paul Manning, eds. *The Zombie Renaissance in Popular Culture.* New York: Palgrave, 2015.

Jeffries, Stuart. "The Superb *In the Flesh* is a Timely Allegory of Racism, Intolerance — and Zombies." *The Guardian* 5 May 2014. Web. 21 June 2016.

Jowett, Lorna, and Stacey Abbott. *TV Horror: Investigating the Dark Side of the Small Screen.* London: I. B. Tauris, 2013.

Kane, Tim. *The Changing Vampire of Film and Television: A Critical Study of the Growth of a Genre.* Jefferson, NC: McFarland, 2006.

Keith Grant, Barry. *Film Genre: From Iconography to Ideology.* London: Wallflower, 2007.

Lauro, Sarah Juliet. *The Transatlantic Zombie: Slavery, Rebellion, and Living Death.* New Brunswick, NJ: Rutgers University Press, 2015.

Mellor, Louisa. "*In The Flesh*: Celebrating BBC Three originals." *Den of the Geek.* 1 January 2016. Web. 20 June 2016.

Neale, Steve. "Genre and cinema." *Popular Television and Film.* Ed. Tony Bennett. London: BFI Publishing, 1981. 6-25.

Poniewozik, James. "Review: In *The Returned*, the French Zombie Drama Deepens." *The New York Times* 28 October 2015. Web. 24 June 2016.

Schatz, Thomas. *Hollywood Genres: Formulas, Filmmaking, and the Studio System*. Philadelphia: Temple University Press, 1981.

Silver, Alain, and James Ursini. *The Vampire Film: From Nosferatu to True Blood*. 4th ed. updated. Montclair, NJ: Limelight, 2011.

Stanley, Alessandra. "*The Walking Dead*: The Undead Are Undaunted and Unruly." *The New York Times* 28 October 2010. Web. 21 June 2016.

Tenga, Angela, and Elizabeth Zimmerman. "Vampire Gentlemen and Zombie Beasts: A Rendering of True Monstrosity." *Gothic Studies* 15.1 (2013): 76-87.

Tompkins, Joe. "The Cultural Politics of Horror Film Criticism." *Popular Communication: The International Journal of Media and Culture* 12.1 (2014): 32-47.

Van Der Werf, Todd. "In the Terrific New Horror Series *The Returned*, the Monster is an Emotion." *The A.V. Club*. 30 October 2013. Web. 14 June 2016.

Verevis, Constantine. "Redefining the Sequel. The Case of the (Living) Dead." *Second Takes: Critical Approaches to the Film Sequel*. Eds. Carolyn Jess-Cooke and Constantine Verevis. Albany: SUNY Press, 2010. 11-30.

"The Monster at the End of This Book": Authorship and Monstrosity in *Supernatural*

JESSICA GEORGE

The long-running US horror serial *Supernatural*, as we might expect, has engaged repeatedly and in a variety of ways with the monstrous over the course of its eleven-year run. *Supernatural* is also known for its self-reflexive "meta episodes" (10.05 "Fan Fiction"), in which its monster-hunting protagonists, the Winchester brothers, encounter a series of in-universe fictions based on their own lives. Evan Hayles Gledhill has made a convincing argument that this kind of "mocking intertextual awareness" is essential to the popularity of the Gothic, but in foregrounding not only its borrowings from other fictions, but itself as fiction within the text, *Supernatural* goes further than most. Crucially, this in-text focus on writings and rewritings allows *Supernatural* to foreground and interrogate the figure of the author; to question who is, in fact (or in fiction), the author of a text; and to ask whether the author is really a god—or, perhaps, a monster.

What are authors?

The status of the author in literary studies has long been contested. Roland Barthes' seminal 1967 essay, "The Death of the Author," sought to break down notions of the author as Godlike creator or Romantic individual, asserting the incompatibility of literature with the idea of a singular author (142), and suggesting that the unity of a text can be found not in the "passions, humours, sentiments, impressions" of a pre-existing author (147), but only in its reader (148). For Barthes, we are no longer to consider the text as imparting "a single 'theological' meaning (the 'message' of the Author-God)," but as a "multi-dimensional space," a "tissue of quotations" always multiple and contested (146).

199

Two years later, Michel Foucault would respond with his lecture "What Is an Author?" not proclaiming the author's death, but rather designating the author as a "function" that limits meaning rather than a genius who originates it: the principle of the author "impedes the free circulation, the free manipulation, the free composition, decomposition, and recomposition of fiction" (290). Effectively, the idea of the author is the tool we use to limit what a text can be made to mean: it "marks the manner in which we fear the proliferation of meaning" (290). That uncontrolled meaning is something to fear is significant. While, for Barthes, the author must be got out of the way to allow the reader free rein, Foucault recognizes that the author performs a reassuring function. If texts without authors are cause for fear, then texts that deal in fear must surely be tempted to question the status of their authors.

Early film studies did not quite follow the same currents as Barthes and Foucault. Instead, it prioritized the director as *auteur*, "[installing] in the cinema . . . the figure who had dominated the other arts for over a century: the romantic artist, individual and self-expressive" (Caughie 10). This approach was at least partly rooted in a desire to establish film as an art-form worthy of study: if directors were artists, their work must deserve serious academic consideration. Even some recent television criticism suggests that audiences—and cult horror audiences in particular—are still "strongly invested in the idea of director-as-auteur" (Hendershot 149). Television, however, immediately problematizes this centering of a single, identifiable creator. As Jeremy G. Butler points out, TV programs have no single identifiable author. TV directors do not wield the same influence as film directors, the usual subjects of auteurist criticism, sharing the creative process with an army of scriptwriters, actors, production designers, editors, and other contributors. While some critics have sought to install the showrunner in the position of *auteur*, the "corporate and collaborative realities of contemporary television" are at odds with any notion of the *auteur*, or the author, as Romantic individual (Butler 369). Jonathan Gray points to the increased visibility of showrunners in recent TV (108), but also suggests that the fixed, antecedent author that Barthes attempted to kill off in favor of the reader is not particularly relevant to the medium of TV anyway. "Barthes killed the author in order to open the text," he writes, "but a television series is nearly always already open" (Gray 110).

One of the ways in which a TV show may be open is the way in which it responds to audience-created "paratexts" such as online discussions and fan fiction. This interplay of texts becomes a kind of

"The Monster at the End of This Book"

interpretive game—and the serial nature of many TV shows, as opposed to closed texts like standalone novels or films, means that "authors both can and must respond" to the "moves" made by their audiences (Gray 111). Scholars in fan studies have long pointed to the ways in which participatory fandom can challenge authority (or author-ity), with fans engaging in critical dialogue with and even transforming the source text, promoting a multiplicity of interpretations and experiences. While there is clearly an unequal power relationship between fans and staff directly involved in the production of a show, fan texts form part of a wider text that surrounds it. Fans may not be able to control the content of a show, but they can elicit responses to their responses. The show begins to form part of a conversation or collaboration between showrunners, writers, actors, and other production staff, and their audience, inevitably introducing an element of collective authorship that exceeds the production of the show itself. At the same time, fan texts by their nature incorporate and transform existing elements of the show, and fan fiction writers shy away from claims to sole authorship, as demonstrated by the once-common practice of including ownership disclaimers in fanfiction headers. Henry Jenkins wrote about this more open, collaborative relationship in 2006, as part of what he terms "convergence culture," suggesting that "[rather] than talking about media producers and consumers as occupying separate roles, we might now see them as participants who interact with each other according to a new set of rules that none of us fully understands" (3). Participatory fandom is "democratic" (Jenkins 247), not the product of top-down authority—a term that Sheenagh Pugh also uses in her 2005 study of fan fiction, *The Democratic Genre.* Kristina Busse and Karen Hellekson, in the introduction to their 2006 edited collection, *Fan Fiction and Fan Communities in the Age of the Internet,* point to the "ultimate erasure of a single author" in fan discourse (6). Abigail Derecho, drawing on Deleuze in the same volume, also argues for the anti-hierarchical nature of fan fiction, suggesting that fan texts "can have as much weight and affect as the originary texts, once preconceived ideas about what constitutes a complete, whole, or original work are forgotten" (74). Mafalda Stasi points to the "nonhierarchical, rich layering of genres" in fan fiction (119), situating it in a long tradition of "anonymous collective authorship" only recently marginalized by the publishing industry and the notion of the author as Romantic individual (124). If all this talk of anti-hierarchical collaboration sounds a little idealistic, we should not suggest that the participants in these collaborations are always willing.

The "moves" made by TV creators may seek to reinforce their status as authors and authorities, and to warn fans off. The depiction of obsessive fans as villains in *Buffy the Vampire Slayer*, for example, is read by Laura E. Felschow as a "harsh disciplinary action" (6.6).

The fan studies scholars mentioned above are not writing exclusively about TV, but serial TV shows, with their relative long runs and short turnaround times, are in a position to respond to fan texts or fan "moves" in particularly timely fashion. *Supernatural* addresses ideas around authorship, authority, and fandom in ways that sometimes question and sometimes reinforce the notion of the Godlike author, sometimes inviting fan authors to participate in and rewrite the show's text, and sometimes appearing to mock or even to monster them.

What have monsters got to do with it?

The preceding (necessarily incomplete) whirlwind tour through television authorship and the challenges posed to it by participatory fandom, may so far appear to have little relationship to the subject of this volume. So, what have monsters got to do with it?

The author-as-individual is a quintessentially human subject. Joanna Bourke, in her 2011 study, *What It Means to Be Human*, identifies the ways in which thinkers including Aristotle, Mill, and Darwin have prioritized language as a means of distinguishing the human from the animal (7, 29-31). Furthermore, the human faculty for language was tied to the special relationship of humanity to the divine. "Humans were set above the animal precisely because of their intimate ties to the divine. Without language, how could any creature have access to God?" (Bourke 46). The Romantic conception of the author, with his special genius in the faculty of language, is both clearly human, and clearly close to God. It is no coincidence that Barthes identifies the emergence of the author at the same moment "the human person" began to take center stage (143). The author-God, then, is a God created in the image of humanity.

The figure of the monster has long served as a focal point for anxieties around both the perceived benevolence of the Abrahamic God, and the stability and supremacy of the human subject. Stephen Asma points out that monsters, after the rise of monotheism, "became intertwined with the theological question, Why did God create evil?" (63). Surely, a God who allowed the existence of "frightening beasts, deformities and demons" must himself partake of monstrosity (63).

"The Monster at the End of This Book"

For human beings ostensibly created in God's image, the existence of monsters, fictional or real, had disturbing consequences. In the nineteenth century, the emergence of evolutionary theory brought with it a new set of anxieties surrounding human supremacy. No longer endowed with divine resemblance, humans were simply the product of an indifferent and sometimes chaotic natural process, and might someday be dethroned by a competitor better fitted to occupy the top of the evolutionary "ladder." Monsters "became part of the rallying cry of the radical atheists against a perfect, purposeful nature" (Asma 165). They could embody the threats posed to human supremacy by other, fitter species, or by evolutionary degeneration. Equally, they could blur the boundaries between human and animal—and, later, between human and machine. As Jeffrey Jerome Cohen puts it, the monster implies the impossibility of a defined, unified "human." Rather, the "incoherent body" of the monster "may well be our own" (Cohen 9). Monsters defy categorization. They are "liminal [beings]" (Asma 40); "disturbing hybrids" who "[refuse] to participate in the classificatory 'order of things'" (Cohen 6).

If the existence of monsters challenged the authority of the God thought to have created them, what might monster texts then do to the authority of their creators? Bearing in mind the uncategorizable nature of monsters, perhaps the tissue of coexisting fan texts — in which characters exist as simultaneously good and evil, queer and straight, male and female; take paths closed off by the show's storyline; or even swap roles between monster and monster-hunter—takes this a step further. Participatory fandom can be argued to celebrate multiple perspectives and multiple identities, even the loss of identity posited by Barthes (142). The multiple possibilities offered by fan texts may be read as both monstrous and liberating. These fictions do not simply talk back to the source text, but participate in an ongoing conversation forming part of the wider text of fandom. *Supernatural* incorporates, represents, and misrepresents this multiplicity in a number of ways.

When is a monster not a monster? When it tells you a story.

This brings us to the monsters of *Supernatural*. The show focuses on the lives of two brothers, Sam (Jared Padalecki) and Dean Winchester

(Jensen Ackles), who are "hunters," seeking out suspicious murders and dispatching the supernatural culprits. As well as "Monsters of the Week," monstrous characters appear as recurring antagonists or allies, and later seasons of the show feature the angel Castiel (Misha Collins) and the demon Crowley (Mark R. Sheppard) as secondary leads. (In *Supernatural*'s mythology, angels appear as monstrous more often than not.) The show often plays with the apparent humanity of its monsters, sometimes reinforcing an apparently safe boundary between human and monster, and sometimes threatening to break it down. *Supernatural*'s early seasons set up a dichotomy between the Winchester brothers. Dean, the older brother, holds a black-and-white view of monsters, asserting, "If it's supernatural, we kill it" (2.03 "Bloodlust"). Sam, the younger brother, puts across a slightly more nuanced view, insisting that their "job is hunting evil. And if these things aren't killing people, they're not evil" (2.03 "Bloodlust"). For Sam, what makes a monster is the danger it poses to humanity. Of course, this sometimes means that even sympathetic monsters have to be killed. For example, in season 4, Jack Montgomery attempts to resist his horrific transformation into a cannibalistic *rugaru*, Sam urging him, "You don't have to be a monster" (4.04 "Metamorphosis"), but eventually succumbs after being attacked by another hunter in his home, forcing Sam to kill him before he attacks Dean. Similarly, the Winchesters initially let the "vegetarian" vampire Lenore go free after learning that she does not kill humans (2.09 "Bloodlust"), but she later asks to be killed after losing her ability to resist human blood (6.19 "Mommy Dearest"). Even monsters who initially appear sympathetic, such as Ruby, the demon who claims she remembers what it is like to be human (3.09 "Malleus Maleficarum") may eventually reveal themselves to be untrustworthy and have to be destroyed (4.22 "Lucifer Rising").

At other times, however, monsters redeem themselves or prove capable of living peacefully among humans. The demon Meg, a major antagonist during the show's first season, later becomes an ally and eventually sacrifices herself to allow Castiel and the Winchesters to escape Crowley (8.17 "Goodbye Stranger"). Castiel eventually becomes so completely humanized that the other angels no longer recognize him as one of them (9.22 "Stairway to Heaven"), while Benny Lafitte, a vampire who befriends Dean in Purgatory, renounces human blood and sticks to it. Significantly, it is when the monster tells its story that it becomes sympathetic and enters into the human community, and *Supernatural*'s genre-savvy monsters are often very aware of this. Benny is allowed to

"The Monster at the End of This Book"

tell his backstory in full, relating how he renounced the murderous ways of his fellow vampires after he fell in love with a human woman and "started seeing something in humanity" (8.05 "Blood Brother"). Dean likens the story to a clichéd romance novel, asking, "Was Fabio on the cover of that paperback?" (8.05), but nonetheless believes it. Similarly, Amy Pond, a *kitsune* who turns out to have been a childhood friend of Sam, becomes sympathetic when allowed to explain that she has been killing people only to save her sick son (7.03 "The Girl Next Door"), and Dean's decision to kill her at the end of the episode is cast in a dubious light. Even Lucifer attempts to garner sympathy by retelling the Genesis story from his own point of view, casting himself as a victim punished for speaking out against human destructiveness (5.04 "The End"). It is at the intersection of narrative and humanity that the monster redeems itself. Benny values humanity, insisting, "I drink blood, I don't drink people" (8.05 "Blood Brother") and eventually proves himself a hero, staying behind in Purgatory to allow Sam's safe escape. Amy remains sympathetic because her desire to protect her son is understandable from a human point of view: Sam argues that "in her position, we'd probably do the same thing" (7.03 "The Girl Next Door"). Lucifer's rejection of humans as "hairless apes," on the other hand, ensures that he remains a villain (5.04 "The End"). Galen A. Foresman and Francis Tobienne, Jr. have argued that monsters "offend human sensibilities . . . by threatening to undermine the value we place on ourselves" (24). *Supernatural*'s monsters achieve redemption when they rescind their challenges to human exceptionalism and reinforce it instead.

The existence of these sympathetic, more-or-less human monsters makes Sam and Dean themselves appear more or less monstrous. Nathan Stout points out that Amy Pond "is clearly a member of the moral community," and that when Dean kills her, "the viewer finds this objectionable precisely because Amy is an example of a moral monster" (14). For Stout, the Winchesters' "apparent disregard for the lives of the moral monsters they hunt . . . should leave us questioning whether or not Sam and Dean are really good" (15). It is not only their ability to kill with little remorse that aligns the Winchester brothers with the monsters they hunt, however. Their other actions often find echoes in those of the monsters. We are aware on some level that the difference between Jack Montgomery's craving for human flesh and Sam's addiction to demon blood, or Amy Pond's killing people to cure her son and Sam and Dean's willingness to risk lives to save one another, is simply the fact that they are the protagonists of this story. Heather L. Duda has discussed the monster hunter as a figure who necessarily holds much in common with the monsters he or she kills, existing on the margins of society (13), and this is certainly true of the Winchesters, who are excluded from normative definitions of home and family (in the earlier seasons they hop from motel to motel, eventually moving into a secret bunker, while neither of them is able to maintain a long-term romantic relationship), rely on credit card fraud to live, and often act in a moral gray area. Perhaps something similar is true of the monster's chronicler.

"You're not a god, Chuck!"

When Chuck Shurley, in the season 4 episode, "The Monster at the End of This Book" (4.18), declares, "I'm definitely a god. A cruel, cruel, capricious god," the statement appears deeply ironic. This episode introduces the show's story-within-a-story, the *Supernatural* book series, based on the lives of the Winchesters. Chuck, the book's author, does not know that the subjects of his stories are real people; Sam and Dean appear to him in dreams, and he has made a living writing up his visions as a series of pulp horror novels. Sam and Dean discover the books while on a case, and promptly seek out the writer, whom they believe to be a psychic. Castiel eventually explains that Chuck is a prophet, and the Winchesters attempt to use his visions to defeat the demon Lilith. According to Castiel, Chuck's novels will one day be known as "the Winchester Gospels"; they are, quite literally, Word of God (4.18 "The Monster at the End of This Book"). The author himself, however, is a pathetic figure. We first encounter him passed out on his couch, disoriented by a vision. His house is in disarray, he drinks too much, and he appears isolated, his publisher describing him as "very private . . . like Salinger" (4.18 "The Monster at the End of This Book"). Even in the stories he writes — which turn out not to be his own creations at all — he is marginalized as a bit player. Dean and Castiel are able to use him to rewrite his own prediction: taking advantage of the fact that prophets are protected by an archangel, they force him at gunpoint to accompany them to the confrontation with Lilith, where the archangel promptly appears and scares her away. At the end of the episode, we see Chuck experience another vision, about which he wants to tell the Winchesters, but the angel Zachariah warns him away, saying, "people shouldn't know too much about their own destiny" (4.18 "The Monster at the End of This Book"). The angels, Zachariah threatens, will stop him

"The Monster at the End of This Book"

if he tries to warn the Winchesters, and will not allow him to commit suicide to escape his visions. In despair, Chuck asks what else he is supposed to do. The response is, "What you always do. Write" (4.18 "The Monster at the End of This Book").

The idea of the author as God seems here to be brought up and summarily dismissed. Chuck is not a monster, but he is far from being a god. Writing, rather than imbuing him with divine authority, is the only act left to a helpless man. Even though his visions are apparently divine in origin, Chuck is unable to ensure that they come to pass. His characters rebel and his stories are subject to rewriting by outside forces. Though the only fan character to appear in the episode is Chuck's publisher, who enables his authorship rather than producing her own fiction, and slash fan fiction gets a passing, jokey mention, the specter of the fan author lurks in the background. Fan fiction writers create alternate universes or "AUs" by having characters make different choices and take different roads, and here, Chuck's characters effectively reject his storyline and write their own AU. Authors who believe themselves to be gods, the episode suggests, are vain and deluded. There is no originality: Chuck discovers that he has only been able to write real events. Once a story makes its way into the wider world, meanwhile, its author has little hope of controlling it. In fact, Godlike authority may not even be desirable. In the wider mythos of *Supernatural,* Heaven is a dystopia, God "[just] another deadbeat dad" (5.16 "Dark Side of the Moon"). The representative of divine authority in this episode is Zachariah, a sleazy businessman-type who appears to Chuck only to threaten him. Indeed, his appearance at the very end of the episode suggests that God himself may be the "monster" at the end of the book.

"We get to be Sam and Dean": Anxieties of participatory fandom

"The Monster at the End of This Book" introduced Sam and Dean to the online fandom for the *Supernatural* books, with the brothers observing that "for fans, they sure do complain a lot" and expressing their bafflement at the existence of erotic slash fiction depicting them in an incestuous relationship (4.18 "The Monster at the End of This Book"). Sera Siege, Chuck's publisher and fan, is presented as a comedic character, firing questions at Sam and Dean—who are posing as journalists writing a profile of Chuck—to determine whether they are real fans, and displaying an anti-demon-possession tattoo (the same design sported by the Winchesters) on an intimate part of her body. She does not, however, really seem to be a participatory fan, working to distribute Chuck's novels rather than writing her own fiction.

Season 5 introduced the character of Becky Rosen, the *Supernatural* books' "number one fan" and a writer of the aforementioned incest— or "Wincest"—stories (5.01 "Sympathy for the Devil"). Becky uses the screen name "samlicker81"; she behaves inappropriately toward Sam when they meet in person; and her insistence that she "[knows] the difference between fantasy and reality" is shown to be paper-thin: she takes Chuck's words at face value as soon as he tells her the books are real (5.01 "Sympathy for the Devil"). Fan reactions to the show's explicit inclusion of fandom—and fic-writing fandom in particular— varied. Deepa Sivarajan suggests that while some fans experienced references to Wincest fiction as an affectionate joke, they "caused pain to fans who did not want their already controversial practices to be further exposed" (4.2). For Laura E. Felschow, "'The Monster at the End of This Book' highlights the tenuous power cult fans actually possess and how the show's creators can both misrepresent and disempower them just as easily as they can do the opposite" (1.3). Even if the representation of fandom in "The Monster at the End of This Book" is a joke, accompanied by some fun poked at the show's scriptwriters (both Sera Siege and Chuck's pen-name, Carver Edlund, are made up of the names of *Supernatural* writing staff), Felschow points out that it is a joke made from a position of power. Fans may be able to express their discontent via online postings, but cannot alter the text of the episode itself. In this way, "The Monster at the End of This Book" is "a reminder to *Supernatural* fandom, delivered with a smile, of exactly who is in charge" (6.6). For Felschow, however, the later introduction of Becky illustrates that this "was not a gesture of ill will" (6.7). Indeed, in her first appearance, Becky is allowed to participate in the Winchesters' storyline, passing on a message from Chuck that will lead Sam and Dean to discover the part that the angels intend them to play in the upcoming Apocalypse.

Lorna Jowett and Stacey Abbott have argued that *Supernatural*'s success is partly attributable to the way it combines elements of episodic horror, epic myth, and soap-like family drama, "[heightening] the sense of intimacy . . . between characters and audience" (53). Becky is certainly emotionally invested in Sam and Dean's story, but the

"The Monster at the End of This Book"

intimacy she feels with the characters also has a sexual component. The show usually portrays this as comedic, but it eventually begins to verge on the monstrous. Becky displays inappropriate, sexualized behavior, touching Sam's chest without his permission and refusing to stop when he asks (5.01 "Sympathy for the Devil"). The incident is played for laughs, and at first glance, it appears far removed from the kind of "violent and destructive" fan behavior referred to by Joli Jenson in her 1992 article on media and academic representations of pathological fandom (23). Jenson is highly critical of studies and articles that seek to portray fans as "abnormal 'others'" who have "crossed that line between what is real and what is imaginary" (24). Becky's behavior may not be violent, but it is violating, and her grasp on that line seems tenuous. She does not differentiate between the Sam in the books and her fantasies and the real person whose lack of consent she ignores. This crossing of boundaries continues in her next appearance (5.09 "The Real Ghostbusters"), in which she steals Chuck's phone and invents an emergency in order to lure Sam and Dean to a *Supernatural* convention, where fans attend panels, dress up as characters from the books, and take part in a LARP (Live Action Role Play) event where they play the parts of the Winchesters and solve an imaginary case. Her intervention draws the Winchesters away from their ongoing quest to kill Lucifer and avert the Apocalypse. Becky does not know that there is a real haunting at the convention hotel, so effectively, she privileges the fictional games played at the convention over the apocalyptic scenario currently taking place in the wider world. She again flirts heavily with Sam, and seems oblivious to the fact that he does not return her interest. At the end of the episode, when she decides to date Chuck instead, she takes Sam aside and apologizes to him, declaring, "We had undeniable chemistry, but like a monkey on the sun, it was too hot to live" (5.09 "The Real Ghostbusters"). This moment is once again played off as comedic, and Sam humors her, but Becky's inappropriate behavior escalates in her last appearance to date (7.08 "Season Seven, Time for a Wedding!"). Here, she uses a love potion to convince Sam to marry her, knocks him out and ties him to her bed when the spell begins to wear off, and comes perilously close to selling her soul to a demon—a path that inevitably leads to the victim eventually becoming a demon too—to ensure that he stays with her. Though Becky is eventually persuaded to help trap the demon instead, her fannish behavior here is certainly pathological, and serves to place her on the path to monstrosity.

Jessica George

Other fans are presented in a more positive light. "The Real Ghostbusters" also gives us the characters of Demian and Barnes, a same-sex couple who act the parts of Sam and Dean while LARPing at the convention. Though "terrified" when they encounter the real ghosts haunting the hotel, Demian and Barnes insist on helping when they realize the convention attendees are in real danger "because that's what Sam and Dean would do," and are able to banish the ghosts, saving Sam, Dean, and their fellow fans (5.09 "The Real Ghostbusters"). Unlike Becky, Demian and Barnes require proof that the supernatural events are real, insisting, "We're not really digging up graves . . . we're just playing a game" until they see a ghost with their own eyes (5.09 "The Real Ghostbusters"). Even after helping with a real ghost hunt, they retain an awareness that the world of the *Supernatural* books does not really belong to them, instead providing escapism from their mundane lives. "In real life," Demian points out, "he sells stereo equipment. I fix copiers. Our lives suck" (5.09 "The Real Ghostbusters"). Demian and Barnes do not expect to be included in Sam and Dean's world; nor do they display excessive attachment to the characters. Indeed, when Dean objects to his life being consumed as entertainment, insisting that his and Sam's "pain is not for your amusement," a bemused Demian assumes he is an over-invested fan and responds, "I don't think they care, because they're fictional characters" (5.09 "The Real Ghostbusters").

The gendered and sexual implications here are impossible to miss. Becky's investment in the *Supernatural* books is explicitly sexualized, and she writes the characters into scenarios that fulfill her erotic fantasies, eventually attempting to alter the narrative of *Supernatural-*the-show by having Sam fall in love with her. Demian and Barnes, in contrast, show no sexual interest in the characters: they play at being Sam and Dean, not at having sex with them. There is an inevitable hint of incestuous subtext in having a couple roleplay as the brothers, but the episode steers carefully clear of bringing this to the forefront. Demian and Barnes show no romantic affection when in character as Sam and Dean, only revealing that they are a couple at the end of the episode, after Dean wrongly assumes they are "friends" (5.09 "The Real Ghostbusters"). "Good" fans are likely male, and they certainly do not view Sam and Dean as sex objects.

More importantly, however, they do not attempt to alter the canon narrative: they may be invited to play in the world of *Supernatural*, but they recognize the ultimate authority of its creators. A particularly pedantic male fan who pokes holes in Chuck's plotlines ends up dead

210

"The Monster at the End of This Book"

because he refuses to believe the ghosts haunting the hotel are real, responding as though they are a dubious special effect (5.09 "The Real Ghostbusters"). In a later episode, the narrative of the "good" fan who recognizes writerly authority plays out again, though at a remove from the *Supernatural* books. The Winchesters' friend Charlie Bradbury, a computer hacker, finds herself trapped in the nightmarish world of a video game which she once copied from a game company's server and "reprogrammed . . . to reflect [her] flamingly liberal politics" (8.20 "Pac-Man Fever"). A few episodes later, however, she wins an invitation to visit the Land of Oz alongside Dorothy, not for rewriting the story to her own tastes, but because she has successfully deciphered the clues left in the Oz books by L. Frank Baum, uncovering the author's true intent (9.04 "Slumber Party"). The fan who respects writerly authority is rewarded; the fan who seeks to undermine it is potentially monstrous, and must be domesticated or punished.

The Monster is God

This anxiety around fannish rewriting reaches its zenith in the season 9 episode "Meta Fiction" (9.18). This episode itself reworks the theme of an earlier episode, season 4's "Monster Movie," in which a murderous shapeshifter morphs into the monsters from his favorite classic horror movies, preferring to act the part of a Bela Lugosi-style Dracula than to face real life. "Life," he declares, "is small. Meager. Messy. The movies are grand. Simple. Elegant. I have chosen elegance" (4.05 "Monster Movie"). The difference, he declares, is that this is his story, and this time, "the monster wins" (4.05 "Monster Movie"). The episode's humor relies on bathetic intrusions of real life into the monster movie setup: the Gothic castle where "Dracula" traps his victims is a flimsy set, the mummy's coffin turns out to be a theatrical prop, and the shapeshifter's attempt to electrocute Dean is interrupted by the arrival of a pizza delivery boy (4.05 "Monster Movie"). This monstrous fan is a pathetic fantasist, and his attempt to rewrite the monster movie narrative is ultimately unsuccessful. Jamie, the girl he has been attempting to seduce, shoots him dead, and he must finally admit that "this is how the movie should end" (4.05 "Monster Movie"). The shapeshifter's identification with movie monsters has its roots in his feelings of marginalization: "everywhere I tried to hide," he says, "people found me . . . attacked me, called me freak, called me monster"

211

(4.05 "Monster Movie"). Fans, the episode suggests, are welcome to identify with fictional monsters, but should not attempt to rewrite their narratives and center them as heroes. Genre-savvy monster hunters like the Winchesters already know "what happens at the end of every monster movie," and recognize that the monstrous fan lacks the authority to change it (4.05 "Monster Movie").

Season 9's major villain is the angel Metatron, the former Scribe of God and an avid consumer of human fiction who has taken it upon himself to rewrite God's "epic story" (9.10 "Road Trip"). The episode is framed by Metatron's narration, and by shots of him sitting at a typewriter in his library. In his opening speech, he asks—apparently addressing the viewer—"[Who] gives a story meaning? Is it the writer? Or you? Tonight, I thought I would tell you a little story and let you decide" (9.18 "Meta Fiction"). This statement seems to open up transformative possibility, since the viewer may choose what kinds of meaning to attribute to a story, effectively rewriting it with each interpretation. As the episode unfolds, we follow Castiel as he encounters Hannah, an angel who claims to have been threatened by Metatron's second-in-command, and has a vision of the archangel Gabriel, a fan favorite character who was killed off several seasons earlier. Gabriel, also known as the Trickster, is a skilled illusionist, the possibility that he faked his own death offers ample opportunity for fan "fix-its." (The online fan fiction archive Archive of Our Own, or AO3, at the time of writing features 271 *Supernatural* stories tagged with "Gabriel Lives.") When we learn that the vision is an illusion created by Metatron, he is allied with fan fiction writers. Castiel wakes up from the vision and finds himself bound and gagged in Metatron's library. Metatron proceeds to explain the new story he is writing, framing himself as the hero and urging Castiel to lead the other angels against him because "[every] hero needs a villain" (9.18 "Meta Fiction"). Here, it becomes clear that from Metatron's point of view, *he* is the one who gives the story meaning. He rejects Castiel's interpretation of events, in which he, not Metatron, is the hero, and throws one of Chuck Shurley's books onto the fire, indicating that he wishes to replace, not merely rewrite or add to, existing narratives (9.18 "Meta Fiction").

From the point of view of the audience, who have already seen Metatron order the murders of two sympathetic characters, the angel Abner and the prophet Kevin Tran, the absurdity of his narrative is obvious. Metatron is the monster here, and he is a monster sorely lacking in self-awareness. When we learn, at the end of the episode,

"The Monster at the End of This Book"

that he has acquired the powers of God through the angel tablet (one of the few surviving examples of the Word of God), his monstrosity is compounded. He is now the biggest threat facing the protagonists, and, like any other fictional villain, must be dispatched. There seems, then, to be a clear anxiety here around fannish usurping of writerly authority. *Supernatural's* God has been absent for many years, essentially abdicating his authority, but "Meta Fiction" suggests that if the author is no longer God, he *should* be; and the fan writer who seeks to insert him or herself into his place in his absence is monstrous.

The development of the Metatron storyline through the end of season 9, however, suggests a slightly different angle to the show's treatment of authorship. The season finale compounds Metatron's monstrousness when he kills Dean, albeit temporarily (9.23 "Do You Believe in Miracles?"). Immediately after this, however, Castiel and Hannah are able to defeat Metatron by broadcasting to his followers a private conversation in which he reveals his contempt for his audience, describing them as "frightened little sheep following my crook wherever it leads" (9.23 "Do You Believe in Miracles?"). Metatron's positioning of himself as Godlike author is given an ironic twist here: he announces he is certain that he will win, because unlike him, Castiel has "never learned how to tell a good story." Castiel responds, "But you did," and reveals that the conversation has been played to the rest of the angels (9.23 "Do You Believe in Miracles?"). Here, then, Metatron's monstrousness consists not just in his usurpation of Godlike authority, but in his inability to recognize the independence of his audience. Metatron ascribes to a dated view of media audiences as passive and receptive but, like active participatory media fans, Castiel and Hannah recontextualize his narrative. They move it from one medium to another and widen its intended audience, ensuring in the process that the other angels will ascribe a new and less favorable meaning to the "epic story" Metatron has been telling them.

Significantly, however, they do not themselves seek to take his place. Later in the episode, Castiel protests that he is "no leader" (9.23 "Do You Believe in Miracles?"). The conclusion of the Metatron storyline, then, seems to qualify the season's earlier condemnation of fan fiction, suggesting that fan authors are only monstrous when they seek to replace the original author. At the same time, it issues a warning to authors who consider themselves Godlike: underestimate your audience, and you risk losing your authority for good.

213

"Some differences of opinion"

In contrast, the Season 10 episode "Fan Fiction" seems to take a celebratory overall view of fan texts. The episode shows the Winchesters investigating the disappearance of a drama teacher at an all-girls high school. When they arrive, they discover that the students are putting on a musical production based on the *Supernatural* books, adapted by Marie, a student who is also a fan. While the first half of the show covers the events of the books (and therefore the show) with added song and dance numbers, the second act is pure fan fiction, featuring robots, outer space, and "Destiel," the slash fan fiction pairing of Dean and Castiel (10.05 "Fan Fiction"). Dean in particular at first reacts to this retelling with indignation, particularly where the inclusion of non-canon elements and homoerotic relationships is concerned. He insists that there is "no singing" and "no space in *Supernatural*," and demands to know why the actors playing Sam and Dean are standing so close together. When Marie replies, "subtext," he requests that they "take a sub-step back there" (10.05 "Fan Fiction").

Members of the musical's cast begin to disappear, and at first, Sam and Dean believe that the monster taking them is a *tulpa*, a thought-form created when a sufficient number of people believe something—usually an urban legend—to be true (1.17 "Hell House"). In this context, the *tulpa* suggestion implies fan investment turned truly monstrous, with an inability to tell fantasy from reality like that demonstrated by Becky. The *tulpa* theory, however, proves wrong, and we eventually learn that the monster is the Muse, Calliope, who feeds off storytelling—specifically, off authors. She has been kidnapping people who intend to block the production, in order to ensure that Marie's vision is "realized," at which point she plans to enact a quite literal death of the author by eating Marie. The Winchesters must work alongside Marie and the other teenagers in order to defeat her, and in doing so, Dean learns to appreciate Marie's particular interpretation of the *Supernatural* story. He acknowledges that he has had "some differences of opinion regarding this particular version of *Supernatural*," but retracts his earlier criticisms, urging the girls to "stand as close as she wants you to, and . . . put as much sub in that text as you possibly can" (10.05 "Fan Fiction"). He acknowledges that "[this] is Marie's *Supernatural*"; perhaps not the definitive version, but one she has every right to express (10.05 "Fan Fiction"). Over the course of the episode, Dean learns to accept that there

"The Monster at the End of This Book"

is space for multiple interpretations in the wider text of *Supernatural* and its fandom, embracing a democratic version of fan authorship. References to canonical authorship, meanwhile, are tongue-in-cheek. Ms. Chandler, the missing teacher, displays in her office a poster of cult TV showrunner Joss Whedon dressed as Shakespeare (10.05 "Fan Fiction"), a lighthearted touch that serves both to celebrate the TV *auteur* and to suggest that any such self-aggrandizement is a little absurd.

Marie herself does not seek approval from Sam and Dean, or accord them any particular authority. Dean relates to her the events of the most recent seasons, claiming, since she does not yet know he is the "real" Dean, that his insider knowledge comes from reading Chuck's unpublished manuscripts. Rather than accepting his version of events as definitive, however, she treats it as just another piece of fan speculation, dismissing it as "some of the worst fan fiction that I've ever heard" (10.05 "Fan Fiction"). She does, however, prove to value authorial approval when it comes from a verified source. When the Winchesters first arrive on set, she eagerly asks, "Are you guys from the publisher?" and when Chuck appears in the audience at the end of the episode, she runs excitedly up to him to ask his opinion (10.05 "Fan Fiction"). While fan fiction in general is met with approval, or at least acceptance, here—Chuck smilingly admits that Marie's take on his books is "not bad"—we once again see an opposition between "good" and monstrous fans. Calliope wishes to destroy or subsume the author completely, while Marie insists on the validity of her interpretation but does not seek to impose it as the only one, accepting that, in the end, the story still belongs to Chuck. When she realizes Chuck is in the audience, she wonders whether "Calliope came for me or for—?" (10.05 "Fan Fiction"). Marie is immediately willing to cede author status to Chuck, instead taking her place as one of many fan authors, equally valid but unable to be definitive.

"Call me Chuck": The author is God after all?

Chuck's appearance in "Fan Fiction" was his first since the finale of season 5, at the end of which he vanished into thin air, leading fans to speculate that he was, in fact, God (5.22 "Swan Song"). This theory is finally confirmed in season 11, when Chuck, aware that his sister, Amara, intends to destroy his creation, makes himself known to a now-human Metatron (11.20 "Don't Call Me Shurley"). This episode

215

literalizes, and in some ways celebrates, the notion of the author-God. Chuck asserts his authority over his creation by asserting his authorship, saying, "This isn't [Amara's] story. It's mine" (11.20 "Don't Call Me Shurley"). Though he is in hiding when Metatron first encounters him, aware that Amara is just as powerful as he is and may be able to destroy him, he is gradually persuaded to join the fight. Chuck's movement toward reaccepting his place as God is intimately bound up with his authorship. He summons Metatron to his hideout, an imaginary bar, in order to help edit his biography. Initially, Metatron is critical, telling him that he has given too much space in the book to "that chapter about being Chuck" and not enough to "juicier stuff" about the creation of life and mythology of the archangels (11.20 "Don't Call Me Shurley"). He also takes aim at Chuck's decision to hide from Amara instead of protecting his creation, saying "I was a crappy, terrible God . . . but at least I was never a coward!" (11.20 "Don't Call Me Shurley"). The Chuck shown on previous episodes of *Supernatural* was a fairly pathetic figure, at the mercy of his characters and subject to harsh criticism from his fans. The God whom Metatron remembers, on the other hand, is a "total badass" who has "some stories to tell" (11.20 "Don't Call Me Shurley"). Metatron encourages Chuck to recapture his Godly self by writing "for an audience of one — you" (11.20 "Don't Call Me Shurley"). Authorship is here explicitly defined as singular, considerations of fan opinion as needless distractions from the realization of the author-God's vision. The episode ends with Chuck handing Metatron the final pages of his manuscript — the latest installment of the Word of God — and seeking out Sam and Dean, with the implication that he will now help them deal with Amara. The ending of the episode takes on a celebratory tone, with an injured Sam and a number of townspeople being miraculously cured at Chuck's appearance. Significantly, this episode is also where Metatron takes his first steps toward redemption, admitting that he was "a terrible writer" and "[a] worse God," content instead to play midwife to Chuck's creations (11.20 "Don't Call Me Shurley"). In the next episode, he will accept that he is disposable and sacrifice himself in the fight against Amara (11.21 "All in the Family").

Despite this apparent celebration of Godlike authority, the monstrous implications of Chuck's behavior before this point are impossible to escape. There is no indication that he was suffering from amnesia during his previous appearances on the show, and when Metatron asks why he took on the persona of Chuck, he replies, "I like front row seats . . . plus, you know, acting is fun" (11.20 "Don't

"The Monster at the End of This Book"

Call Me Shurley"). He has stood by and allowed angels and demons to slaughter many innocent people and to attempt to bring about the Apocalypse, apparently for his own entertainment. We return to the questions mentioned by Stephen Asma: how can a God who creates monsters, and allows their monstrous actions to go unchecked, be anything but monstrous himself? However, the episode allows both Chuck and Metatron to redeem themselves by working together, with Metatron asking the questions that allow Chuck to realize his vision more thoroughly, and not seeking to impose his own version of events. Metatron becomes a domesticated, "good" fan, while Chuck rewards his help with approval, but asserts his own authority. We even find an Easter egg for "good" fans at the end of the episode, where scenes of Sam, Dean, and the townspeople being saved and Metatron approvingly reading the final manuscript are intercut with Chuck singing and playing his guitar onstage at the bar. Fans who spend the large amounts of money necessary to attend *Supernatural* conventions, where actor Rob Benedict regularly performs with his band, are rewarded with an onscreen reminder of concerts they may have attended, and an inside reference opaque to casual viewers. Those fic-writing fans who reject canonic *Supernatural* storylines in favor of their own, on the other hand, are subject to a gentle reminder of precisely whose storyline this is. As long as they recognize the ultimate authority of the show's writers, they, like Metatron, can avoid monstrosity. Of course, sometimes these fans are the same people, and fans may engage in "good" and "monstrous" fan behaviors at different times. Watching the show, buying associated merchandise, attending conventions, and supporting charity campaigns promoted by its stars does not rule out rewriting storylines in fan fiction or vocally criticizing decisions made by the show's creative team—or, indeed, clearly inappropriate fan behaviors like harassing cast and crew members and other fans on social media. Rather, like Metatron, we are all more or less monstrous at different times. "Don't Call Me Shurley" encourages fans to maintain their distance; to respect the ultimate authority of the author.

Of course—as indicated earlier, with reference to Butler—this is a problematic suggestion when it comes to a TV serial, particularly one as long-running as *Supernatural* which, at the time of writing, is heading into its twelfth season under its fourth showrunner. Indeed, this position proves unsustainable, and the season 11 finale goes some way toward questioning it. Chuck, the Winchesters, and a motley collection of allies have been unsuccessful in their attempt to imprison Amara, and

217

plan to destroy her instead, with Dean — by whom she is particularly fascinated — acting as a suicide bomber. However, when Dean goes off-script and attempts to talk her around instead of killing her, he is able to persuade her to abandon her plan to destroy the world. Despite Chuck having earlier asserted that this "isn't her story," he eventually reconciles with his sister and accepts that they are equals (11.23 "Alpha and Omega"). The season ends with Amara and Chuck together leaving his creation behind, Chuck reassuring Dean that "Earth will be fine" without him (11.23 "Alpha and Omega"). It seems significant that this episode also marked the end of Jeremy Carver's tenure as showrunner. *Supernatural*'s "authors" may come and go, but their story will "be fine" in the hands of its creative fans. The story is, however, ongoing, and will no doubt continue to engage with authors and fans — monstrous and otherwise — in future seasons.

God or monster?

In *Supernatural,* then, it appears that authorship may be equally redemptive or monstrous. Both the author as God, and the fan as author, may become monstrous. The difference, it seems, is that the fan-author becomes monstrous when he or she seeks to claim too much authority; the author-God when he claims too little. While *Supernatural* engages with its fanbase onscreen to a greater extent than many TV shows, its message seems still to be ultimately conservative. Via the unifying figure of Chuck, it seeks to reinforce a version of authority that bears little resemblance to the actual process of TV authorship, or the way the story is experienced by fans. The very appearance of fans onscreen, however, speaks to the untenable nature of the figure of the author-God, and it is this tension between notions of authorship — unitary and Godlike, or multiple and contentions — to which the show obsessively returns. Like *Supernatural*'s nonhuman creatures, fan authors may be ridiculed, monstered, or portrayed as "good" only when they accept the rule of the author-God, but they cannot be kept out of the sandbox.

Works Cited

"All in the Family." *Supernatural*. The CW. 11 May 2016.

"Alpha and Omega." *Supernatural*. The CW. 25 May 2016.

Asma, Stephen T. *On Monsters: An Unnatural History of Our Worst Fears*. Oxford: Oxford University Press, 2009.

Barthes, Roland. "The Death of the Author." *Image Music Text*. Trans. Stephen Heath. London: Fontana, 1977. 142-148.

"Blood Brother." *Supernatural: The Complete Eighth Season*. Writ: Ben Edlund. Dir: Guy Norman Bee. Warner Brothers, 2013.

"Bloodlust." *Supernatural: The Complete Second Season*. Writ: Sera Gamble. Dir: Robert Singer. Warner Brothers, 2007.

Bourke, Joanna. *What It Means to Be Human: Reflections from 1791 to the Present*. London: Virago, 2011.

Busse, Kristina and Karen Hellekson. "Introduction: Work in Progress." *Fan Fiction and Fan Communities in the Age of the Internet: New Essays*. Eds. Karen Hellekson and Kristina Busse. Jefferson, NC: McFarland, 2006. 5-32.

Butler, Jeremy G. *Television: Critical Methods and Applications*. 4th ed. London: Routledge, 2012.

Caughie, John. "Auteurism: Introduction." *Theories of Authorship*. Ed. John Caughie. London: Routledge, 1981. 9-16.

Cohen, Jeffrey Jerome. "Monster Culture (Seven Theses)." *Monster Theory: Reading Culture*. Ed. Jeffrey Jerome Cohen. Minneapolis: University of Minnesota Press, 1996. 3-25.

"Dark Side of the Moon." *Supernatural: The Complete Fifth Season*. Writ: Andrew Dabb, Daniel Loflin. Dir: Jeff Wollnough. Warner Brothers, 2010.

Derecho, Abigail. "Archontic Literature: A Definition, a History, and Several Theories of Fan Fiction." *Fan Fiction and Fan Communities in the Age of the Internet: New Essays*. Eds. Karen Hellekson and Kristina Busse. Jefferson, NC: McFarland, 2006. 61-78.

"Do You Believe in Miracles?" *Supernatural: The Complete Ninth Season*. Writ: Jeremy Carver. Dir: Thomas J. Wright. Warner Brothers, 2014.

"Don't Call Me Shurley." *Supernatural*. The CW. 4 May 2016.

Duda, Heather L. *The Monster Hunter in Modern Popular Culture*. Jefferson, NC: McFarland, 2008.

"The End." *Supernatural: The Complete Fifth Season*. Writ: Ben Edlund. Dir: Steve Boyer. Warner Brothers, 2010.

"Fan Fiction." *Supernatural: The Complete Tenth Season*. Writ: Robbie Thompson. Dir: Phil Sgriccia. Warner Brothers, 2015.

Felschow, Laura E. "'Hey, Check It Out, There's Actually Fans': (Dis)empowerment and (Mis)representation of Cult Fandom in *Supernatural*." *Transformative Works and Cultures* 4 (2010). Web. 27 May 2016.

Foresman, Galen A. and Francis Tobienne, Jr. "Aristotle's Metaphysics of Monsters and Why We Love *Supernatural*." *Supernatural and Philosophy: Metaphysics and Monsters… for Idjits*. Ed. Galen A. Foresman. New York: Wiley-Blackwell, 2013. 16-25.

Foucault, Michel. "What Is an Author?" *The Book History Reader.* 2nd ed. Ed. David Finkelstein and Alistair McCleery. London: Routledge, 2006. 281-291.

"The Girl Next Door." *Supernatural: The Complete Seventh Season.* Writ: Andrew Dabb, Daniel Loflin. Dir: Jensen Ackles. Warner Brothers, 2012.

Gledhill, Evan Hayles. "Fan Girls and Fangbangers: Gender and the Gothic Audience." *The Gothic Imagination.* University of Stirling. 7 February 2015. Web.

"Goodbye Stranger." *Supernatural: The Complete Eighth Season.* Writ: Robbie Thompson. Dir: Thomas J. Wright. Warner Brothers, 2013.

Gray, Jonathan. *Show Sold Separately: Promos, Spoilers, and Other Media Paratexts.* New York: New York University Press, 2010.

"Hell House." *Supernatural: The Complete First Season.* Writ: Trey Callaway. Dir: Chris Long. Warner Brothers, 2006.

Hendershot, Heather. "*Masters of Horror*: TV Auteurism and the Progressive Potential of a Disreputable Genre." *Flow TV: Television in the Age of Media Convergence.* Eds. Michael Kackman, Marnie Binfield, Matthew Thomas Payne, Allison Perlman and Bryan Sebok. London: Routledge, 2011. 144-163.

Jenkins, Henry. *Convergence Culture: Where Old and New Media Collide.* New York: New York University Press, 2006.

Jenson, Joli. "Fandom as Pathology: The Consequences of Characterization." *The Adoring Audience: Fan Culture and Popular Media.* Ed. Lisa A. Lewis. London: Routledge, 1992. 9-29.

Jowett, Lorna and Stacey Abbott. *TV Horror: Investigating the Dark Side of the Small Screen.* London: I. B. Tauris, 2013.

"Lucifer Rising." *Supernatural: The Complete Fourth Season.* Writ: Eric Kripke. Dir: Eric Kripke. Warner Brothers, 2009.

"Malleus Maleficarum." *Supernatural: The Complete Third Season.* Writ: Ben Edlund. Dir: Robert Singer. Warner Brothers, 2007.

"Meta Fiction." *Supernatural: The Complete Ninth Season.* Writ: Robbie Thompson. Dir: Thomas J. Wright. Warner Brothers, 2013.

"Mommy Dearest." *Supernatural: The Complete Sixth Season.* Writ: Adam Glass. Dir: John F. Showalter. Warner Brothers, 2011.

"Monster Movie." *Supernatural: The Complete Fourth Season.* Writ: Ben Edlund. Dir: Robert Singer. Warner Brothers, 2009.

"Pac-Man Fever." *Supernatural: The Complete Eighth Season.* Writ: Robbie Thompson. Dir: Robert Singer. Warner Brothers, 2013.

Pugh, Sheenagh. *The Democratic Genre: Fan Fiction in a Literary Context.* Bridgend: Seren, 2005.

"The Real Ghostbusters." *Supernatural: The Complete Fifth Season.* Writ: Eric Kripke, Nancy Weiner. Dir: James L. Conway. Warner Brothers, 2010.

"Road Trip." *Supernatural: The Complete Ninth Season.* Writ: Andrew Dabb. Dir: Robert Singer. Warner Brothers, 2014.

"Season Seven, Time for a Wedding!" *Supernatural: The Complete Seventh Season.* Writ: Andrew Dabb, Daniel Loflin. Dir: Tim Andrew. Warner Brothers, 2012.

"The Monster at the End of This Book"

Sivarajan, Deepa. "Tlön, Fandom, and Source Text: The Effect of Fan Works on the Narrative of *Supernatural*." *Transformative Works and Cultures* 4 (2010). Web. 27 May 2016.

"Slumber Party." *Supernatural: The Complete Ninth Season*. Writ: Robbie Thompson. Dir: Robert Singer. Warner Brothers, 2014.

"Stairway to Heaven." *Supernatural: The Complete Ninth Season*. Writ: Andrew Dabb. Dir: Guy Norman Bee. Warner Brothers, 2014.

Stasi, Mafalda. "The Toy Soldiers from Leeds: The Slash Palimpsest." *Fan Fiction and Fan Communities in the Age of the Internet: New Essays*. Eds. Karen Hellekson and Kristina Busse. Jefferson, NC: McFarland, 2006. 115-133.

Stout, Nathan. "Are Monsters Members of the Moral Community?" *Supernatural and Philosophy: Metaphysics and Monsters… for Idjits*. Ed. Galen A. Foresman. New York: Wiley-Blackwell, 2013. 7-15.

"Swan Song." *Supernatural: The Complete Fifth Season*. Writ: Eric Kripke, Eric Gerwirtz. Dir: Steve Boyum. Warner Brothers, 2010.

"Sympathy for the Devil." *Supernatural: The Complete Fifth Season*. Writ: Eric Kripke. Dir: Robert Singer. Warner Brothers, 2010.

NOTES ON CONTRIBUTORS

Dr **Cristina Artenie** is a *Dracula* expert. She is the author of *Dracula: A Study of Editorial Practices* and *Dracula Invades England*, the editor of *Gothic and Racism* and *My Own Land's Sins: An Anthology of Victorian Poetry*, and the co-editor of *Dracula: The Postcolonial Edition*. She researches and publishes on all aspects of gothic literature and film, with an eye on postcolonial approaches to classic and contemporary gothic works.

Alissa Burger is an Assistant Professor of English and Director of Writing Across the Curriculum at Culver-Stockton College. She teaches courses in research, writing, and literature, including a single-author seminar on Stephen King. She is the author of *Teaching Stephen King: Horror, The Supernatural, and New Approaches to Literature* (Palgrave, 2016) and *The Wizard of Oz as American Myth: A Critical Study of Six Versions of the Story, 1900-2007* (McFarland, 2012).

Erin Casey-Williams is an Assistant Professor of English at Nichols College in Dudley, Massachusetts. She specializes in early modern literature, gender studies, and political theory, as well as monsters and the monstrous in literature and popular culture. She recently completed her dissertation, *The Queen's Three Bodies: Representations of Sovereignty in Early Modern Women's Writing, 1588-1688*, at the University at Albany, SUNY, and is currently working on bodies and embodiment and on how women's bodies in particular exist within political and literary structures. Her favorite class to teach at Nichols College is "Zombie (R)Evolutions," a current issues symposium that focuses on critical reading, research, and writing.

Jennifer Collins is a reference and instruction librarian at The State University of New York campus at Delhi though she more often refers to herself using the title of Franken-librarian. Her work with students and faculty as the humanities and social sciences liaison covers

223

information literacy instruction, collection development, instructional design and service learning. Her research interests include scholarly communications, early modern Europe and interesting ephemera.

Erika Cornelius Smith is an Assistant Professor of History and Political Science at Nichols College in Dudley, Massachusetts. She specializes in twentieth-century U.S. history, comparative politics, citizenship studies, and gender studies. Recently, Dr. Cornelius Smith completed additional studies in cultural diplomacy through the Institute of Cultural Diplomacy in Berlin. Her recent research focuses on volunteer networks and global citizenship in the twentieth century, and she is currently completing a manuscript examining transitioning economies and political institutions in central and eastern Europe.

Coco d'Hont is currently completing her PhD at the School of Art, Media and American Studies at the University of East Anglia (UK). Her project explores transgression in the fiction of Bret Easton Ellis, Chuck Palahniuk and Poppy Z. Brite. Other research interests include but are not limited to horror, queer theory, popular culture, and biopolitics.

Heather L. Duda, Ph.D. is an Associate Professor of English at the University of Rio Grande in Rio Grande, OH. Her academic areas of interest are American literature and film studies, in particular adaptation studies and the horror genre. She has published both a book on monstrous monster hunters—*The Monster Hunter in Modern Popular Culture*—and an article on vigilantism in Michael Cox's modern gothic novel *The Meaning of Night*.

Alberto N. García is an Associate Professor of Film and Television Studies at the School of Communication and researcher for the Institute for Culture and Society (University of Navarra, Spain). He has been Visiting Scholar at the University of Stirling and Universidad de los Andes, Chile. His work has appeared in *Post Script*, *Communication and Society*, *Zer* and *Analisi*. He is co-editor of *Landscapes of the Self: The Cinema of Ross McElwee* (2007), author of *El cine* *de no-ficción en Martín Patino* (2008) and editor of *Emotions in Contemporary TV Series* (Palgrave, 2016). He has also written essays about *The Wire, The Shield, Breaking Bad, Supernatural* or *In Treatment*. He is currently researching about emotions, narrative and TV Series.

Jessica George received her PhD from Cardiff University in 2014. Her doctoral research focused on the uses of evolutionary theory in the weird fiction of Arthur Machen and H. P. Lovecraft, and she is currently working on developing it into a monograph. She has published on Machen, Lovecraft, and Neil Gaiman, and has additional research interests in Gothic authorship, literature and science in the long nineteenth century, Welsh writing in English, utopian and dystopian fictions, and adaptations and transformative works.

Kristine Larsen is Professor of Astronomy at Central Connecticut State University, where her teaching and scholarship focus on the intersections between science and society. She is the author of *Stephen Hawking: A Biography,* and *Cosmology 101*, and co-editor of *The Mythological Dimensions of Neil Gaiman* and *The Mythological Dimensions of* Doctor Who. She is widely known in Tolkien scholarship for her work on astronomical mysteries and motifs in Tolkien's works, and has published and presented on aspects of the *Harry Potter* and *Witcher* series of novels, the works of C.S. Lewis, Robert Heinlein, and Philip Pullman, the television series *Land of the Lost, Lost, Dominion, Highlander, Doctor Who*, and *Game of Thrones*, and the *Resident Evil* series of films, among others.

Dr. **Marylou Naumoff** is an Assistant Professor in Communication Studies, Coordinator of the Fundamentals of Speech Program and Supervisor of the Public Speaking Resource Center in the School of Communication and Media at Montclair State University. Her specialization is rhetorical studies, cultural studies, gender studies, and popular culture. Dr. Naumoff's research focuses on citizenship, race, and masculinity, specifically examining popular culture as a site of national discourse where citizens look to understand and construct American identity, as well as form a sense of community.

She is currently working on a book manuscript that examines the impact of hip hop on American masculinity and national identity.

Tatiana Prorokova is a Doctoral Candidate in American Studies at Philipps University of Marburg, Germany. Her Ph.D. project analyzes the representation of U.S. interventionism from 1990 onward and the culture of U.S. imperialism in film and literature. She is an academic editor at Pod Academy (UK). Her article "Documenting Vietnam: Verisimilitude, Political Propaganda, and Manipulation in Peter Davis's *Hearts and Minds*" was recently published in *the quint: an interdisciplinary quarterly from the north* (Canada) and her essay "Madness and Imagination in Washington Irving's 'The Adventure of the German Student'" was published as a chapter in *Hermeneutics of Textual Madness: Re-Readings/ Herméneutique de la folie textuelle: re-lectures* (ed. Mary Jo Muratore) in 2016. Her book and film reviews have appeared in U.S., Canadian, British, and German academic journals. She has presented her papers in various academic conferences worldwide, including the recent PCA/ACA conference in Seattle, WA, the USA. She has also participated in the Salzburg Global Seminar (Austria, 2015) devoted to the problem of America's changing role in the world. Her research interests include U.S. literature and culture, film studies, war studies, genocide studies, documentary film, visual culture, race studies, gender studies, and American exceptionalism.

Brooke Southgate is a doctoral candidate at Wilfrid Laurier University in Waterloo, Ontario. She has previously published on monstrosity in comic book heroes and presented on Gothic monsters in contemporary urban fantasy. Her current research focuses on the dinosaur as allegory in American science fiction.

Ashley Szanter (M.A.) is an adjunct instructor in Weber State University's English Department. She frequently publishes and presents on monsters in popular culture, more recently with a focus on the evolving role of the zombie. She is currently co-editing two essay collections with her colleague, Jessica K. Richards, on zombies in pop culture: the first volume, *Romancing the Zombie*, deals

226

with the growing influence of romance and love in the zombie genre—the second is a text specific collection on the The CW series *iZombie* **as** well as the Vertigo comics series of the same name. Her work can be found in the *Journal of Dracula Studies, The Victorian*, and *The Supernatural Revamped* (2016), as well as *Albeit. Journal* where she is the On-Staff Book Reviewer.

Tracey Thomas is a PhD student at York University in Toronto, Canada. Her research focuses on DC comics, the relationship between the superhero and the city, and on how the city's design (historical, culture, ethnic, architectural) plays an important part in building a specific need and reception for a superhero. She explores the graphic novel representation of the city in the CW show *The Flash* and in its parent program, *Arrow*, and challenges why one city applauds heroes while the other denigrates them. Her interests include other CW television shows, *Teen Wolf*, comic books and manga, and Japanese anime. Tracey predominantly explores concepts of identity and culture in her research.

CPSIA information can be obtained
at www.ICGtesting.com
Printed in the USA
LVHW020706080523
746255LV00001B/5